Cricket

The Dales

A celebration of the Golden Anniversary of the
Dales Council Cricket League, 1955-2005.

By Barry Foster

With the foreword from Sir Tim Rice

Published by The Dales Council Cricket League

ISBN 0-9548372-0-7

PREFACE, or to put it another way, a kind of early pitch inspection

THERE is an obscure little record which has appeared annually in the Dales Council league handbook since 1981 which makes it that much harder for me to understand why I came to be invited to put together the following story which tracks the first half century of the league's existence.

Until 2002 when New Farnley joined them by being dismissed for six, New Wortley stood on their own as the club to have one of its teams on record with the lowest score in an innings by any Dales Council side. The handbook shows New Wortley's six and out day fell on 10 August, 1980, at High Eldwick. It was a day the former league president Les Thompson remembers well. He opened for New Wortley that day and was joint top scorer with two caught off the bowling of one B. Foster. Nearly twenty years on when late in his tenure as president, he brought up that afternoon again during drinks at one of the league's annual dinners held at Yorkshire's headquarters at Headingley. Forgiven, but with that 1980 moment not forgotten, he asked me to think about putting such events together in book form to help mark the 50th birthday of the league which was, in manner of speaking, just around the corner. Knowing that I had chased sporting stories for a lifetime all over the country and Europe I suppose he thought it was a good idea at the time and, reasonably, after that day at High Eldwick ~ even though it was Wilf Anderson who did most of the damage for Eldwick ~ he had a favour coming his way.

So this is the result, though without a great deal of help from Dales Council enthusiasts it would have been an impossible task, particularly difficult too, without all the league handbooks to work from. But at one stage it looked as though the most important of these annual publications, one covering the first season, had never made it to the printers. Knowing how the league's father, Jack Shuttleworth, used to work I should never have doubted that he would have ensured one was produced but it took over three years to dig up a copy.

Cricket in The Dales, however, is not a tale about the game in the wide sense, just an account of a little league's journey through 50 years. I may have missed cricketers who should have been mentioned and written too much about others, missed team exploits that deserved space and given too much space to others and for that I apologise in advance. Yet it would be nice to think the general picture is just about in focus and I have added a little to the ongoing story of sporting life in the county.

Barry Foster, November, 2004.

The story so far........

Late Sep 1955	A preliminary meeting about the possible formation of a new league is held
05–Oct–55	The Dales Council is born at the White Cross Hotel at Guiseley
05–Oct–55	Jack Shuttleworth, 'father' of the league, appointed first secretary.
30–Nov–55	Kenneth Hodgson (Tong Park) confirmed as the league's first president
28–Apr–56	Dales Council first league games played
28–Apr–56	FIRST hat-trick: K. Wilkinson (Pool Paper Mills)
19–May–56	FIRST century: S, Newton (Ross Mills)
08–Sep–56	End of first season
	FIRST Champions: Green Lane
	FIRST season batting averages leader: A. Carrick (Smiths Sports)
	FIRST season bowling averages leader: G. Milner (Crompark)
	FIRST 100 wicket league wicket haul: G. Sample (Green Lane), (111 wkts)
Summer 1957	FIRST Cup winners: Green Lane
15–Jun–57	FIRST all 10 wickets in an innings haul: G. Sample (Green Lane)
1960	FIRST League and Cup double winners: Green Lane
1967	FIRST Bradford Area Cup final success for the Dales Council
02–Aug–75	FIRST innings of 300-plus: Smiths Sports (323-8 dec in A Div league game)
14–Dec–77	FIRST former Dales Council player to play for England: G.Cope v Pakistan.
21–Feb–96	'Father' of the league Jack Shuttleworth dies
23–Aug–97	FIRST double century: P. Slater (Nat West Bank), (200 in "A" Div match)
01–May–99	FIRST 250: J. Collier (Motivators), (253n.o. in "C" Div match)
05–Feb–01	Geoff Cope, (Leeds Zingari, Yorkshire & England) appointed league president
05–May–02	FIRST innings of 400-plus: New Wortley, (428-6 in 40-over Cup tie)
Summer 2003	June 14: N. Oram (New Farnley) hits A Division highest individual score of 208
	August 2: S. Dobson (Meanwood) sets new bowling record with 10 for 4 return
	August 23: Mount hit highest score in an innings in league games of 398 for 3
05–Oct–04	Dales' 50th year opens today
Late April 2005	Dales Council's Golden anniversary season opens
05–Oct–05	Dales Council is 50 today

Sir Tim Rice, President, M.C.C. 2002-2003

Dales Council Cricket League

Cricket in The Dales

Foreword

Fifty years of cricket for the Dales Council Cricket League – a magnificent milestone! I am delighted to have been asked to provide the foreword to this production of the League's history. Club cricket is an essential part of the infrastructure of the sport in England, and it is marvellous to know that Leagues such as the Dales Council competition are flourishing.

The future well-being of the game depends upon the identification and nurturing of raw talent. With the Dales Council League having produced 17 County players in its short history, most notably England's opening bowler Matthew Hoggard, it is clear that this League is providing a great platform for aspiring cricketers.

When reading this history, it is particularly pleasing to note the expansion that has taken place in the League from its formation of 18 clubs. Club Cricket can only flourish by the continued support of all those who love the game – groundsmen, scorers, coaches, umpires, tea providers and many others, all have a great part to play in the continuation and development of the game.

The Dales Council League has had a solid foundation for its first fifty years – now I wish you all the best on your way to a century.

Sir Tim Rice
President, M.C.C. 2002-2003.

BATTING ORDER (Contents)

INTRODUCTION

OVER the years cricket has been good to me. There have been high points, there have been low points but overall it has been smashing to be so deeply involved with the game and there are any number of people and organisations I can thank for helping me along the way. They make up a list, I am grateful to say, that is a long one.

And very high on it is the Dales Council. It's where I started to think about and play the game seriously. My first contact with the league goes back to pre teenage days. I have fond memories of those formative times. Yorkshire and even England might have been part of a youngster's dreams but a love of the game had to develop in the right surroundings and I found them in the Dales.

So you can imagine how thrilled I was just into the new Millennium to be invited to be President of the Dales Council. I knew at the time that the 50th anniversary of the league was just around the corner and looked forward to playing a part in the celebrations to mark the milestone.

This book is part of those celebrations. It details what has gone into the making of our league and I hope you will enjoy looking back and looking forward with it. The league has already given thousands of cricketers moments to treasure and I trust there will be many more in the years ahead.

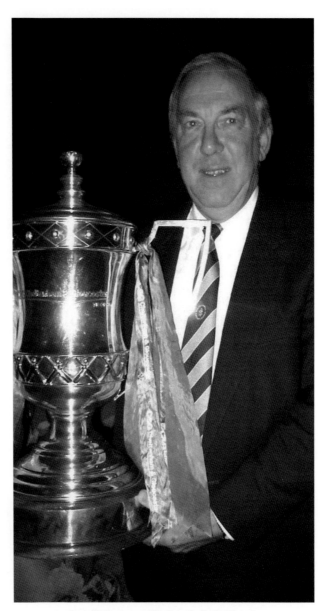

Geoff Cope with the C & G Trophy won by Yorkshire in 2002.

Geoff Cope, Dales Council President, November 2004.

Jack Shuttleworth, 19 September, 1911 – 21 February, 1996.

"The father of the Dales Council Cricket League"

Cricket in The Dales

Chapter One: Opening a new game

IT was an extraordinary summer for English cricket particularly if you happened to be a Yorkshireman. It was the summer of 1956.........when Frizinghall-born Jim Laker re-wrote the record books and when, somewhat down the batting order in the wider picture maybe, a new local league was playing its first matches in the great bowler's old backyard.

Laker's never-to-be-forgotten bowling miracle came well into that special season. By late July when he was creating a legend over the Pennines by destroying the Australians in the Fourth Test at Old Trafford the new league - The Dales Council - was building up for the climax to its initial campaign.

In fact, while what has become known throughout the cricketing folklore as "Laker's Match" was being decided, back in Laker's native dales there was a game in progress which, in its small way, was every bit as intense for the Saturday afternoon players involved as England's Ashes confrontation.

Around the time the lethal off-spinner was setting about bringing the Australians to their knees by following his nine for 37 with his all ten for 53 in the greatest display of Test match destruction ever witnessed, at grass roots level in Yorkshire the players of title-chasing Green Lane were in the thick of a juicy derby encounter with Esholt in the new Dales Council. Small beer perhaps alongside the pitch-shattering exploits in Manchester but a big deal in that little corner of the Aire Valley that weekend.

It was one of nine first team fixtures in the fledgling competition's rain-hit scheduled programme as the still young format continued to evolve and along the way build a reputation in a county where local cricket had long been a way of life. "Matches between Green Lane and Esholt were always cracking games in those early days," recalled Malcolm Franks, an all-rounder who made an early input into the league's record book. But on that day, player of the match for Green Lane, and for that matter for much of their season, was the new league's first star Gordon Sample - better known for reasons explained in a later chapter as Gloss.

In those days when the local weekly newspapers like the Wharfedale and Airedale Observer and the Shipley Times and Express covered the area for just three old pence, Sample provided plenty of copy. On this particular Saturday he captured seven wickets for 42 off 14.4 overs as Esholt fell for 78 then hit an unbeaten 36 in Green Lane's 80 for two to ensure a victory which gave the champions-to-be a seven-point cushion over the then second placed Tong Park with six matches to go in their 21 game programme.

In Laker-like fashion on the same afternoon, Norman Hartley took four wickets in four deliveries to finish with eight for 23 for International Harvesters but it was not enough to stop Ives Sports claiming a one wicket win. Meanwhile the unplayable Laker, who incidentally knew all about local cricket in West Yorkshire and at one point played in the Bradford League with Saltaire, was looking beyond the storm lashed weekend in Lancashire and forward to finishing the Australians off on the following Monday and Tuesday when as history now shouts England roared on to an innings and 170 runs victory.

It was an unsurpassed achievement, massive in every respect but, as local history now insists, in its way so was what was going on in the dales that weekend – a still new local cricket programme adding further significant moments in what was all part of the founding of what has proved to be an enduring little league.

As its season count nudges and strokes its way to beyond a first 50, the Dales Council is still batting comfortably and those who love the league readily maintain it is still scoring well. It may be a comparatively small operation at the side of the senior leagues which operate around it but back in the mid-fifties it set out to provide an alternative to its higher profile neighbouring organisations and in reaching a first half century confirms there was, and still is a place for such competition.

And in underlining its position in the county's cricketing marketplace the Dales Council has provided a stepping stone for a string of clubs to grow into leading sides in West Yorkshire not to mention providing a launching pad for the careers of nearly 20 county players, some of whom went on to become international performers like the Dales President Geoff Cope and latterly Matthew Hoggard.

From a league of 18 clubs (18 in a first elevens division with six of them providing teams for a second elevens competition) back in the days when the Surrey favourite from Bradford was arguably the best bowler in the world, the Dales Council has developed into a league of three/four divisions. It peaked with 46 teams in the 1980s and in the decade running up to its golden milestone numbers have hovered round the 30 mark in clubs generating 40 or more teams.

above left: Gordon 'Gloss' Sample.
centre: Jack Shuttleworth and Malcolm Franks in the mid 50s.
above right: Jim Laker in action.

Just one club has survived the whole of the league's half century though around a dozen have left the fold and returned and in odd cases left and returned a second and then a third time. However, Crompark are the great survivors but their tenure has not been especially rewarding in terms of trophies.

They have picked up their share of championships in the lower divisions, notably winning both the B and D division titles in 2002, but their single league title was way back in the league's second season, 1957.

New Farnley and Otley Town, two of the clubs to have left and returned to the Dales, have the best track records though the Otley club appears in the list of clubs under three differing names, Town, Otley Mills and Grove Hill. Both clubs have 10 major trophies to their credit, Otley with seven league titles and three cup winning campaigns, New Farnley with six league wins and four in the cup. Green Lane took seven titles (three as cup winners) in their dominance of the early seasons then Esholt and Smith Sports had their best years while Meanwood, Mount and New Wortley have all made their mark in the run up to the Millennium and the early part of this new century.

Not surprisingly, in and amongst all this there have been some spectacular individual performances, many of which will be featured as the story of the league's 50 seasons unfolds but a couple of long serving efforts should be mentioned now – Mick Edwards for, remarkably, playing in every single season from 1956 until 2004 and Malcolm Franks' run which saw him play in each of the five decades to the league's golden year.

Of course, the Dales Council does not pretend to be the best league around. The 1967, 2000 and 2003 Bradford Area Cup titles are the most notable achievements going the Dales way at league level but for many cricketers who have played their part in its half-century, it has become a way of life. And in standing the test of time in a period when other bigger brothers have had to call it a day, it continues to emphasise the faith shown in the future by the handful of cricket lovers who set up the new venture back in the mid fifties.

It all began as a dream of the Esholt pair Jack Shuttleworth and his brother Ralph and their friends who were convinced there was room in West Yorkshire for a new competition to be run on a smaller scale to the big and established leagues in the Aire and Wharfe valleys. So as the 1955 season was closing a group of them sat round a pub table in Guiseley and started drawing up a batting order for the proposed new venture.

"Jack and Ralph called the meeting, I remember it was all a bit 'hush hush' at the time," said John Whiteley of Pool Paper Mills who was to be on the executive committee and serve as the league's second President throughout its second decade. "It was at the White Cross Hotel where all the committee meetings were held for quite a while."

That first meeting on that September night, however, was starting point of quite a few ripples in local cricket circles in the ongoing winter months. The new league was the subject of a string of stories in the Observer but it was soon clear that the Shuttleworths and their fellow players meant business and they sent down their first overs in determined fashion.

Chapter Two: The first deliveries

THE first public hints that a new league was being planned came in late September, 1955. The Wharfedale and Airedale Observer of September 30 disclosed under a headline stating 'Move to form new cricket league' that a preliminary meeting of invited clubs had been held and a second meeting was scheduled for the White Cross Hotel the following week.

"At this meeting it is anticipated that support for the new idea will be ascertained and a definite decision made as to whether the league will be formed," the Observer reported. "Prime mover behind the scheme is Mr Jack Shuttleworth of Baildon, a playing member and committee man of the Esholt club for 25 years.

"He said this week that 14 clubs were invited to the initial meeting. Most of these were Wharefedale League clubs with the addition of two from the Yorkshire Council and a Bradford Amateur Council club. Twelve were represented at the meeting.

"Mr Shuttleworth said the majority of the representatives favoured the formation of a new league. 'Our object is to get better cricket and encourage better cricketers,' he said. 'Some of the grounds of the junior clubs in the district are not worth playing on.'

The following Friday the Observer announced: "A new cricket league came into being this week and it will be known as the Dales Council, comprising clubs in the Wharfedale and Airedale area. The decision was made at a meeting of 14 club representatives at the White Cross Hotel at Guiseley on Wednesday and it was also decided that the league should begin operation next season."

The same day the local evening newspaper, the Telegraph and Argus, ran a three sentence story about the move. "A new league, The Dales Council, has been formed to cater for junior Dales cricket next summer. Mr Jack Shuttleworth, of Baildon, a member of the Esholt cricket club for 25 years, has been elected secretary. The new league, largely a breakaway from the existing Wharfedale League, has an initial membership of 14 clubs."

So the new venture was up and running albeit a long way from seeing the first batting order. The names of the clubs involved, for instance, were still under wraps because, said the Observer, "most of them are still connected with other leagues, principally the Wharfedale League and will have to be given clearances before they can make this change."

It was hardly surprising that Shutt, as he was affectionately known, was appointed as the first official of the new league and another Esholt player Stan Hughes from Rawdon was made treasurer. An executive was formed to draw up rules for circulation to the clubs who would be called together again in around six weeks' time to approve their efforts and consider amendments. "It's all a long time ago but I can remember us all getting together in the bar at the White Cross to talk it through," said Mr Hughes almost 50 years later.

"We wanted an alternative to the Aire-Wharfe. The two Shutts (Jack and his brother Ralph) whose roots were basically with Esholt were the keenest, especially Ralph," he said. "I seem to recall one of the biggest debates we had was what to call the new league but we settled on the Dales Council taking it from the Yorkshire Council and that we were going to play in the dales. It was a name that reflected the essence of the area really."

John Whiteley, who was to become the league's second president, believed the new name came from Dales as in Wharfedale League and Council because there were players coming out of the Yorkshire Council involved. "I think Jack probably thought up the name beforehand through canvassing the rest of us," he said. Whichever way it went the name Dales Council stuck.

A further month on saw the Observer reporting on November 11 that eleven clubs had resigned from the Wharfedale League whose president Fred Wheatley told their annual meeting "I have never had a blow like this in my 60 years of cricketing." He listed Pool Mills, Green Lane, Netherfield Sports, Ives Sports, Esholt, Ross Mills, Otley Mills, Otley Wesley, Wilson and Mathieson's, Smiths (Rodley) and Bramley Moriah as the clubs to have tendered resignations though Moriah pointed out that they had not resigned for the same reason as the others. The meeting eventually agreed that the resignations should be accepted provided all financial obligations had been met.

"Mr J Shuttleworth said he was the instigator of the new league adding 'We did not do anything against Yorkshire Federation rules. I notified the league and if they had wanted to do anything about it they had the opportunity'." On December 2 the Observer revealed that the newly formed Dales Council "is now 18 teams strong."

Mr C. K. Hodgson of Tong Park was elected as President of the new venture and Mr H Sugden of Netherfield Sports was made vice-president. League rules were confirmed and a list of umpires was to be drawn up. By February 24 it was being reported that the search for more umpires was being widened while the secretary had secured a silver cup to be known as the William Hill Trophy "and there was a distinct probability other trophies would be given to the league."

On April 20 the Wharfedale League chose the Rawdon Baptist ground for the May 23 meeting with the Dales Council in the Bradford Area Council Cup, a cup tie which was to be dominated by Sample and won by nine wickets by the new boys. Before that, however, the Dales Council clubs had to negotiate the initial league programme, but with two days to go before their first matches, the weather bowled a googly at the newcomers: pitches were covered with snow! It was not enough to stop them though and on 28 April, 1956, the first overs were bowled and the Dales Council was up and running.

Chapter Three: The first day....the first season

THE Dales Council's first day in business proper could not be undermined even by the elements. It had been a long winter of negotiation and organisation so the weather was not going to stand in the way of the planned opening right at the last moment.

But when April 28, 1956, did arrive it was on the back of snowfalls in West Yorkshire on the run-up days to the new league's initial fixtures. The weather prospects were of such concern, in fact, that the new cricketing ventures likely or otherwise progress found space in the local paper. "Snow covered pitches within two days of the opening of their first season has been an unexpected hazard for the clubs in the new Dales Council but there is enough optimism in the league to sustain such a setback," the Wharfedale and Airedale Observer reported 24 hours or so before wickets were pitched for the first time. The conditions were not great but the opening overs in the Dales got under way on schedule regardless.

The opening programme, with scores, was:

Netherfield Sports 57, Pool Paper Mills 112.
Green Lane 128, David Brown Tractors 39.
Butterfield Sports 56, Smiths (Rodley) 62.
Wilson & Mathiesons 54-3, Thackley 51.
James Ives Sports 56, English Electric 57-8.
Crompark 68, Tong Park 69-5.
Ross Mills 93-5, International Harvesters 91.
Laisterdyke 114, Esholt 115-9.
Otley Mills 57, Otley Wesley 82

Best bowling: H. Grice, (Eng. Elect.) 8-11, K. Wilkinson, (PPM) 7-15.

Obviously, the day was a pivotal moment for the league and its officials. Machinery was being tested for the first time, no-one knew for sure whether everything would fall into place but the programme went without hitch or complaint.....as they say bowlers bowled and batsman batted.

It turned out to be a low scoring afternoon but not without its moments with the first record (in the form of a hat-trick) being achieved and the odd tight finish......ironically involving the Shuttleworths' club Esholt. Though there have been counter claims in recent years about who performed that first hat trick, league and newspaper records at the time insist that the milestone belongs to Ken Wilkinson of Pool Paper Mills. "There will be others later but this is a record that cannot be improved on," the Observer said.

Wilkinson came on at Netherfield when they were 36 for one chasing the Mills' total of 112 and in his third over he claimed his three victims in three deliveries going on to lead his side home with seven wickets for 15. Meanwhile Billy Russell of Wilsons and Mathieson's with seven for 28 and a knock of 31 against Thackley was already showing he would be a major force to be reckoned with in the league while Esholt were reduced to sending in their last man still wanting 14 to win at Laisterdyke - Alan Walker, unbeaten on 29, proving to be their match winner. Esholt stalwart Jack Shuttleworth must have been delighted not only with Walker but also with the league's launch as a whole.

Wearing his other hat for the league handbook, the league secretary had produced a list of eight requests for those involved with his fledgling competition finishing with his most insistent plea: "Please enjoy your cricket and help others – players, umpires, spectators and workers – to enjoy theirs." Another request: "Please read, digest and adhere to all rules." For the record, these revealed among other pointers to the times that there was an entrance fee for any club newly admitted to the league of £1. 1s. in old money with an annual subscription of £2. for a first eleven and £1. for a second eleven. The league committee "shall meet at such times as the business of the league may require" with clubs not represented fined 5s.

In fact, club and player fines seem to have been a fair source of income for the league in those early days. "I remember that in the first few seasons the league made more money than little from fines for late starts, misconduct, not playing, not sending in results and the like. Fines were possibly our biggest source of income," commented the first treasurer Stan Hughes years later.

It was four weeks into that first campaign before the Dales Council had a centurion. Holiday Saturday, May 19, proved to be a run feast for Sidney Newton of Ross Mills who, in reaching the milestone against Butterfield Sports, picked up 19 fours (no sixes in those days) in his unbeaten 107 (140 mins) out of 199 for eight, Mills going on to win by 65 runs. On the same day, Len Morant (six wickets for seven for Wilson and Mathieson's) reduced Netherfield Sports to an all out score of just 21, taking the last four wickets in five deliveries (all bowled and including the hat-trick).

In mid August, Russell, who had been building up a handy total of runs, picked up an eight wickets for nine runs return to emphasize his ability with the ball as well as the bat. Alongside Green Lane's towering performer Gordon Sample, he set the benchmark for all-rounders from that point on. Russell finished joint second in the league's batting averages and sixth in the bowling list. Russell's runs total for the season of 476 (at an average of 29.75) was the league's highest, almost 90 ahead of his nearest rival, while his 80 wickets at 6.4 runs apiece was 23 wickets ahead of the third highest haul of the first campaign registered by Peter Forkin of Ives Sports. But when it came to taking wickets no-one compared with Sample.

Sample, who finished sixth in the batting averages, simply demolished the heart of Dales Council batting throughout the season to build a record which has stood longer than any other in the league's history. But although his 111 victims cost him just a mere 5.45 runs each the effort was not quite good enough to leave him top of the bowling averages. That accolade went to Geoff Milner of Crompark whose total of 32 wickets from 94 overs cost him just 160 runs for an average of 5. And to underline the point Milner did it again the following season when he played a key role in Crompark's only championship winning campaign. Amazingly, his second successive bowling prize was achieved with an identical average to the first of 5 but the second time around he claimed 48 wickets conceding 240 runs.

Russell apart, the first season's batting honours went to Smith's Sports players Archie Carrick and David Pearce who finished first and joint second respectively. Carrick was an all round sportsman who also played soccer for the works team and who had a special fan in those days.

Carrick topped the 1956 batting average with 31.70 – 317 runs from 14 times to the crease. And it is more than likely that most of his knocks were watched by the then four-year-old Phil Carrick. While his dad was in the middle, often partnered by Pearce, who was to become one of the new league's most influential characters both on and off the field, the young Carrick used to play by the boundary edge at the Coal Hill Lane ground at Rodley maybe dreaming of the days ahead when he would become captain of Yorkshire.

But in that opening season Green Lane's powerful charge to the league's first championship dominated most Saturday afternoons with Sample's exploits overshadowing everything else. He went through the 100 wickets mark for the campaign in the penultimate programme with a nine for 33 return against Crompark and rounded it off in a nine wicket win with six for 24 return against Wilson and Mathieson's who had finished the season as runners-up in the title race.

The season was completed in mid September with a fixture between the champions and The Rest and guess what? Green Lane won in comfort with that man taking another five wickets. Kenneth Hodgson, the president, presented the league trophy making the point that one man could not carry a team to the title. "Green Lane have shown a fine team spirit," he said but adding that Sample's 111 haul would be marked with a trophy from the league in recognition of his outstanding record. Enough said.

Geoff Milner.   *Archie Carrick.*   *Ken Wilkinson.*

Chapter Four
Gloss & Matt, two artists who are the first and latest stars of the Dales Council

GLOSS and MATT could have been the catchy name for a firm of painters on another surface on another day but on the surface of a cricket field the pair are proven artists with the ball and can justly claim to be known as the first and latest of the stars of the Dales Council.

Green Lane's Gordon Sample, known wherever he played the game in West Yorkshire as Gloss, set the Dales Council on fire in its opening season with a bowling feat which has never been matched while Matt – Matthew Hoggard – who started his cricketing life as a youngster with Pudsey Congs jumped into the first five of the world's top bowlers behind such celebrated players as McGrath, Muralitharan, Pollock and Warne as the Golden anniversary of the league came into sight.

The two strike bowlers are the initial and most recent of the players on a list of cricketers who, over the years, have made big names for themselves via the Dales Council – Gloss by dominating the league at its birth and going on to play in senior leagues and Matt, who started his career in the Dales nearly four decades later, who has gone on to establish himself on county and international fields.

Gordon 'Gloss' Sample with his framed record of the viaduct throw.

So why Gloss as a name? It might be reasonable to assume that the nickname had something to do with Sample's prowess with the ball but in fact it had nothing at all to do with cricket. "I was born in Coventry but we were bombed out in the war and so I came to live with my grandparents in Yorkshire. That's where I met Hildred Jackson, a life-long pal who gave me the 'Gloss' tag because on our six weeks summer school holidays we used to go up to Yeadon aerodrome where we'd we watch the Gloucester Gladiators doing their stuff," he said. "The gloss had nothing to do with a shiny new cricket ball, it came from Gloucester and it's stuck ever since."

Gloss was a quick right arm bowler who used an economic six strides to the wicket and opening bat in a Green Lane side that swept almost everything before them as the Dales Council established itself on the local scene. His 111 wickets record in the league's first season was followed up in the 1957 campaign with an all ten haul for 28 against Ross Mills and an eight for 10 performance against Newlands. He was unstoppable.

But after army service he went into the Bradford League with Yeadon and then on to a spell in the Aire-Wharfe with Rawdon where he was captain before becoming professional with Rastrick, Gomersal and Lacelles Hall in the Huddersfield League.

It was while he was playing with Rastrick that his reputation for throwing the cricket ball caught the imagination and more than a 1,000 people turned up on September 1, 1962, when it was announced he was going to have a go at throwing a ball over the high and mighty viaduct near the Lockwood ground. "I didn't go in for keeping cuttings but one thing I can remember is that particular afternoon," he said. "The Press was there and everybody wanted me to try before the game but I was Rastrick's pro and the game had to come first so they all had to wait.

"The last person to do it before me I was told was Jack Krum in 1935 when he had thrown a ball over three times straight. I managed it four times. We estimated the viaduct was 130 feet high and 30 feet across so the ball had to reach around 180 feet high to clear it."

Gloss still has the ball that was inscribed and his son Mark (who played professionally in the Bradford League) prepared a painting as a memento of the feat. "I particularly remember my days in the Dales Council. It was a brilliant time really," said Gloss who had to cut short his career in his early 40's after a serious illness had seen him 17 days in the intensive care ward at Otley Hospital. But what cricket lost, golf gained for Gloss went on to be a more than useful club golfer.

Matt's association with the Dales goes back to the early 90's and in the 1993 season along with Chris Taylor from nearby Pudsey St Lawrence, he won the Dales Council's Young Cricketer of the Year accolade. That season the 16-year-old Hoggard finished fourth in the league bowling averages bowling nearly 300 overs and taking 58 wickets at 10.68 apiece. (The two bowlers immediately above him in the averages were also Pudsey Congs players Brian Newall with 37 wickets at 9.73 and Mick Jones, 45 at 10.31).

"I owe a big debt to the Dales Council for getting me started and particularly to the people at Congs like Brian Newall, Derek Reason and Mick Hirst," said Hoggard. "They were great days for me and I'll always look back on them with pride. Fondest memory? I did the hat-trick in a six for 14 but I cannot recall now who it was against." (Congs v. Adel on 6 June, 1992 when he returned 18overs, 10mdns, 14runs 6 wkts at Fulneck in a nine wkt Congs win). He made his debut for Yorkshire three years later and was awarded his cap in 2000 helping the county to the County Championship title in 2001 and the Cheltenham and Gloucester Trophy at Lord's in 2002 when many regarded his five wickets for 65 every bit as important to the cause as Australian Matthew Elliott's unbeaten 128. But it has been on the international field where the Leeds born Matt has really made his name.

He got his first call up for England even before the award of his county cap in June, 2000. By then aged 23 and with a couple of winters playing for Free State in South Africa behind him, he was getting stronger and faster all the time but he admitted to be taken aback yet also delighted about being called into the squad for the 100th Test at Lord's. "Everybody strives to play for his country and I am glad my opportunity has arrived but getting the England call has come sooner than I expected," he said when selected.

Mike Atherton commented at the time that Hoggard was sitting as the ninth wicket unfolded with a stern look on his face broken only by the first sign of a smile when the scores were level and he realised he might not have to go in and win the game for England after all. England won by two wickets in what was one of the most exciting victories seen at headquarters.

But Matt's days at the crease at the death were to come. The following May he claimed his first Test wicket when he trapped Younis Khan lbw without playing at the ball finishing with England's best figures of three for 79 as Pakistan went to a massive 403 on day two at Old Trafford. It was enough to see the second Test looking for a result into the last session of the last day which turned out to be a sunlit evening at the famous old ground. The situation and conditions suited Pakistan and the upshot was that Matt had to go in as England collapsed to try and help Darren Gough save the day.

"I went down the wicket to him before I took strike and he just said 'Basically, don't get out' and with what seemed the whole Pakistan team breathing down my neck, I tried my best to just do what Darren had asked," he said surviving the last ball of four-wicket Saqlain's 47th over. But when Gough was caught in the covers off Waqar in the next over, Pakistan completed a 108 runs victory and England, after losing eight wickets for 60 runs after tea, had to make do with a series tied. But there was a happier outcome in Galle as 2003 was drawing to a close.

Matt found himself in a familiar situation this time facing the hungry Sri Lanka attack with Muralitharan on fire. The tricky wizard of spin had taken 7-46 in England's first innings and four in the second and, as Sri Lanka moved in for the kill, Matt had to go out to join Ashley Giles as England slumped to 208 for nine. But this time the pair hung on until poor light brought the curtain down and the match was drawn.

It is part of a tail-end fast bowler's lot to have to bat in a crisis but the real magical moments come more often than not with ball in hand. For Matt they included claiming the wicket of Sachin Tendulkar twice in the winter tour of 2001 of India and the seven for 63 he picked up against New Zealand in March, 2002 – the best figures for a Yorkshire cricketer playing for England since Chris Old's seven for 50 against Pakistan in 1975. He then saw Nathan Astle smack the fastest double hundred in Test history but plugged away to get the big hitter and see England home by 98 runs.

On August 2, 2002, he jumped into the top five bowlers in the world list on the back of decisive performances in England's series win over Sri Lanka and the first Test against India when he again picked up Tendulkar and then Sourav Ganguly in consecutive deliveries. Yet it was not all champagne days for the former Pudsey Congs speed merchant and, in fact, he went through a difficult run the following winter on the Ashes tour of Australia.

He bounced back, however, and in the final Test in Sydney, where Gough had claimed a hat-trick on the previous tour, he had a two in two deliveries in a four for 92 return which included the prize wicket of Australian captain Steve Waugh who had just hit 102 to equal Don Bradman's total of 29 Test 100s. But maybe Hoggard's biggest moment came just six months before the start of the Dales golden anniversary year opened in October, 2004.

In early April it was his turn for a Test match hat-trick – only the 10th time it had been achieved for England and the first since Gough's effort in Sydney. He knocked over Ramnaresh Sarwan, Shivnarine Chanderpaul and Ryan Hinds to set up the completion of England's first series win in the West Indies since the winter of 1967-68, finishing with 4-35 as the Windies crumbled to an all out second innings total of 94, England going on to an eight wicket victory in the Third Test in Barbados.

Nevertheless, in the middle of all this international excitement he still found time to show he had not forgotten his roots for when he was around and not away on tour he was on hand with the then Yorkshire cricket chairman and Dales Council president Geoff Cope to present the league's prizes at the annual dinner. Local lads make good.

Matthew Hoggard and our president Geoff Cope show off
Yorkshire's County Championship title winning trophy
at the league's annual dinner, 2001.

Chapter Five:
A First Team with a Jack of all trades in command.

LEADING the way as the Dales Council posts its first half century is the former Yorkshire and England bowler Geoff Cope. He took over as President of the league soon after the new Millennium arrived, the eighth to take on the role and the most readily recognised official the league has had.

But that is not to say the Dales Council has not been blessed with administrators of great presence and personality. The list of officers who have guided the league to its golden year overflows with cricket lovers of rare dedication.

They make up what can reasonably be termed the league's first team with one name standing out above all the rest, the father of the league Jack Shuttleworth. He was there from day one as the main voice behind the league's formation and in one capacity or another served it for more than 30 years.

He was a busy man with a ready and wicked smile and while he may not have been instantly recognisable on the international stage like today's leader he was nevertheless widely known in Yorkshire local cricket circles even though he never strayed too far from his beloved Esholt and Baildon.

In fact, he was associated with the cricket club at Esholt for 75 years as a scorer, player, captain, umpire, committee member, chairman and finally president and heavily involved with the Yorkshire Federation (Under 18) sides in the 1960s and 70s. But it was as Jack of all trades in the Dales Council that he made one of his biggest impacts.

He was the voice behind the birth of the league and was voted in as the league's first secretary when it was formed in the winter of 1955/1956. He was to continue in the office for a quarter of a century

left: The Dales chairman and treasurer, David Smith
centre: The Dales secretary Alan Wardle and past president Les Thompson.
right: The Dales Results/Fixture secretary Steve Raistrick.

before serving a further three years as the league treasurer following that with two years as president. No wonder then that he was the league's guest of honour at the 40th anniversary dinner a few months before he died at the age of 84 in February, 1996.

The stories about his passion for cricket, the league and Esholt, where, fittingly, he was president during the club's centenary year in 1995, are many. He was the man who would not take a no thank you when he was raising money for the game, especially by way of raffle tickets; he was always ready for a lift back up to his home of 59 years in Brantcliffe Drive, Baildon, where his children David, Anne and Graham were nightly called upon for nets on the lawn once school homework was done. "I remember, too, there was a strict rule that the telephone could not be used at home until after eight on Saturdays because the league results would be coming in until then," said his son David. That is a situation which still persists but nowadays it is at the home of Steve Raistrick, the league's Results and Fixtures secretary, who with secretary Alan Wardle and chairman/treasurer David Smith form the backbone of today's admin team. Wardle's reign goes back to 1987; Smith joined him four years later and Raistrick in 1995. The trio burn a great deal of midnight oil on behalf of cricket in the area and take great pride in seeing the Dales through to its major landmark.

Overseeing much of their tenure in office was Les Thompson, the Dales Council president who took the league into the new millennium to cap his 11 years in charge. Though now retired from a front line role he is still active for the league behind the scenes but he will be particularly remembered for his leadership through the nineties which saw a determined effort to increase the number of clubs in the league. "I saw it as a way to ensure the league survived at a time when other leagues were falling by the wayside," he said later.

"I've enjoyed my stint with the league of 21 years on the committee and 11 as president," he said responding to a standing ovation when he stepped down at the league's annual dinner in October, 2000. "I've done over 50 years in cricket since becoming a club secretary when I was 18 and enjoyed every minute of it but I think it's the right time to let someone else have a go. Since I took over as president the League has grown and now we have over 40 teams and four divisions.

"The last decade was one of progress for us despite league cricket's decline to a certain degree," said the veteran who played in the Leeds Wednesday Half Holiday League at 14 and was a founder member of the New Wortley club in the late 1960's where he was a useful opening batsman and wicketkeeper.

For Thompson now read Cope but between them and Shutt there have been more than enough officers to make-up several pretty useful teams both on and off the field. At the outset, Shutt was joined by another Esholt player in Stan Hughes who was the league's first treasurer; a role he held for 18 years, an innings and half in itself.

The league's first president was Kenneth Hodgson who held office for the first eight formative years before being succeeded by John Whiteley, one of the original committee members from the Pool Paper Mills club who is still one of the league's vice-presidents. After a decade at the helm he handed over the office to Stan Handford, the Otley secretary for 21 years, then in 1979 Peter Marsh from Pudsey Congs became the league's fourth president before Shutt stepped in.

Stan Hughes, the league's first treasurer

John Whiteley

Long serving umpire Jack Toothill.

Colin Bentley

But the list of officers and committeemen is packed with names that evoke many memories. Cyril Chapman, the Bramley official and umpire, Jack Shutt's brother Ralph, Les Heaton, the Esholt batsman, umpire Jack Toothill, Colin Bentley, Ron Mackenzie, fellow scribe John Morgan, who provided the league with its Young Cricketer and Umpires awards via the Yorkshire Evening Post, and that man of many wickets Derek Hawley, from Otley, who was treasurer for seven years in the 1970's, are just a few. But there is one other name which jumps out – that of David Pearce.

He was an extraordinary player and administrator. The league's top run scorer, a canny spin bowler, great close in fielder, captain of both his club sides and the league side and for four years in the 1980's the league president, he was a man of many parts. Both on and off the field he was a major player among those who have carried the league through to its 50 year landmark. A list of all the major players is a dangerous item because there is always someone left out who should be included – or who thinks he/she should be mentioned. But this is as near complete as seems possible.

The four/five major offices have been filled as follows:

President.	Secretary.	Treasurer.	Fixture/ Results Sec.
C.K. Hodgson. (1955-63)	J. Shuttleworth. (1955-80)	G.S. Hughes. (1955-73)	J. Marshall. (1987)
J.H. Whiteley. (1964-73)	S.M. Swallow. (1981-84)	D.R. Hawley. (1974-80)	D.A. Young. (1988)
S. Handford. (1974-78)	J. Marshall. (1985-86)	J. Shuttleworth. (1981-83)	L. Thompson. (1989-92)
P. Marsh. (1979-83)	A. Wardle. (1987-)	P.G. Richardson. (1984-90)	P. Dews. (1993-94)
J. Shuttleworth. (1984-85)		D. Smith. (1991-)	S. Raistrick. (1995-)
D. Pearce. (1986-89)			
L. Thompson. (1990-00)			
G. Cope. (2001-)			

The league introduced a new office of chairman from 2001. David Smith was elected and now combines the appointment with that of treasurer.

Vice Presidents: A.L. Heaton, G.S. Hughes, J.H. Whiteley, G. Griffiths, C. Bentley, R. Mackenzie, J. Morgan, D.Smith.

Auditor: R. Mackenzie.   **Solicitor:** M. Burns.

Life Members: M. Cryer, S. Handford, D. Clark, D.R.Hawley, P. Richardson, M. Franks, G. Hewitt, G.S. Hughes, P. Marsh, L. Thompson, S.M. Swallow, J.H. Whiteley, L. Heaton, M. Wright.

AT THE DOUBLE......No 1.

IN our AT THE DOUBLE feature national/county/local personalities write specially for the Dales Council. Their articles appear alongside profiles on some of the leading Dales Council cricketers of the league's first half century. The opening partnership focuses on the former Yorkshire, Lincolnshire and England offspinner Geoff Cope who, incidentally, started his league cricket career as an 11-year-old in the Dales Council and is now Operations Director at the Yorkshire County Cricket Club and the Dales Council league's president. He opens alongside the Dales Council's leading run scorer and a former league president, the late David Pearce.

They wrapped me in cotton wool

Says the former Yorkshire, Lincolnshire and England off-spinner Geoff Cope who is now the Operations Director at the Yorkshire County Cricket Club – and the President of the Dales Council.

IT took me no time at all to accept the invitation to become the president of the Dales Council, it was a great honour to be asked and I felt it was an opportunity to help something that means a lot to me. But to get down to grass roots of the matter, I took it on first and foremost for Ernest Smelt and Norman England and second for the Leeds Zingari cricket club.

You see that's where it all began for me from a cricketing point of view – guided in particular by Mr Smelt, who sadly is no longer with us, and on the field by Mr England. They were my mentors though I could add a few other names and probably should mention Arthur Swallow and Ken Fletcher. They wrapped me in cotton wool and started my cricket life as an 11-year-old in the Dales Council in the proper way. I cannot emphasise enough how much I have always felt that what they did for me amounts, in my view, to be the perfect example of how a youngster coming into an

Geoff Cope.

David Pearce.

established senior side should be brought along – I cannot imagine many who would adopt someone like they did.

Mr Smelt, who played for Durham earlier in his cricket career, was my headmaster at Manston junior school and he taught me the basics of cricket and life. He always insisted on calling me Geoffrey ('That's your proper name, lad') and he was a stickler when it came to doing things the right way, which included always turning up for fixtures with a full team.

I have one fond memory of him coming along to a game with his wife after he had retired (I think Zingari played at Crompark that day). We had turned up with 10 men and to him that was a cardinal sin, it was the first time it had happened.

He had a tea appointment which he could not break but he said 'Geoffrey, go to my car and please bring me my bat and pads'. He duly opened the innings for us wearing brown trousers, a green shirt and pumps and hit the perfect 60-plus out of 87 but at 5.20pm said 'I'm sorry but I really have to leave you now and join my wife' as he chipped a ball to a surprised fieldsman. It was the best innings I ever saw.

Memories of those days with the Dales are rich, though. As a 10-year-old, I'd already had a 10-for helping our school win the Leeds Schools under 11 final before I got my first chance to play for Zingari at Ives Sports. That would be in 1958 when I'd be 11. I remember I got some wickets and when I was 12 or 13, I managed a four wickets in four balls spell at Netherfield.

They were wonderful times but the seasoned cricketers around me never let me get into deep water. Mr England was a lecturer at Leeds College and our wicketkeeper and he would carry mints in his pocket on the field and promise me one if I could really spin the ball or even for a wicket or two. But they never put pressure on me at Zingari. In fact, Mr Smelt would only allow me to play in the fixtures that he believed were right for me at the time.

We had Jack Walkington who played for Hunslet and Great Britain at Rugby League as our president, John Sharpe who always bowled with his cap on and sleeves rolled down (he was approaching 60 and to my young eyes looked 90) and Des Finn, a batsman of some quality among the players in a team mainly made up of college and school teachers. They were a special breed and definitely put me on the right road long before it was time to move on to the Leeds club in the Yorkshire Council, Yorkshire and ultimately England. Happy, happy days.

Geoff Cope, October, 2004.

At the Double partner..............David Pearce

The man who hit a mountain size number of runs.

DAVID PEARCE was not the kind of cricketer to mess about. He was a tough customer; a dedicated batsman, bowler, fieldsman – and winner.

He loved cricket and his teams. The Dales Council Handbook is littered with the records either he achieved or players who played alongside him managed. Team-mates Kenny Booth, Arnie Beech and Roy Webster all figure strongly alongside the mountain of runs down to Pearce. His 11,809 total in competitive Dales games stands alone; 158 of those runs coming in the record breaking second wicket stand with Tony Metcalfe for Smiths against Farnley Estate in May, 1977, a partnership record which stood for 26 years.

"If you were playing against him he was a right sod but I can tell you he was one of the best cricketers I've known and it was great to be on his side. His heart and soul was steeped in the game, he was Mr Smiths Sports, a great organiser and if he had been able to run – he had a bad knee – he would have got many more runs to add to his all-time Dales scoring record," said Metcalfe.

Metcalfe, father of the former Yorkshire batsman Ashley Metcalfe, remembers that record-breaking stand of more than a quarter of a century ago as though it was yesterday. He said: "He smashed his way to 150 odd while I pushed my way to 49 and then a little beyond. If there had been sixes then the stand would have been worth many more, in fact had there been sixes in Dales cricket for most of the time he was playing his run aggregate would have been phenomenal – he was a big, heavy man who hit the ball a long, long way."

Record breaking wicketkeeper Webster, who enjoyed some great times with Pearce at Smiths, was in awe of his captain's batting skill. "In all the time I played I never saw any to match him when it came to hitting boundaries. He hit many more than anyone I knew and had he been able to run, well, who knows how many more runs he would have finished with," said Webster.

I can vouch for the power and timing Pearce employed at the crease. I recall him once lifting one of my deliveries over my head, over the long on boundary and way out of the field at the Coal Hill Lane ground at Rodley, which at the time was about the longest boundary in the area. I must have done something right with Esholt that day in the late sixties though because soon afterwards the invitation came along to join what was becoming a powerful Smiths side under his leadership.

Bowling to him always presented a rare challenge but batting against him and his side was something else. He would use the bowler he knew you did not care for and field right on the bat end; a kind of Dales Council version of Brian Close and there was no question of doing the gentlemanly thing if you killed the ball at your feet when batting and tried to bend down and hand it over. The stern faced Smiths captain would immediately growl: "Leave it. Don't touch that ball," and you knew he was playing for keeps. He was more than a bit different, too, when he bowled himself. It was slow and looked innocuous enough from the pavilion but out there facing him (as his regular appearances in the league bowling averages underlines) it was another matter – for instance, if there was little happening he would go for the unexpected and sometimes bowl from a yard or so backward of the umpire.

He was always a deep thinker about the game. And left little to chance when it came to organising his forces. I remember when I was picked to play under his captaincy in the league side being astonished a couple of days before the game to get a letter from him detailing where I would be fielding for any one particularly bowler, when I was likely to bowl, the position I was likely to go in – and when we played I found the rest of the team had also had their written instructions and by and large he stuck to his game plan.

He was a rare servant for the Smiths and Farsley Celtic clubs and the league and eventually became its president. There is no doubt that he left an indelible mark on all those who played with and against him and on the Dales Council.

The Smiths Sports 1973 Cup winning side.
Back row left to right: Margaret Foster (scorer), L. Herbert, A. Beech, B. Rhodes,
A. Longley, I. Parker, B. Foster;
Front row: B. Cooke, K. Booth, C. Janney, D. Pearce (capt)., K. Kay.

Chapter Six
1956 to 1965.
Green Lane dominate the first decade

WITH a successful opening season behind it, the Dales Council settled down to a future which was to fulfil most of the dreams of the men who had launched the new league with the first champions, Green Lane, going on to become the team to beat for much of the first decade.

It was a time when standards were set, a time upon which a golden anniversary has been built. But, initially, it was a time that belonged to Green Lane with four of the first six league championships and three of the first four cup titles going to the club, a run that included the first double winning season in 1960.

Malcolm Dibb, who finished fifth in the league batting averages in the opening campaign of **1956**, and Gloss Sample were, perhaps, the players who stood out for Green Lane in those early days. But to underline the club's strength in depth, two of Green Lane's second team, which finished as runners-up to Wilson and Mathiesons in the 2nd X1's competition in that first season, batsman B. Lilley and bowler F. Hudson, finished second and top, respectively, in the league second team averages.

Top of the second team batting averages in 1956, incidentally, was Wilson and Mathiesons' Pete Seaman who finished their title winning campaign with his top score, a splendid unbeaten century in their home game with Otley Wesley on September 1. By coincidence, his partner, J. Lawrence, had started the season with his highest score – he opened against Esholt on April 28 and made 64 before being the last man out.

Archie Carrick, whose son Phil played in the Dales long before his call up to the Bradford League and the county side, was top batsman of 1956 playing in a Smiths Sports side which often saw the well loved former Rugby League referee Matt Coates among his team-mates. Geoff Milner (Crompark), Sample and R. Lowis (David Browns Tractors) took the first three places in the top bowlers list, all three turning in an average of below 6.

The **1957** season was special for Crompark, the only club among the league's original 18 members to survive every season of the golden 50. With International Harvesters, Wilson and Mathiesons and Green Lane hard on their heels they went to the title on the back of 17 victories in 21 games losing fewer (two) games than any other side in the competition.

It was a performance the club have never been able to emulate over the years despite some notable efforts in the lower divisions, a performance that saw two of the side claim the top batsman and top bowler prizes for the season. Derek Pinder's high point in a season in which he hit a record 520 runs at an average of 57.7 was an unbeaten 111 while Milner, a giant of an opening bowler at around 6ft. 6ins, repeated his league bowling prize winning effort of the opening season with another campaign's average of exactly 5 – his 48 wickets coming from 105 overs.

George Stocks, with almost 400 runs at an average of 23.11, finished just behind Pinder in the club's batting list and seventh in the league list, another top performer in a season which even opened on a memorable note for the club. Their first game was at Netherfield Sports and after hitting 161, Crompark then whipped out their neighbours for a record low score for first teams of just 10 with Derek Nicholson capturing six wickets for three runs. But 1957 was not all about the exploits of Crompark and its players.

That man Sample, inevitably, weighed in with the first ten wicket haul when Ross Mills batsmen had to suffer, the Green Lane all-rounder finishing with 10 for 28 as the Mills side were shot out for 52 chasing 132. And Smith's bowler Gerald Hardaker took nine Otley Mills wickets for a mere eight runs as bowlers made their mark in that campaign.

There was the growing talent of Malcolm Franks emerging, too. The Esholt all-rounder, who had made his debut for the club in the Wharfedale League as a 16-year-old in the early 1950s, finished in eighth place in the league's batting averages and sixth in the bowling list, an effort which included the league's new highest individual score of 129 hit on the last day of August against Tong Park and a seven for 11 effort against the same side the previous week.

The century represented the lion's share of a league record fourth wicket stand which has turned out to be the most enduring of any of the highest partnerships for any wicket in the league's history, Franks sharing that special moment of glory with his captain, Ralph Shuttleworth.

"I can remember we were eight for three when I went in to join Ralph. We just seemed to settle

Crompark's championship winning side of 1957.
Back row left to right: S. Hudson, D. Newell, D. Nicholson, G. Milner, scorer,
Alan Baxter, N. Bickley, D. McNare.
Front row: H. Dean, G. Stocks, D. Pinder (capt)., G. Hewitt, B. Exley.

in together and I think he made 50-odd as the stand just grew and grew," said Franks more than 45 years later. "It was a good time for me, I'd had a few wickets against the same side only a week before so they must have really loved me at the time."

But, of course, Green Lane could not be kept out of the picture and they duly became the first winners of the Pool Paper Mills Cup in that second campaign, the trophy having been donated by executive committee man and PPM chief John Whiteley in remembrance of his father. And in the **1958** season Green Lane again hit the spotlight.

They roared to their second league title five points clear of International Harvesters with their batsman Denis Exley grabbing the league batting prize with an average of marginally under 50. Harvesters' S. Farquason, with 65 wickets at 5.63 apiece including one return of nine for 20 was the top bowler with Pool Paper Mills taking the cup home for the first time. In the second teams competition, runners-up International Harvesters A side went to Esholt for their penultimate fixture and flattened them, A. James returning figures of six overs, five maidens, one run and eight wickets as Esholt managed just seven runs.

But Esholt's first eleven turned out to be top dogs in **1959**. They edged beyond Green Lane by a point to win what was to be the first of their five league championships by winning 14 games - more than any other side in Section A. There were two points for a tie that season, Esholt's tied game giving them that extra point which saw them over the winning line. Green Lane could not be kept from the silverware though for they took the Pool Paper Mills Cup for a second time and their second team romped away with the second teams' title. Pool Paper Mills lifted the highest score by any

Green Lane's all-conquering side of 1958/59.
Back row left to right: Roy Tillotson (scorer), J. Driver, G. Sample, B. Graham,
K. Yeadon, B. Coultas.
Front row: N. Cousins, M. Dibb, A. Kay (capt), R. Walker, G. Marshall, D. Exley

eleven when they hit 281 for seven off the Ives Sports attack in mid May while P Hargreaves of Wilson and Mathiesons became the second bowler after Sample to pick up a ten wicket haul, his victims costing him 36 runs and Green Lane's opening pair Dibb and C. Denison posted a new record first wicket partnership of 144 against Ross Mills.

Two new highest partnership records helped Esholt's run to the title, too: Ernest Barker and Terry Dudley put on 88 for the eighth wicket against Laisterdyke and W. Cox and John Taylor had a 55 run last wicket stand against Green Lane. But it was back to title winning ways again in **1960** with a vengeance by Green Lane.

They swept to the first League and Cup double in style. After claiming the cup they went on to pick up the league title six points ahead of Smiths Sports with Gerald Marshall and Edward Lennon creating a new fifth wicket record with their unbeaten stand of 101 against Crompark.

Sowerby Bridge marked their final campaign in the league by taking the B Section title by a five point margin over Leeds Zingari while the second teams' title was taken by English Electric who finished 10 points ahead of Green Lane. It turned out to be a memorable season, too, for S. Farquason who finished sixth in the league batting averages and second in the bowling averages with 73 wickets, which included a four in four deliveries spell. The International Harvesters' all-rounder also shared in a first wicket partnership of 198 with A Walker in a cup game against English Electric, Harvesters going on to make 227 for 3 in just 30 overs.

The **1961** season marked the end of Green Lane's first spell in the Dales. They finished as they started as champions, taking the title with an eight point advantage over International Harvesters who had handsome consolation by winning the cup. The Lane's two leading bowlers L. Roberts and Peter Forkin picked up 129 wickets between them in finishing second and third respectively in the bowling averages but it was J.Bartle's efforts which really caught the eye. The Harvesters' all-rounder topped the bowlers' list with 45 wickets at an average of 5.09 and was third in the batting averages.

There was a third all ten wickets performance, too, when Leeds Zingari's John Sharpe also managed to perform the hat-trick in his 10 for 23 haul in mid May against Smiths Sports but the accolade of club of the season had to go to Bramley Sports.

They bounced back from relegation in 1960 to win the B Section by nine clear points while their second team took the second teams title by a similar margin. Tony Imeson's 87 B Section wickets left him with a new record average. He bowled 198 overs, 82 maidens, conceded just 328 runs to

Gerald Hardaker.

Harry Dean.

Derek Ellsworth.

leave him with the league's lowest season's bowling average of an incredible 3.77. On the same day, May 13, that Sharpe was destroying Smiths, Imeson was running riot against Thos. Waides taking seven for seven and he finished off the season with a seven for eight return against Netherfield.

The Dales reverted to one first teams division and one second teams division in **1962** with Esholt and English Electric the respective champions. Franks finished ninth in the league batting list and sixth in the bowling averages in Esholt's title run with their opening bowler Jack Walker eighth in the list with 48 wickets at an average of 7.85.

One remarkable return, however, was managed by P. Jones of Ives Sports in June when he picked up five wickets against Reuben Gaunts without conceding a run. Gaunts did make their mark with their only Dales title that season though when they won the cup. The averages, however, were dominated by Bramley Sports players with W. Dacre and L. Smith topping the first and second team bowling lists and Derek Elsworth taking the second teams batting prize.

The 1963 and 1964 seasons saw the Dales reduced to fewer teams and clubs than at any time in the league's history, 13 clubs and 17 teams in 1963 and 12 clubs providing 16 teams the following season. In **1963** first and second elevens competed in the same division with the Otley Mills "A" side taking the title and the Bramley Sports demon bowler Imeson claiming the bowling prize with 62 wickets at a cost of 4.98 runs apiece. And he was quickly into his stride too – on the second Saturday of the season playing against Reuben Gaunts he underpinned a 54 run win when he claimed all 10 wickets for 16 runs off thirteen overs.

Crompark's Harry Dean, who was later to spend several successful seasons with Esholt, was a popular winner of the batting title with an average of 34.23 from 17 visits to the crease. It was also the start of an unprecedented run in the Pool Paper Mills Cup by Wilson and Mathiesons, the first of a hat-trick of wins in the competition.

The **1964** campaign saw two divisions return with eight teams in Section A and eight in Section B. Otley Mills made it a league title double while Section B also went the Otley way, this time Otley Wesley making their mark. Mills took the title by the huge margin of 17 points from Ives Sports while Wesley were five points clear of Netherfield. Mills players B. Bolton and K. Gawtry carried off the league batting and bowling awards.

The first decade came to an end with the Dales in a slightly better position in numbers. In **1965** there were 14 clubs and 19 teams involved, a situation, which, over the following years was, apart from the odd setback, to see the league grow and grow in numbers. The decade closed with Esholt as champions and league newcomers Holbeck Bethel winning promotion from the B Section as champions with 50 points. Bolton followed his batting prize success of 1964 by repeating the feat while the burly Otley Wesley bowler Francis Quinn, who was to claim over a 1,000 wickets in the Dales with his quick cutters off a short run up, collected the bowling award with 47 wickets costing a straight six runs apiece.

Wesley's ground was out on Wharfe Meadows overlooking the River Wharfe back then. The league handbook suggested to get there players should take a bus to Otley, go down Bridge Street, over River Bridge, turn right through the Park and turn left past the first tennis courts; continue up through the woods. That amounted to a bit of a trek with cricket bags and other gear.

But that was the norm for many Saturday afternoon cricketers at the time for few had their own transport, everything and everyone piled onto the local bus. It may be commonplace nowadays to pick up a lift from a team-mate: there is always someone with his or her own wheels but in 1965 it was a different story.

Franks unlocked this point with a tale about Esholt's game at Netherfield on May 1 that year. For the record, May 1, 1965, was the day Leeds United finally made it to Wembley for the first time. They met Liverpool in the F A Cup final going down 2-1 after extra-time having missed the League title in their first season back in the top division by 0.686 of a goal, statistics which underline the intense interest in the Elland Road side at the time.

"I remember we were playing at Netherfield (not Wesley by any means in terms of walking distance to the ground yet still not on the beaten track)," said Franks. "It was Cup Final day and we were pretty desperate to watch the game at Wembley on tele but, of course, cricket had to come first despite Leeds being in their first final and the wonderful season they had had on the football field.

"However, we managed to whip out Netherfield for 8 (they had eight men) and I opened with Billy Foster who promptly hit three fours in the first four deliveries and we were on our way. But it was not just a matter of piling all the pads and bats into our own vehicles and racing off home to try and catch what was left of the final.

"There were no cars then among our lot so we had to leg it with all our gear to the nearest bus stop at the White Cross Hotel at Guiseley about half a mile away. But it must have been our day for a bus came nearly straight away and when we got down to Shipley there was another ready to pull out for Wrose where Terry Naylor and a couple of the other lads were wanting to join me at our house to watch the game.

"It was amazing how the buses fitted together that day. We could hardly have done much better with a car but nevertheless we were a breathless lot when we sat down in front of that tele...... just in time as Leeds went out for the second half."

With the way the final went, he would not be drawn on whether all that huffing and puffing had been worth it. But, in fact, Esholt's match at Netherfield was the only one played in the Dales Council that Saturday. The following Wednesday the Shipley Times and Express reported: "An innovation for the league was that clubs were allowed to play their matches on Sunday due to the interest in the F A Cup final and the only game played on Saturday was at Netherfield where Esholt were the visitors. Evidently the Netherfield players were more Cup final minded for they had only eight players."

The report went on to record the all out for eight scoreline calling it "the all time low score" but, of course, it did not find a definitive place in the record book because Netherfield had not fielded 11 men. There would be other occasions when single figure scores would be made by sides with fewer than11 players though two second teams would eventually fall for just six runs when fielding a full eleven to find unwanted spots in the league's records list.

But back to the Netherfield game. For the stats., it should be mentioned that Bill Mason, with 4-1, and Jack Walker, 3-6, did the damage. It was an afternoon that would launch Esholt to much bigger things for, fittingly, as one of the original 18 clubs, they went on to round off the league's first decade in pole position.

THE CHAMPIONS AND CUP WINNERS, DECADE BY DECADE

The top three in each division and their records plus the Cup winners....the first decade, 1956-65.

League	Winners (Win 3pts, Tie 2pts, Draw 1pt)	P.	W.	L.	D.	Pts.	Year	Pool P M Cup	Cawthorne Cup
1st X1s	Green Lane	21	17	2	2	53	1956		
	Wilson & Mathiesons	21	14	3	4	46			
	Tong Park	21	12	4	5	41			
2nd X1s	Wilson & Mathiesons	20	14	3	3	45			
	Green Lane	20	13	3	4	43			
	Esholt	20	8	9	3	27			
1st X1s	Crompark	21	17	2	2	53	1957	Green Lane	
	International Harvesters	21	15	3	3	48			
	Wilson & Mathiesons	21	15	3	3	48			
2nd X1s	Wilson & Mathiesons	20	12	5	3	41			
	Green Lane	20	11	8	1	34			
	Leeds Zingari	20	10	6	4	34			
Sec A	Green Lane	22	14	2	6	48	1958	Pool Paper Mills	
	International Harvesters	22	13	5	4	43			
	Crompark	22	12	5	5	41			
Sec B	Otley Mills	18	15	0	3	48			
	Reuben Gaunts	18	11	2	5	38			
	Netherfield Sports	18	8	6	4	28			
2nd X1s	Wilson & Mathiesons	18	11	1	6	39			
	International Harvesters	18	11	3	4	37			
	English Electric	18	8	7	3	27			

Notes:

League games format:
1956-1967: Time games: Start 2.45pm, end 7.30pm.
1968-1971: 40 overs.
1972 onwards: 45 overs.

Cup competitions:
Pool Paper Mills Cup: from 1957.
Cawthorne Cup: from 1961.

Boundaries:
Fours only 1956-1977.
Fours & Sixes 1978 onwards

League	Winners	P.	W.	L.	D.	Pts.	Year	Pool P M Cup	Cawthorne Cup
Sec A	Esholt (* 2pts for tie)	22	14	5	3*	46	**1959**	Green Lane	
	Green Lane	22	13	4	5*	45			
	English Electric	22	13	5	3	42			
Sec B	Bramley Sports	21	14	5	2	44			
	Smiths, Rodley	21	13	5	3*	43			
	Leeds Zingari	21	13	6	2	41			
2nd X1s	Green Lane	18	14	2	2	44			
	English Electric	18	13	5	0	39			
	Pool Paper Mills	18	11	6	1	34			
Sec A	Green Lane	22	14	4	4	46	**1960**	Green Lane	
	Smiths, Rodley	22	12	6	4	40			
	Otley Mills	22	11	5	6	39			
Sec B	Sowerby Bridge	22	13	5	4	43			
	Leeds Zing. (*2pts for tie)	22	11	7	4*	38			
	Wilson & Mathiesons	22	11	6	5	38			
2nd X1s	English Electric	20	18	1	1	55			
	Green Lane	20	15	5	0	45			
	Esholt	20	10	7	3	33			
Sec A	Green Lane	22	16	1	5	53	**1961**	Int. Harvesters	English Electric
	International Harvesters	22	13	3	6	45			
	Esholt	22	11	4	7	40			
Sec B	Bramley Sports	22	15	1	6	51			
	Eng Elect. (*2pts for tie)	22	10	1	11*	42			
	Ives Sports	22	11	5	6*	40			

League	Winners	P.	W.	L.	D.	Pts.	Year	Pool P M Cup	Cawthorne Cup
2nd X1s	Bramley Sports	18	14	1	3	45			
	English Electric	18	11	4	3	36			
	Green Lane	18	10	4	4	34			
1st X1s	Esholt	20	15	2	3	48	1962	Reuben Gaunts	English Electric
	Bramley Sports	20	14	3	3	45			
	International Harvesters	20	13	4	3	42			
2nd X1s	English Electric	16	13	3	0	39			
	Otley Mills	16	12	4	0	36			
	Bramley Sports	16	11	3	2	35			
1st X1s	Otley Mills "A" (*2pts-tie)	20	14	3	3*	46	1963	Wil. & Math's	
	Ives Sports	20	13	4	3	42			
	R. Gaunt (# inc. 2 ties)	20	11	3	6#	41			
Sec A	Otley Mills	21	14	0	7	49	1964	Wil. & Math's	Otley Mills
	Ives Spts. (*2pts for tie)	21	8	6	7*	32			
	Esholt	21	9	9	3	30			
Sec B	Otley Wesley	21	13	4	4	43			
	Netherfield	21	11	5	5	38			
	Turner Sports	21	11	5	5	38			
Sec A	Esholt	22	12	1	9	45	1965	Wil. & Math's	Holbeck Bethel
	Otley Mills	22	12	2	8	44			
	Ives Sports	22	12	3	7	43			
Sec B	Holbeck Bethel	20	16	2	2	50			
	Turner Sports	20	15	2	3	48			
	Pool Paper Mills	20	10	7	3	33			

AN AVERAGE VIEW

Season by season leaders of the averages ~ the first decade, 1956–65.

The Batsmen   The Bowlers

League	Name/Club	Ins.	NO	H.Sc n.o.*	Rns.	Av.	Year	Name/Club	Ovs.	Mdn	Rns.	Wks.	Av.
1st X1s	A. Carrick, Smiths	14	4	47*	317	31.7	1956	G. Milner, Crompark	94	37	160	32	5
	W. Russell, W&M	16	0	81	476	29.8		G. Sample, Green Lane	251	63	605	111	5.5
	D. Pearce, Smiths Sp	15	3	60*	375	29.8		R. Lowis, David Brown	93	28	189	32	5.9
	J. Otty, P.P.M.	13	1	84*	342	28.5		W. Dacre, Smiths Sp	193	56	342	55	6.2
	M. Dibb, Green Lane	16	1	71	389	25.9		P. Forkin, Ives Sp	173	62	362	57	6.4
	G. Sample, Green Lane	18	3	69	367	24.5		W. Russell, W&M	247	79	512	80	6.4
2nd X1s	P G Seaman, W&M	12	1	104*	318	28.9		F A Hudson, Green L.	95	19	238	43	5.5
	B. Lilley, Green Lane	15	3	39	265	22.1		J. Crossland, W&M	115	44	304	49	6.2
	G. Petch, W&M	15	3	45*	229	19.1		G. Petch, W&M	177	55	367	57	6.4
1st X1s	D Pinder, Crompark	15	6	111*	520	57.7	1957	G Milner, Crompark	105	30	240	48	5
	W. Russell, W&M	18	5	60	463	33.5		N. Hartley, Int. Harv.	258	86	466	80	5.8
	G. Sample, Green Lane	18	3	77	418	27.9		H. Wigglesworth, W&M	71	18	182	31	5.9
	M. Dibb, Green Lane	17	1	81	442	27.6		J. Driver, Green Lane	112	30	255	43	5.9
	R. Shuttleworth, Esholt	18	3	68*	409	27.3		D. Jagger, Esholt	113	39	214	36	5.9
	G. Marshall, Green Ln.	16	5	62	284	25.8		M. Franks, Esholt	120	47	240	39	6.2
2nd X1s	L Greenhall, W&M	13	7	57*	241	40.2		P Robertson, Nether'ld	91	26	180	36	5
	E. Thornborrow, Esholt	15	5	57	241	24.1		J. Crossland, W&M	118	34	225	34	6.6
	G. Adams, W&M	16	3	45	306	23.5		S. Danskin, Otley Wes.	86	22	208	30	6.9

League	Name/Club	Ins.	NO	H.Sc	Rns.	Av.	Year	Name/Club	Ovs.	Mdn	Rns.	Wks.	Av.
Sec. A.	D Exley, Green Lane	12	8	53*	198	49.5	1958	S Farquason, Int. H.	184	49	311	65	5.6
	D. Pinder, Crompark.	15	7	100*	366	45.8		D. Carter, English Elec.	160	61	285	50	5.7
	G. Marshall, Green Ln.	17	7	117*	339	33.9		L. Morant, W&M	212	80	316	52	6.1
	M. Dibb, Green Lane	18	0	64	504	28		L. Roberts, Green Lane	139	48	230	37	6.2
	R. Patch, Tong Park	13	1	75	240	20		J. Driver, Green Lane	107	23	262	41	6.4
	K. Bolton, Laisterdyke	18	3	66*	296	19.8		G. Perkins, P.M.M.	162	65	244	38	6.4
Sec. B.	G Bland, Otley Mills	12	7	80	242	48.4		T W Hudson, R. Gaunts	233	91	335	76	4.4
	J. Holdsworth, R. Gaunt	16	5	78*	351	31.9		B. Gawtry, Otley Mills	178	49	340	55	6.2
	J. Hamer, Otley Mills	16	3	67*	385	29.6		T. Cropper, R. Gaunts	169	70	258	38	6.7
2nd X1s	J Walton, W&M	10	1	100*	259	28.6		P Renton, Eng. Elec.	61	20	114	27	3.9
	R. Temple, Netherfield	15	2	72*	299	23		L. Greenhall, W&M	105	29	184	37	5
	G. Adams, W&M	12	2	65*	197	19.7		H. Kay, Int. H.	84	25	186	36	5.2
Sec. A	M. Dibb, Green Lane	20	3	101*	716	42.1	1959	D Harkness, Eng. El.	101	34	190	32	5.9
	J. Holdsworth, R. Gaunt	18	2	60	489	30.6		S. Farquason, Int. Harv.	215	38	566	77	7.4
	D, North, Ross Mills	19	0	116	494	26		E. Goldthorpe, Esholt	158	35	349	47	7.4
	K. Bolton, Laisterdyke	17	2	72	384	25.6		N. Hartley, Int. Harv.	183	46	429	57	7.5
	D. Nicholson, Crompark	19	0	66	484	25.5		J. Taylor, Esholt	114	39	238	31	7.7
	G. Bland, Otley Mills	21	2	62	463	24.4		J. Inman, P.P.M.	171	40	463	60	7.7

League	Name/Club	Ins.	NO	H.Sc	Rns.	Av.	Year	Name/Club	Ovs.	Mdn	Rns.	Wks.	Av.
Sec. B	N England, Lds. Zingari	18	3	82*	524	34.9		T Thorpe, Smiths Sp.	67	13	169	26	6.5
	J. Lawrence, W&M	18	2	130*	468	29.3		W. Dacre, Smiths Sp.	286	108	523	79	6.6
	S. Firth, Illingworth	12	0	92	310	25.6		E. Brown, Bramley Sp.	153	44	349	49	7.1
2nd X1s	K Yeadon, Green Lane	12	4	40	278	34.8		C. Long, Green Lane	83	30	151	27	5.6
	K. Wilkinson, P.P.M.	14	4	64*	339	33.9		J. Chew, Green Lane	118	39	209	35	6
	G. Soden, Eng. Elec.	13	3	47	253	25.3		H. Padgett, Int. Harv.	116	39	223	37	6
Sec. A	G Bland, Otley Mills	19	8	61*	422	38.4	1960	G Stuart, Green Lane	144	46	269	44	6.1
	B. Bolton, P.P.M.	19	8	69*	356	32.4		S. Farquason, Int. Harv.	201	57	459	73	6.3
	G. Marshall, Green La.	20	5	102*	463	30.9		E. Goldthorpe, Esholt.	114	29	298	42	7.1
	D. Pearce, Smiths Sp.	13	2	66	319	27.2		P. Hey, Esholt.	153	47	384	54	7.1
	R. Farquason, Int. Harv.	12	0	87	316	26.3		W. Dacre, Smiths Sp	225	63	554	75	7.4
	S. Farquason, Int. Harv.	18	1	106	436	25.6		T.W. Hudson, R.Gaunt	239	60	526	69	7.6
Sec. B	E Smelt, Lds. Zingari	11	4	51	267	38.1		J Sharpe, Lds Zingari	324	94	623	83	7.5
	P. Seaman, W&M	12	2	74*	309	30.9		R. Haigh, Ives Sports	89	23	246	31	7.9
	D. Knapton, W&M	19	3	61	492	30.8		F. Quinn, Otley Wesley	117	31	300	35	8.6
2nd X1s	B Graham, Green Lane	12	2	119*	289	28.9		J Chew, Green Lane	100	28	228	39	5.9
	J. Robinson, Esholt	16	3	77	335	25.8		T. Brooks, Green Lane	91	31	155	26	6
	R. Walker, Green Lane	14	2	52*	283	23.6		N. Mattocks, Int. Harv.	84	18	191	31	6.2

Year	Name/Club	Ovs.	Mdn	Rns.	Wks.	Av.
1961	J Bartle, Int. H.	156	63	229	45	5.1
	L. Roberts, Green Lane	188	71	299	57	5.2
	P. Forkin, Green Lane	232	85	410	72	5.7
	W. Dacre, Smiths Sp.	265	92	488	78	6.3
	J. Sharpe, Lds. Zingari	147	52	313	45	6.8
	B. Smailes, R. Gaunts	172	60	362	49	7.4
	A. Imeson, Bramley Sp	198	82	328	87	3.8
	D. Carter, Eng. Elec.	146	56	256	47	5.4
	D. Holmes, Ives Sports	187	59	367	64	5.7
	C Moores, Eng. Elec.	75	23	153	37	4.1
	G. Withers, Bramley Sp	78	27	130	28	4.6
	T. Vickerman, Esholt	88	28	176	33	5.3
1962	W Dacre, Bramley Sp.	102	48	189	32	5.9
	T.W. Hudson, R Gaunts	171	51	376	58	6.5
	A. Imeson, Bram. Sp.	171	51	376	58	6.5
	M. Cryer, P.P.M.	197	54	380	54	7
	D. Holmes, Ives Sports	214	54	426	60	7.1
	M. Franks, Esholt	134	45	260	35	7.4

League	Name/Club	Ins.	NO	H.Sc	Rns.	Av.
Sec. A	B Bolton, Pool PM	17	6	124*	532	48.4
	A. Walker, Int. Harv.	16	2	53	346	24.7
	J. Bartle, Int. Harv.	14	2	44	241	20.1
	R. Dawson, Crompark	15	1	105	262	18.7
	D. Knapton, Int. Harv.	18	3	54	257	18.3
	G. Marshall, Green Ln.	16	1	68	271	18.1
Sec. B	E Hodgson, Eng. Elec.	12	4	67	225	28.1
	A. Short, Bramley Sp.	16	2	70	323	23.1
	P. Marsh, Eng. Elec.	14	2	66*	249	20.8
2nd X1s	B Holmes, Bramley Sp.	11	2	48	178	19.8
	W. Rhodes, Netherfield	13	1	50	226	18.8
	F.Jackson, Bramley Sp	14	0	63	251	17.9
1st X1s	E Hodgson, Eng. Elec.	16	5	52	398	36.2
	B. Bolton, P.P.M.	17	2	65	515	34.3
	R. Baldwin, Ives Sports	17	3	96	455	32.5
	D. Knapton, Int. Harv.	17	7	69	322	32.2
	N. England, Lds Zingari	14	3	101*	322	29.3
	A. Short, Bramley Sp.	15	6	102	257	28.7

League	Name/Club	Ins.	NO	H.Sc	Rns.	Av.	Year	Name/Club	Ovs.	Mdn	Rns.	Wks.	Av.
2nd X1s	D. Elsworth, Bram. Sp.	11	6	105*	241	48.2		L Smith, Bramley Sp.	166	47	313	56	5.6
	F,H.Jackson, Bram. Sp	11	0	47	194	17.6		H. Padgett, Int. Harv.	110	30	259	46	5.6
	R. Hird, Eng. Elec.	14	0	51	230	16.4		W. Rhodes, Netherfield	101	34	200	31	6.5
1st X1s	H Dean, Crompark	17	4	57*	445	34.2	1963	A Imeson, Bramley Sp.	182	68	309	62	5
	K. Cowgill, W&M	18	4	79	466	33.3		J. Fletcher, Ives Sports	166	55	303	53	5.7
	J. Holdsworth, R. Gaunt	18	3	75	430	28.6		B. Farrington, Otley M.	159	49	343	50	6.9
	B. Bolton, Otley Mills	16	3	70*	369	28.4		W. Stott, Bram.Sp."B"	213	55	434	63	6.9
	P. Cooper, Bram. Sp.	15	1	93	357	25.5		P. Summersgill, Eng. E	195	63	396	57	7
	T. Hughes, Crompark	15	3	65*	305	25.4		D. Holmes, Ives Sports	228	70	456	65	7
Sec. A	B Bolton, Otley Mills	12	3	79	277	30.7	1964	K Gawtry, Otley Mills	110	41	199	32	6.2
	J. Lawrence, W&M	15	3	73*	351	29.3		J. Sharpe, Lds Zingari	152	38	305	49	6.2
	D. Wilkinson, Otley M.	14	2	36	307	25.5		B. Smales, R. Gaunts	177	70	333	43	7.7
	A.L. Heaton, Esholt	17	4	50	331	25.5		T.W. Hudson, R. Gaunt	109	23	279	36	7.8
	G. Perkins, Otley Mills	15	5	56	246	24.6		K. Cowgill, W&M	148	11	291	36	8.1
	B. Farrington, Otley M.	13	4	72*	221	24.5		J. Bailey, Bramley Sp.	166	56	354	43	8.2
Sec. B	B Metcalfe, Crompark	14	3	102*	250	22.7		K T Hack, Bramley Sp	101	27	234	40	5.9
	G. Robertson, Neth'ld.	15	5	52*	224	22.4		G. Bona, Otley Mills	104	37	222	31	7.2
	M. Warren, Turner Sp.	15	2	57	282	21.7		N. Lightfoot, Otley Wes.	228	67	423	57	7.4

League	Name/Club	Ins.	NO	H.Sc	Rns.	Av.
Sec. A	B Bolton, Otley Mills	14	4	47*	324	32.4
	J. Holdsworth, Ives Sp.	18	6	57*	349	29.1
	G. Waite, Netherfield	15	2	49*	309	23.8
	J. Cockshott, Smiths S.	18	2	92	368	23
	W. Mason, Otley Mills	12	6	27	135	22.5
	E. Mason, Esholt	13	3	54	223	22.3
Sec. B	N Smallwood, Pool PM	14	2	73*	415	34.6
	K. Smith, Turner Sports	12	2	70	276	27.6
	T. Drury, Holbeck Beth.	16	1	60	345	23

Year	Name/Club	Ovs.	Mdn	Rns.	Wks.	Av.
1965	F Quinn, Otley Wesley	164	68	283	47	6
	E. Mason, Esholt	191	71	381	58	6.5
	J. Fletcher, Ives Sports	229	74	473	73	6.6
	G. Perkins, Otley Mills	162	56	288	41	7
	C. Sayer, Crompark	170	56	298	41	7.3
	D. Holmes, Ives Sports	248	67	501	68	7.4
	K Belsham, Holbeck B	108	40	195	43	4.5
	D. Foulkes, Holbeck B.	130	59	232	50	4.6
	D. Thornton, Holbeck B.	123	44	236	42	5.6

Award Winners, Decade by decade, 1956–1965

Trophy winners of the league's miscellaneous awards over the years.

Year	Wicketkeeper	Fielder	Fast 50
1956	Nil recorded		
1957	Nil recorded		
1958	"A" J Evans, Eng. Elec "B" G Foulds, Illingw. 2nds. C Proctor, W&M	"A" B Hannam, Int. H.	
1959	"A" W Cox, Esholt	"A" J Inman, PPM "B" D Elsworth, Bram Sp.	
1960	"A" D McNair, CromP. "B" N England, Lds Zing.	"A" K Morritt, Eng Elec "B" A. Hollings, NetherF. 2nds A L Reeve, Esholt	
1961	Nil recorded		
1962			1st X1 B. Exley, CromP. 2nd X1 J Morley Bram Sp.
1963	M Free, Esholt	F. Rose, Otley M A Parnham, Esholt	P Cooper, Bram Sp. A. Walker, Ives Sp.
1964		W Davidson, Turner Sp.	J Fenton, Turner Sp
1965	J Cockshott, Smiths Sp.	A Holmes, Otley Wes.	(Unnamed) Bramley Sp.

AT THE DOUBLE......No 2.

The Dales Council - a Yorkshire jewel
By former Yorkshire and Notts opener Ashley Metcalfe.

MY association with the Dales Council League is at best tenuous but for all that strikingly memorable – after all, the cricketing experiences gained as a youngster sowed the seeds and certainly helped inspire future success.

It is a league I can only recall playing in on a couple of occasions but much of my early interest was encouraged by many hours of scoring - or watching my father play in the Dales Council, first for Esholt and then for a much longer period at Smiths Sports at Rodley (later Farsley Celtic).

Esholt was the club most responsible for my early ventures into cricket. I was fortunate that my father and fellow stalwart, Brian Reeve, both qualified as coaches and greatly encouraged by a grand old man of the league and the Esholt club, the late Jack Shuttleworth, who launched a junior section at the club. As a nine-year-old playing in the Under 14s progress at times I am sure was slow and very frustrating for all associated, but the experience gained definitely stood us all in good stead.

Undoubtedly my best memories of the Dales are during the period my father played with Smiths. I remember him – and I'll bet many of his day will as well – as a most dour batsman who had little to do with any ball if it was not straight. However he did put some pundits to flight when I watched him hit his one and only century against Pool Paper Mills at Rodley. I was also watching when he and David Pearce broke the second wicket record for the League.

Ashley Metcalfe

Keith Smith

Later I often wondered why two of Smith's top stars of the day, prolific batsman Pearce and fearsome bowler Kenny Booth (both sadly no longer with us) played in the Dales Council. From my point of view as a cricket mad but impressionable youngster, the opportunity to watch and learn as well as practice against two of the best players in the league was invaluable and certainly helped speed my progress.

As time has gone by I have seen far worse performers in higher leagues and I have often wondered what kept them in the Dales League?

Picturesque grounds, competitive cricket, great teas, a love of the League and its characters – why would you want to play elsewhere? There could be no greater accolade – it is unashamedly one of Yorkshire's many cricketing jewels.

Finally, I would like to congratulate the league, and the clubs and, most importantly, the players for all their achievements over the last 50 years and wish them every success in the future.

Ashley Metcalfe, September, 2003.

At the Double partner.................Keith Smith

Ordinary name – extraordinary talent

RIGHT at the height of the time when he was terrorising Dales Council bowlers, in particular, and batsmen, too, for that matter, a film came out that smashed its way to the forefront. Get Carter was the tough, in your face, thriller of the day.

So too was Keith Smith. An ordinary, everyday type of name maybe, but an extraordinary talent on the cricket field and from the middle sixties to the middle seventies when he was operating in the league, his scalp was one of the most prized by any opposition. So when Get Carter hit the screens in 1971 it was an easy step to translate the title into Get Smith on Saturday afternoons. But he did not mind being the prime target at all. In fact he relished the challenge and most of the time he came out on top as his record in the Dales underlined time and time again.

"I played with some good lads in the Dales but I knew that in most games I was the target for the opposition. I didn't mind, in fact I loved it - the bigger the odds the better I played. It never bothered me, anyway we were a works team and went out on Saturday afternoons to enjoy ourselves," he said.

He first hit the Dales averages in 1964 when, in his middle teens, he finished fourth in the batting averages and sixth in the bowling in the "B" Section. The following season he was second in the batting and fourth in the bowling lists in Turner Sports' promotion season. Modest, by his standards but it was the relative quiet before the storm.

In his first season in the top division he was second in the batting averages and by coincidence eighth in the list was one G. Carter (Geoff) of Bramley Sports, the team Smith was soon to join. But in 1967 the Smith era really got under way. He topped the batting list an incredible six times in eight seasons, a feat yet to be matched in the Dales.

His record ran: **1967,** top, average 58.7; **1968,** top, 51.3 and third in the bowling averages with 67 wickets at 6.5; **1969,** top, 57.00; **1970,** 2nd, 41.8 (3rd in the bowling, first season with Bramley Sports); **1971,** top, 47.00; **1972,** did not figure; **1973,** top, 37.9; **1974,** top, 47.70.

After that he moved up into the Bradford League with Pudsey St Lawrence where he also made a big impact going on to help the famous club win six titles and the Priestley Cup and scoring close to 10,000 runs along the way before giving way to his sons Stewart and James in the side – and having short spells with Farsley Celtic, back in the Dales, and Horsforth in the Aire-Wharfe.

"People used to say why didn't I go into the Bradford League earlier, I got a lot of pressure from people saying 'you should be playing in a higher grade' but I enjoyed every minute of my time in the Dales. There were some poor pitches at times but the experience I got on them was invaluable and I made a lot of friends in the Dales. I used to love playing at Otley. In particular I loved playing against the Danskins and Derek Hawley and would stay over there at times on Saturday nights after games," he said.

Otley's captain of those days and opening bowler with Francis Quinn was Billy Mason. "I can remember those weekends like yesterday," he said. "He used to come up to Quinny and me before the game and say with a smile right in your face to one or the other of us 'right then, it's your turn to get a clattering this week' and he invariably gave his victim a good hiding hitting the ball to all corners of the park."

Then there was Smiths Sports and David Pearce. "It was always big game when we played there," said Smith. "They were the games I used to look forward to every season. The rivalry was always intense but we had some great times." Maybe never more so than on the day Pearce declared against Turners with 192 on the board.

John Fenton, captain of Turners at the time and himself a class act with both bat and ball, remembers it well. "I can see Dave now calling in his troops from the boundary edge and saying they had got enough. But we knocked them off with Keith cracking a fast ninety-odd," he said. "Before the days of sixes in the league there was one afternoon he put six successive deliveries in a game against Ives Sports onto the railway bank next to our ground, too.

"But there was one fine innings he played for us against Bramley Sports, the side he would soon join, which might not have lasted as long as it did but for an admiring umpire. We were playing at Rodley and Keith had not scored when he went for a juicy square cut. I was his partner at the other end and it seemed to me he had taken the skin off the ball which was duly caught by Derek Isles standing up at the wicket – but Keith was judged to be not out. The umpire told me he had come a long way that day and loved watching Keith bat from close quarters and so could hardly give him out for something like that," smiled Fenton.

So after so many big demonstrations of his power, what happened to the cavalier of the crease in 1972 when there was no Smith in the averages? "That must have been the season I started with five ducks, three first ballers. It takes a lot to come back from that," said the mighty hitter. But of course he did – with bells on!

Chapter Seven
1966 to 1975
The second decade: The Dales Council comes of age - and finds a new hero

THERE is a line in The Village Blacksmith (1842) that reads, "The smith a mighty man is he". It was a line both batsmen and bowlers alike had good reason to acknowledge during the second decade of progress in the Dales Council.

The Smith in question was as well built and strong as your traditional blacksmith but this one used his muscular forearms for firm hitting, flashing stroke play and pretty quick bowling in his days with Turners Sports and Bramley Sports in the sixties and the seventies. In fact, history shows that Keith Smith came into the spotlight at just the right time for the still aspiring young league - making an impact just when the Dales needed a new hero.

Towards the end of the first ten-year period, club and team numbers had wobbled. The league had established itself well enough but there was a need to move on, a time for the new league to come of age, so to speak. The second decade had to be a period when the league would not merely consolidate its position in the area but step up a gear. And apart from a hiccup in 1967 when the number of clubs slipped back to 13 generating 19 teams, the Dales not only achieved as much but has marched forward ever since.

Yet that second ten-year spell needed to be decorated with some solid team efforts and some eye

Derek Best

Holbeck Beth captain Terry Drury receives the PPM Cup in 1968.

catching individual performances to underscore the league's credibility in West Yorkshire. The clubs that led the way in this important period of development in terms of success were Otley, under various names, New Farnley and Smiths Sports with players like Smith, Francis Quinn and David Pearce dominating the scene in much the same way as Green Lane and Gloss Sample had done in the opening seasons of the league's existence.

Smith's eye for the ball enabled him to pick it up early and his powerful, stocky frame did the rest. He used to smack bowlers to all quarters of the field giving many captains headaches trying to find a way to contain him. He was so successful in the time slot under review that he topped the averages six times, in fact six times in the space of just eight seasons.

Meanwhile, Quinn was helping himself to a barrow load of wickets in most of the seasons while Pearce was putting together a formidable side at Smiths Sports and at the same time accumulating the meat of what was to become the highest run aggregate in competitive Dales Council matches on record with many displays of dedication to the cause of building of big scores.

Otley, New Farnley and Smiths were just as prominent on the major trophy scene taking 12 of the senior league or cup titles between them in the decade. And so by the end of the second ten-year spell it was fair to insist that the Dales Council had truly arrived.

But all-rounder Terry Drury deserved much credit for giving that second decade such a great lift-off when he turned in an individual performance so special that it has never been matched. The statistics show that Otley Mills were champions of **1966** but the team to follow them to the winning post, Holbeck Bethel, had the player of the season.

Drury finished top of both the batting averages (Smith was second) and the bowling averages – the first and so far only time such a double has been achieved in the top division. He took the batting prize with 375 runs at an average 31.2 and his 34 wickets at 4.3 runs apiece was just enough to pip his Holbeck team-mate Denis Foulkes to the bowler's prize – by just .6.

It was a double year, too, for Otley for they picked up the Pool Paper Mills Cup to add to their "A" Section title while Leeds Zingari registered their first trophy success by winning the other knock-out competition which in later years took the title of the Cawthorne Cup. Otley's success was the pinnacle of a great run in the Dales, their double underpinned by an all-round performance from Billy Mason who finished sixth in the league batting averages and third in the bowler's list - and in a career spanning over 20 years with the Otley sides he went on to claim 1,000 wickets plus.

Yet though 1966 was not a season notable for new records, the Esholt pair Ernest Barker and Jim Spivey did lift the 10th wicket partnership record to 83 - at the expense of Crompark bowlers in mid July.

It was Esholt's year in **1967** – they went to their fourth league title in nine seasons with Holbeck Bethel bridesmaids for the second successive season after their promotion in 1965. This time Esholt got home by just a single point with Les Heaton, regularly their leading run scorer in the late sixties and early seventies, finishing in fourth place in the averages and also leading the league side to the first of its three successes in the Bradford Area Council Cup.

Smith Sports, now in their second spell in the league, won their first trophy, the PPM Cup. It turned out to be the first of seven league and/or cup wins in 14 seasons when Pearce's men were flying. Meanwhile, the second eleven of the original league members Crompark carried off the "B" Section championship with Otley Mills seconds just behind them but as second teams they could not be promoted so the third and fourth placed sides Leeds Zingari and Reuben Gaunts moved up.

Smith's 411 runs at an average of 58.7 set up a new high average record and he again averaged 50-plus in topping the charts in **1968**, this time accumulating 513 runs. Smith also claimed 67 wickets to finish third in the bowling list but it was second place all the way for Smiths Sports – runners up in the league and in Pearce, they had the runner-up in both the batting and bowling averages.

New Farnley took pride of place. League champions for the first time, they liked the feeling. They did it again in the next campaign and once more in 1972 with Mick Holmes and Paul Chadwick key bowlers for them. The Otley Mills second string achieved a notable double carrying off the "B" Section and Cawthorne Cup titles while the premier cup, the PPM trophy, at last gave Holbeck Bethel their moment of glory. Mills' first team had one of the quirkier afternoons of the campaign on the very first Saturday when they whipped out Leeds Zingari for just five with Francis Quinn claiming a five wickets for one run return. But their 10 wicket victory did not really qualify them for the record book as such. The fact was that Zingari had managed to muster only nine players that day.

New Farnley's **1969** title success was on the back of a formidable attack. John Ridley's pace up in the top corner of the Farnley Hall playing field was hardly one of the experiences many of the useful batsmen of the time (not to mention those down the batting order) looked forward to dealing with while Holmes and the nippy Barry Finch, who got bounce and speed off the shortest of run-ups, were also a handful. The trio took the top three slots in the bowling averages, Holmes finishing just ahead of Ridley, with the Grove Hill (Otley) pair Quinn and Mason fourth and fifth.

Otley Mills captain Billy Mason receives the PPM Cup in 1966 from league president John Whiteley.

Smiths Sports captain David Pearce receives the PPM Cup from league president John Whiteley in 1973.

In another corner of the Farnley Hall playing field, Derek Best and Colin Barraclough were starring in the "B" Section for Farnley Hill, Best's unbeaten 111 helping him finish top of the averages on 30.9 while Barraclough also finished top dog with a bowling average of 4.42 having claimed 66 victims. The Wibsey pair B Yeadon and D Shepherd, on 4.56 and 4.64 respectively, pushed Barraclough hard and Keith Robertshaw, with 51 wickets at 5.67, was fifth in the bowler's table, three good reasons why Wibsey took the title in a tight finale from Farnley Hill who, nevertheless, had had their moment taking the Cawthorne Cup earlier in the campaign.

By **1970**, Smith had joined Bramley Sports which turned out to be hard on Esholt who had to try and deal with him in the PPM Cup final. Inspired by Smith, Bramley made the most of the tight Grove Hill field to win their only Cup final. The league title went to Grove Hill, but Farnley Hill, in their first season in the top division, surged into second place with their paceman Barraclough following up his first place in the lower division 12 months earlier by claiming top spot in the "A" Section with 75 wickets this time around. Quinn's stint of 90 wickets from 299 overs was a big reason why the Otley side had taken their fourth league championship but his huge bowling effort was only enough in the end to earn him fourth place in the averages.

Smiths Sport's reliable Tony Armitage was top batsman ending a run of three consecutive number one spots by Smith who nevertheless finished second ahead of two more Smiths Sports batsmen Pearce and Brian Rhodes. In the "B" Section yet another top-name-to-be emerged, Ralph Middlebrook winning both batting and bowling awards in a Pudsey Congs promotion winning side. They went up as runners–up to Dales newcomers Oxford Place who had made a stunning impact in their first season. They toppled ten man Smiths Sports second string for just seven in their first match in the league with Ernie Dufton picking up four wickets for no runs from eight deliveries, went on to claim the Cawthorne Cup in mid season and then the "B" Section title to round off the campaign unbeaten. For good measure they provided both runners–up to Middlebrook – Brian Anderson just .1 behind the Congs all-rounder in the batting list and Dufton whose bowling average was a mere .11 higher than Middlebrook's effort. In the same campaign medium pace bowler Robertshaw, who was later to join Oxford Place, recorded a nine wickets for four return off 8.4 overs.

Smith could not be kept out of the spotlight, however, and when he faced his old side Turner Sports he set up a new third wicket record partnership with David Jones. He was back in top place in the batting averages in **1971** well clear of Anderson in second place but an opening partnership at Grove Hill was catching the eye.

Ian Peacock and Don Baker, who, in 11 seasons at Otley clocked up over 5,000 runs in all games, finished fifth and sixth in the batting list scoring approaching 800 runs between them. They finished off the campaign in rare style by creating a new league opening partnership record of 155 at home against Armley. A month earlier Terry Drury and Paul Hurd had taken the bowlers of neighbours Farnley Hill to task by sharing a 155 second wicket stand to equal the record set up 11 years earlier by the Smiths Sports pair G. Holdsworth and D. Williams.

Smiths Sports took the 1971 title with Grove Hill claiming the PPM Cup and yet another debutant Dales side Farnley Estate put a new name on the Cawthorne Cup.

Third place in the "B" Section was enough to win the Estate side promotion, too, and in **1972** their leading batsman John Pullan topped the league's batting averages. New Farnley, ten points clear of the rest, carried off the championship for the third time in five campaigns while Pudsey Congs won the PPM Cup, the first of three cup wins in four seasons. Leeds Zingari bowler Brian Newall picked up the top bowling award in the "B" Section while batsmen Peter Bullock and Des Finn also did well as Zingari won the Cawthorne Cup and also promotion.

Smith topped the averages yet again in **1973** as his Bramley Sports side surged to the title but though he totalled 417 league runs he was no more than third in the aggregate scoring list after Oxford Place's Brian Anderson (428 runs) and Middlebrook (423 runs). Barry Finch, who by this time like Smith had moved on to the Bramley side, topped the bowling list with 77 wickets. But his average of 7.84 was only .01 better than Bill Mason's effort for Grove Hill. It was a season of near misses for the Otley first eleven for they had been runners-up in the league title race though their second string did picked up the Cawthorne Cup.

But Anderson ensured Bramley did not get it all their own way in the run-in to their title for with team-mate David Maltby, the Oxford Place captain had created a new, and undefeated, league seventh wicket partnership at the champions' expense in late August. Oddly enough on that same afternoon, Pool Paper Mills were at Wibsey chasing their first point of the season after 16 consecutive defeats, ending their unhappy run with a 23-run victory – and they won their next game, too. But two victories in their 20-match programme left them well adrift at the end of the campaign and looking at relegation. They bounced straight back the following season though. In the Pool Paper Mills Cup, Smiths Sports picked up the trophy for the third time in seven seasons at Grove Hill while J. Hudson led the way in the "B" Section batting averages to help lift Phoenix Park to their first title of champions of "B" Section.

The **1974** campaign was Smith's swansong and, predictably, he went off to a new challenge in the Bradford League by not only topping the "A" Section batting averages once more but also creating a new league highest individual score of 139 against Phoenix Park. But his Bramley Sports side –

The T & A coverage of the 1967 Bradford Area Council Cup final included a picture of the winning Dales Council side. Back row l to r. K. Smith, N. Smallwood, B. Farrington, T. Drury, C.A. Bloor, D. Foulkes. Front row: F. Quinn, A. Spivey, L. Heaton (capt), A. Wright, G. Perkins. They scored 162-9 against the Bradford Central League who managed 151.

Peter Bullock.

even though Barry Finch included an eight for eight performance in July against Wibsey – managed only a mid table position in a season in which Otley Town left the rest well behind in the championship race.

With their ace attack bowler Quinn picking up 84 wickets, they finished 20 points clear of the field on 91 points – neighbours Farnley Estate were runners-up three points ahead of Oxford Place.

It was a different situation in the "B" Section though where Crompark and Pool Paper Mills produced one of the tightest finishes in the history of the league. They both ended their campaigns on 67 points with Crompark winning a play-off for the title. Mills batsman Colin Bentley, with a batting average of 42.00 was pipped for the top spot in the batting averages, too, by Ian Mortimer of the Leeds YMCA by .83. But there was consolation for him with the fastest 50 of the season award and a century that lifted his run aggregate to 378. The cups went to Pudsey Congs and Otley Mills. The decade closed in **1975**, however, with Pudsey Congs emphasising their appetite for cup knock-out cricket by winning both the PPM and Cawthorne trophies in a season marked by the run scorers. The Otley Town pair Brian Anderson and Don Baker finished first and second in the "A" Section batting list totalling more than 1,100 runs between them while Smiths Sports knocked up a new highest team score of 323 for eight against Pool Paper Mills – the runs coming in just 160 minutes.

It was the first time a team had broken the 300 barrier in the league's history, Smiths topping their own record of 284 of six years earlier, ironically also set against PPM. It was also a special day for their diminutive left hander Tony Metcalfe who hit an unbeaten 101, his first and what turned out to be the only century of his career. After starting the knock backing up opener Colin Janney on his way to a fine 52, Metcalfe then shared 50 partnerships with both Ian Parker and Brian Cooke going to his 100 in the 44th over.

But the wicket turned out to be the real winner on the day for Mills found it played as well for them as it had done for Smiths and they were able to bat out for a draw. Smiths finished the season as runners-up in the "A" Section, Oxford Place winning their first senior title with no second team back-up while Wibsey took the top spot in the "B" Section.

THE CHAMPIONS AND CUP WINNERS, DECADE BY DECADE
Division winners and their records and winners of the Cup competitions................seasons 1966–1975

(Win 4pts, tie 2pts, side scoring faster in drawn game 2pts and 1pt for a drawn match)

League	Winners	P.	W.	L.	D. (2)	D. (1)	Pts.	Year	Pool P M Cup	Cawthorne Cup
Sec. A	Otley Mills	18	13	2	1	2	56	1966	Otley Mills	Leeds Zingari
	Holbeck Bethel	18	13	4	0	1	53			
	Esholt	18	9	3	0	6	42			
Sec. B	Wilsons & Mathiesons	18	15	1	0	2	62			
	Otley Mills	18	11	4	1	2	48			
	Leeds Zingari	18	10	6	0	2	42			
Sec. A	Esholt	18	9	5	0	4	40	1967	Smiths Sports	Reuben Gaunts
	Holbeck Bethel	18	8	3	0	7	39			
	Turner Sports	18	7	3	1	7	37			
Sec. B	Crompark *2pts for tie	16	9	1	1*	5	43			
	Otley Mills	16	9	2	0	5	41			
	Leeds Zingari	16	8	2	1	5	39			
Sec. A	New Farnley	22	14	5	2	1	61	1968	Holbeck Bethel	Otley Mills
	Smiths Sports	22	13	3	2	4	60			
	Otley Mills	22	12	4	1	5	55			
Sec. B	Otley Mills	18	14	0	0	4	60			
	Wilsons & Mathiesons	18	11	2	2	3	51			
	Esholt	18	9	6	1	2	40			

League	Winners	P.	W.	L.		D.	Pts.	Year	Pool P M Cup	Cawthorne Cup
Sec. A	New Farnley	22	13	1	0	8	60	**1969**	Smiths Sports	Farnley Hill
	Grove Hill	22	13	4	0	5	57			
	Smiths Sports	22	12	2	1	7	57			
Sec. B	Wibsey	20	15	1	0	4	64			
	Farnley Hill	20	15	2	0	3	63			
	West Leeds	20	8	6	0	6	38			
Sec. A	Grove Hill	22	17	3	0	2	70	**1970**	Bramley Sports	Oxford Place
	Farnley Hill	22	16	5	0	1	65			
	Bramley Sports	22	14	5	1	2	60			
Sec. B	Oxford Place	22	18	0	2	2	78			
	Pudsey Congs	22	16	4	0	2	66			
	Grove Hill	22	15	2	0	5	65			
Sec. A	Smiths Sports	22	16	4	1	1	67	**1971**	Grove Hill	Farnley Estate
	New Farnley	22	15	5	0	2	62			
	Grove Hill	22	12	3	2	5	57			
Sec. B	Wilson & Mathiesons	22	15	2	2	3	67			
	Grove Hill	22	14	3	2	3	63			
	Farnley Estate	22	14	3	1	4	62			
Sec. A	New Farnley	22	13	2	1	6	60	**1972**	Pudsey Congs	Leeds Zingari
	Oxford Place	22	12	8	0	2	50			
	Wibsey	22	10	5	1	6	48			
Sec. B	Grove Hill "A"	20	13	2	0	5	57			
	Pool Paper Mills	20	9	4	2	5	45			
	Leeds Zingari	20	9	7	0	4	40			

League Winners

(Win 5pts, tie 2pts, draw 1pt with 2 bonus pts for faster scoring in drawn game)

	P.	W.	L.	D.	Pts (1 3)	Pts.	Year	Pool P M Cup	Cawthorne Cup
Sec. A							**1973**	Smiths Sports	Grove Hill
Bramley Sports	20	13	4	3	0	68			
Grove Hill	20	12	4	3	1	66			
Smiths Sports	20	12	7	1	0	61			
Sec. B									
Phoenix Park (1 tie)	20	12	3	3	1	68			
West Leeds	20	12	4	4	0	64			
Bramley Sports	20	12	7	0	1	63			
Sec. A							**1974**	Pudsey Congs	Otley Town
Otley Town	22	17	1	3	1	91			
Farnley Estate	22	13	5	3	1	71			
Oxford Place	22	13	6	3	0	68			
Sec. B									
Crompark	20	13	5	2	0	67			
Pool Paper Mills	20	13	5	2	0	67			
Leeds YMCA	20	12	5	3	0	63			
* Crompark beat P.P.M. in a Play-Off.									
Sec. A							**1975**	Pudsey Congs	Pudsey Congs
Oxford Place	22	16	3	2	1	85			
Smiths Sports	22	14	5	1	2	77			
Otley Town	22	14	5	2	1	75			
Sec. B									
Wibsey	20	15	3	2	0	77			
Pudsey St. Lawrence	20	11	6	2	1	60			
Leeds YMCA (1 tie)	20	9	4	5	1	55			

AN AVERAGE VIEW

Season by season leaders of the averages ~ the second decade, 1966-1975.

		The Batsmen							The Bowlers				
League	Name/Club	Ins.	NO	H.Sc	Rns.	Av.	Year	Name/Club	Ovs.	Mdn	Rns.	Wks.	Av.
Sec. A	T. Drury, Holbeck Beth.	17	5	68*	375	31.2	1966	T. Drury, Holbeck Beth.	75	23	147	34	4.3
	K. Smith, Turner Spts.	12	2	78*	240	24.0		D. Foulkes, Holbeck B.	151	61	214	44	4.9
	J. Hamer, Otley Mills.	14	3	53	262	23.8		W. Mason, Otley Mills	112	42	191	35	5.4
	D. Pearce, Smiths Spts.	13	2	42	247	22.5		A. Chadwick, N. Farn.	118	38	237	43	5.5
	L. Heaton, Esholt.	14	2	57*	240	20.0		J. Sample, Esholt.	173	73	289	51	5.6
	W. Mason, Otley Mills.	12	2	44	200	20.0		G. Perkins, Otley Mills	144	57	232	41	5.7
Sec. B	N. Smallwood, P.P.M.	16	2	85*	381	27.2		E. Fox, Wil & Math	148	46	234	63	3.7
	P. Chegwin, Wil & Math	12	3	54*	235	26.1		B. Jarrett, Wil & Math	102	30	212	51	4.1
	W. Foster, Esholt.	15	1	91*	324	23.1		D. Hawley, Otley Mills	97	32	204	37	5.5
Sec. A	K. Smith, Turner Sports	10	3	100	411	58.7	1967	P. Chadwick, N. Farnley	81	25	167	36	4.6
	A. Wright, Otley Mills	10	3	78*	394	56.3		D. Thornton, Holbeck B.	98	28	222	38	5.8
	P. Seaman, Wil & Math	8	2	52	254	42.3		F. Quinn, Crompark	127	39	248	34	7.3
	L. Heaton, Esholt	11	1	54	282	28.2		A. Walker, Ives Sports	91	27	226	29	7.8
	G. Perkins, Otley Mills	9	1	67*	222	27.7		W. Stott, Smiths Sp.	93	20	227	26	8.7
	S. Broadbent, Smiths S	12	1	50	287	26.0		G. Gornall, Bramley Sp.	110	39	262	30	8.7
Sec. B	P. Barraclough, Crom P	10	2	59*	197	24.6		D. Hawley, Otley Mills	103	31	251	43	5.8
	S. Reyner, Otley Mills	8	0	51	187	23.3		P. Barraclough, Crom P.	110	32	217	33	6.5
	P. Marshall, R. Gaunts	8	3	34	108	19.5		R. Metcalf, Crompark	107	32	217	32	6.7
Sec. A	K. Smith, Turner Sports	14	4	97	513	51.3	1968	F. Quinn, Otley Mills	218	78	423	70	6
	D. Pearce, Smiths Sp.	17	3	69	426	30.4		D. Pearce, Smiths Sp	126	18	251	46	6.1
	A. Armitage, Smiths Sp	14	3	103*	293	26.8		K. Smith, Turner Sp.	232	82	440	67	6.5
	D. Elsworth, Bramley Sp	17	1	73	392	24.5		P. Chadwick, N. Farnley	246	61	487	74	6.5
	J. Fenton, Turner Sports	13	3	60	243	24.3		M. Holmes, N. Farnley	113	35	250	35	7.1
	B. Foster, Esholt	13	1	52	284	23.6		A. Beech, Smiths Sp.	123	31	232	31	7.4

Cricket in The Dales

League	Name/Club	Ins.	NO	H.Sc	Rns.	Av.	Year	Name/Club	Ovs.	Mdn	Rns.	Wks.	Av.
Sec. B	N. Smallwood, P.P.M.	12	2	54	297	29.7		D. Hawley, Otley Mills	115	39	233	46	5
	P.G. Seaman, W&M.	13	4	57	238	26.4		N. Smallwood, P.P.M.	125	51	208	37	5.8
	S. Danskin, Otley Mills	14	5	50	228	25.3		R. Lilley, Smiths Sports	100	22	209	34	6.1
Sec. A	K. Smith, Turner Sports	12	5	114*	399	57.0	1969	M. Holmes, New Farnley	85	25	158	32	4.9
	P.G. Seaman, W&M	14	5	53	320	35.5		J. Ridley, New Farnley	105	29	210	37	5.7
	A. Armitage, Smiths Sp	15	5	78	350	35.0		B. Finch, New Farnley	131	40	281	47	6.0
	A.L. Heaton, Esholt	13	0	73	400	30.8		F. Quinn, Grove Hill	230	89	416	67	6.2
	D. Baker, Grove Hill	14	1	87	389	30.0		W. Mason, Grove Hill	124	25	288	39	7.4
	B. Rhodes, Smiths Sp.	16	2	129	398	28.4		J. Linley, Armley Saxon	178	42	476	63	7.6
Sec. B	D. Best, Farnley Hill	17	7	111*	309	30.9		C. Barraclough, Farn. H	177	64	292	66	4.4
	D. Knapton, Johnson R.	12	2	86	268	26.8		B. Yeadon, Wibsey	89	26	176	39	4.6
	G. Bell, Farnley Hill	18	4	35	349	24.9		D. Shepherd, Wibsey	138	51	246	53	4.6
Sec. A	A. Armitage, Smiths Sp.	13	5	77*	371	46.4	1970	C. Barraclough, Farnley H	245	73	508	75	6.8
	K. Smith, Bramley Sports	15	2	119	543	41.8		B. Finch, New Farnley	203	59	419	59	7.1
	D. Pearce, Smiths Sports	17	2	65*	486	32.4		K. Smith, Bramley Sports	158	43	378	53	7.1
	B. Rhodes, Smiths Sports	17	2	67	406	27.1		F. Quinn, Grove Hill	299	93	673	90	7.5
	G. Perkins, Grove Hill	17	4	60	328	25.1		R. Lilley, Bramley Sports	246	69	568	69	8.2
	A. Wagstaff, Armley	16	1	57*	369	24.6		J. Ridley, New Farnley	168	42	455	55	8.3
Sec. B	R. Middlebrook, Pud. C.	14	6	62*	318	39.8		R. Middlebrook, Pud. C	183	61	412	60	6.9
	B. Anderson, Oxford Place	16	5	86*	437	39.7		E. Dufton, Oxford Place	78	14	237	34	7.0
	A. Barrett, Grove Hill	12	4	71*	283	35.4		D.R. Hawley, Grove Hill	146	34	376	53	7.1
Sec. A	K. Smith, Bramley Sports	14	4	101*	470	47.0	1971	J. Ridley, New Farnley	171	57	349	63	5.5
	B. Anderson, Oxford Place	18	3	73	465	31.0		R. Middlebrook, Pud. C	183	47	390	65	6.0
	D. Pearce, Smiths Sports	20	2	90	523	29.0		B. Finch, New Farnley	240	89	480	79	6.1
	L. Heaton, Esholt	16	3	100*	355	27.3		C. Barraclough, Farnley H	97	35	230	36	6.4
	I. Peacock, Grove Hill	17	3	89	372	26.5		K. Robertshaw, Wibsey	269	109	538	82	6.5
	D. Baker, Grove Hill	18	3	71	396	26.4		W. Mason, Grove Hill	214	75	367	56	6.6

Batting Averages

League	Name/Club	Ins.	NO	H.Sc	Rns.	Av.
Sec. B	E. Hargate, Farsley	15	5	96*	568	56.8
	J. Pullan, Farnley Estate	20	4	64*	765	47.8
	P. Seaman, Wil & Math.	13	4	70*	307	34.1
Sec. A	J. Pullan, Farnley Estate	17	4	48*	413	31.8
	I. Peacock, Grove Hill	13	2	103*	330	30.0
	T. Drury, West Leeds	16	2	84*	418	29.9
	J. Lawrence, Wil & Math	15	2	71	348	26.7
	D. Baker, Grove Hill	17	0	55	427	25.1
	R. Middlebrook, Pudsey C	16	1	74	364	24.4
Sec. B	R. Giles, Farsley	13	5	91*	467	58.4
	E. Hargate, Farsley	14	1	110	534	41.1
	C. Bentley, P.P.M.	14	1	78	452	34.8
Sec. A	K. Smith, Bramley Sports	13	2	100	417	37.9
	P. Jackson, Bramley Sp.	15	5	70	299	29.9
	D. Hunter, Lds Zingari	15	2	53	385	29.6
	D. Jones, Bramley Sports	19	5	41*	371	26.5
	D. Benn, Oxford Place	14	5	50	228	25.3
	A. Cockerham, Grove Hill	15	2	54	311	23.9
Sec. B.	J. Hudson, Phoenix Park	15	4	77	360	32.7
	M. West, Grove Hill	15	4	65*	313	28.5
	R. Waite, West Leeds	12	1	54	289	26.3
Sec. A	K. Smith, Bramley Sports	14	3	139	525	47.7
	R. Askham, Otley Town	13	7	55	272	45.3
	J. Pullan, Farnley Estate	21	5	57	589	36.8
	R. Middlebrook, Pudsey C	18	7	51*	384	34.9
	J. Armstrong, Phoenix P.	18	6	56*	403	33.6

Bowling Averages

Year	Name/Club	Ovs.	Mdn	Rns.	Wks.	Av.
	D. Pullan, Farnley Estate	264	91	450	68	6.3
	M. Warren, Wil & Math.	204	55	458	64	7.2
	M. Cryer, P.P.M.	224	69	423	59	7.2
1972	J. Lawrence, Wil & Math.	115	33	269	38	7.1
	B. Finch, New Farnley	263	89	511	72	7.1
	K. Booth, Smiths Sports	122	46	221	31	7.1
	M. Holmes, New Farnley	92	26	217	30	7.2
	K. Robertshaw, Wibsey	288	103	505	65	7.8
	B. Eager, Oxford Place	158	45	355	45	7.8
	B. Newall, Lds Zingari	118	40	227	33	6.8
	M. Cryer, P.P.M.	197	58	393	51	7.7
	M. Gillingwater, Smiths S	139	37	284	36	7.8
1973	B. Finch, Bramley Sports	285	97	604	77	7.8
	W. Mason, Grove Hill	232	60	534	68	7.9
	R. Middlebrook, Pud C	138	31	325	40	8.1
	J. Ridley, New Farnley	206	58	439	52	8.4
	L. Herbert, Smiths Sports	199	44	517	58	8.9
	A. Beech, Smiths Sports	104	16	306	33	9.3
	D. Foulkes, West Leeds	93	30	168	35	4.8
	D. Hawley, Grove Hill	121	34	199	34	6.1
	E. Edley, Phoenix Par	111	23	257	35	7.3
1974	C. Horner, Wibsey	56	10	146	32	4.6
	D. Benn. Oxford Place	148	51	303	48	6.3
	F. Quinn, Otley Town	296	113	552	84	6.5
	B. Finch, Bramley Sports	209	59	456	52	8.8
	K. Robertshaw, Oxford P.	213	58	466	53	8.8

League	Name/Club	Ins.	NO	H.Sc	Rns.	Av.	Year	Name/Club	Ovs.	Mdn	Rns.	Wks.	Av.
Sec. B	I. Mortimner, Leeds YMCA	16	4	110*	514	42.8		K. Dickens, Pudsey C.	97	30	210	36	5.8
	C. Bentley, PPM.	12	3	101	378	42.0		M. Cryer, PPM.	214	71	391	62	6.2
	M. West, Otley Town	15	3	62	412	34.7		J. Raistrick, Pudsey S.L.	80	27	199	30	6.6
Sec. A	B. Anderson, Otley Town	22	6	93	577	36.1	**1975**	H. Rider, Oxford Place	99	37	197	34	5.8
	D. Baker, Otley Town	22	4	104	534	29.7		C. Oldfield, Pudsey C.			467	63	7.4
	P. Bullock, Lds Zingari	19	4	68*	432	28.8		B. Cawthray, New Farnley	169	54	371	47	7.9
	D. Pearce, Smiths Sports	17	1	95	432	27.0		J. Mahoney, Farnley Est.	120	23	400	49	8.2
	R. Chew, Oxford Place	19	5	67	358	25.6		K. Booth, Smiths Sports	220	65	529	62	8.5
Sec. B	PR Fisher, YMCA	19	5	87*	497	35.5		S. Brear, Wibsey	168	49	356	52	6.8
	M. West, Otley Town	16	3	78	439	33.8		S. Swallow, Pudsey S.L.	190	68	365	52	7.0
	J. Fisher, Smiths Sports	14	2	63	378	31.5		C. Horner, Wibsey	128	32	284	38	7.5

Award Winners, Decade by decade, 1966-1975

Trophy winners of the league's miscellaneous awards over the years.

Year	Wicketkeeper	Fielder	Fast 50
1966	Nil recorded		
1967		J Twinham, Smiths Sp.	R Paley, Crompark
1968	Nil recorded		
1969	Nil recorded		
1970	Nil recorded		
1971	G. Bland, Wibsey	T. Waites, New Farnley	D. Pearce, Smiths Sp
1972	G. Ives, Grove Hill	M. Gillingwater, Smiths Sp	J Cockshott, Farsley
1973	R Webster, Oxford Place	B Cooke, Smiths Sp	K Toomes, Smiths Sp
1974	P Sidebottom	P Heaton, Esholt	C Bentley, PPM
1975	R Isles, Farnley Est.	S Wilkinson, PPM	S Warrington, Pudsey St. Law

AT THE DOUBLE......No 3.

Benaud and potted meat sandwiches
By John Helm, ITV Sports Commentator

LIKE many of you, I suspect, I was weaned on cricket at Park Avenue. Men of my age drool nostalgically about Fiery Fred running in from the pavilion end, shirt sleeves flapping, and rolling over the opposition with fire streaming from his nostrils.

When I was 11 the Australians came to Park Avenue, and good old Mr Jonathan, our form master, decided that was worth a school outing, no doubt because he didn't want to miss the historic occasion rather than anything to do with our education.

I can vividly remember squatting beside the boundary ropes, mum's potted meat sandwiches by my side, goggling at the gods that were Keith Miller, Ray Lindwall, Richie Benaud, and for some reason most of all the baby of the team Ian Craig, just feet away from me.

Miller, he of the film star looks, made 159 not out, and the men in the baggy green caps piled up 453-6 before declaring in that one day. They even had time to ruin the outing completely by dismissing our hero Len Hutton for a duck. Spoilsports!

My love for cricket knew no bounds from that day forth.

Sometimes on a Saturday my parents took me to friends in Horsforth and I always persuaded them that we should go to Hall Park where there just happened to be a cricket match. There always seemed to be a Hitchenor playing.

Baildon was my first love though. It had to be as my neighbours included the county coach Arthur Mitchell as well as the captain of the local side Ronnie Burnet who was to go on to lead the county team as well. I never missed a match and I can recall to this day not just Baildon legends like Wilf Burkinshaw, Tom Tetley and Bill Ellis but the "stars" of Bowling Old Lane, Eccleshill, Yeadon, Queensbury, Idle and the rest.

My perfect Saturday was to play for Salt Grammar School at Esholt in the morning, and then watch Baildon thrash somebody in the afternoon (that was before I grew up and actually played for them!). To this day it doesn't matter where I've been or where I'm going if I see a field occupied by men in white, sometimes running around like headless chickens, I have to stop and take in an over or two.

I've been lucky enough to play on the Test ground at Christchurch, New Zealand, seen matches in the West Indies and South Africa and perhaps best of all went to a dozen or so games at the 1998 Commonwealth Games in Malaysia. I even had the privilege of producing a Test Match special in the days of John Arlott and Brian Johnston, but to me it does not matter whether its Lord's or Pool Paper Mills, a game of cricket is a thing of beauty, something I cannot resist.

There's a special bond between followers of the great game and those who have performed with credit over the years in the Dales Council are just as important as those who have achieved greatness at the highest level. In an all-encompassing sport everyone has a tale to tell be it from inside or outside the boundary ropes and that's what makes cricket so special.

Thank you, Mr Jonathan.

John Helm, September, 2004.

At the Double partner....................Derek Hawley

A case of BACK to the future

IF ever there was a case of BACK to the future in a cricketing sense it has to be the tale of Derek Hawley, an extraordinary wicket-taker who has played major roles both on and off the field in the building of the Dales Council and, in particular, the game in the Otley area.

In his early days it was all about the long run up and the fierce delivery. He was a handful then and a key performer as the Otley Mills side put down the foundations of one of the most successful outfits in the league. But the year after Mills took the league title in 1963, it looked like Hawley's career had come to an abrupt end.

"I did my back in during 1964 and the specialist I went to see removed two discs and told my wife 'your husband will never play cricket again'. I was devastated, I was just 32 and suddenly it was all

John Helm.

Derek Hawley.

over. I spent nine months on my back but was determined to find a way back into the game," he said.

The approach to the wicket was changed to an ambling three to four paces, the action was modified to use the shoulder more and Hawley was on his way again. "It was a whole new ball game, I thought my back had finished me but in fact it opened up a new future in cricket for me," he said.

"The first game back was against Crompark and with my first ball with the new action I got a wicket. I couldn't believe it, I was back in business again." After that the wickets just kept on tumbling for him to place him alongside Otley colleagues Billy Mason and Francis Quinn and the Smiths pair Kenny Booth and Arnie Beech as the league's most prolific wicket-takers – all of them members of the 1,000 victims plus club.

The long hours he spent working on his new action paid off to the extent that he played on a further 33 years after his operation finishing in his mid sixties after playing in the Dales from 1957 to 1979 and then, following a spell in the Leeds League, returning for his final three years in action in the early 1990s. Apart from an odd season at Esholt, he spent his whole career with the Otley sides, Mills, Grove Hill and Town, was a club official for much of that time and took over from Stan Hughes as the league's treasurer for six years in 1974.

One cherished memory was opening the bowling with England's Derek Underwood on a cricket tour in Australia when the Otley stalwart was 60. "I picked up the wicket of an Australian Under 19 player hitting middle stump," he recalled with some satisfaction. His best bowling return was a 9-35 blitz against English Electric in August, 1960, though he did wipe out New Farnley with an 8-12 performance in 1967. His top season for wickets was in 1978 when he picked up 91 in league and cup games but he was not noted as the best batsman and fielder around. "I can't boast about my batting, I never made a 50 in league cricket, my highest was 37 against Bramley Sports. Mind you I did bat at number 11 for almost the whole of my 51 seasons in the game," he said.

Otley captain Billy Mason tells one story about Hawley's fielding exploits that left most people inside the Grove Hill park ground in stitches – except Gloss Sample. The great Green Lane all-rounder had just smashed Mason's first delivery into the bushes beyond square leg and Hawley disappeared in the undergrowth to retrieve the ball. "It came back out of the bushes and I ran up without noticing Derek had not found his way out. But Gloss dispatched the next ball in the same way – and at that moment Derek stumbled back on to the field from nowhere and hung on to the ball for a great catch. Everyone was amazed," he said.

"It probably should have been called since I was no-where when the ball was being delivered. But I came out of the trees and there it was and I managed to make the catch – and a few people smile," said the Otley veteran. Happy days.

Chapter Eight
1976 to 1985
The Third Decade: The "Big Time" arrives.

THE third decade turned out to be a key period for the Dales Council – it was a time when many things got bigger: the number of teams involved and the number of runs scored were maybe the prime examples.

For the first time the number of teams contesting the various divisions in the league went through the 40 mark and for seven of the 10 seasons under review, a 40-plus number of teams involved was the norm in the chase for the various league trophies. Midway through the decade the number peaked at 46, the highest number of teams still recorded for one season in the Dales though in the late 1990's figures were pushing towards similar high marks once more.

It was a healthy state of affairs and competition was good. It was far from uncommon for leading batsmen to hit more than 600 runs for the season and two bowlers managed to smash through the 90 wickets barrier. One factor, however, which probably helped, certainly as far as the batsmen were concerned, was the introduction early in the decade of sixes.

Until the 1978 season batsmen had to manage without the extra two runs for their bigger hits to the boundary which underlines the efforts of top run scorers during the first 22 seasons of the league's existence. When the best you could get for any shot was four there was an obvious disadvantage for the really big hitters and for that matter for bowlers hoping to coax their prey into an error by going for an imprudent big hit.

Andy Maude.

Wilf Anderson.

Kenny Booth.

It is fascinating, for instance, to contemplate though just how many more runs big hitting batsmen of the calibre of Keith Smith and David Pearce might have added to their aggregates had the six been available before 1978. Interesting, too, to wonder just how much more Ralph Shuttleworth and Malcolm Franks might have added to their league record fourth wicket partnership of 190 way back in 1957 with the six option in place. "I can recall around four or five of my boundaries went out of the field," remembered Franks.

Consider, also, that just 12 months before the new six rule was adopted, might Pearce and Tony Metcalfe have lifted their second wicket record for Smiths – not broken again until 2003 - to an even higher mark in 1977? Certainly it is hard to argue against the likelihood of higher scores in such cases since all the other league high scoring records have been toppled following the introduction of the six hit. And as though to underline the point Ian Dobson became the first batsman in the league to hammer six sixes in an over in the final season of the period under scrutiny. His big hitting party piece came for Rodley in a second eleven fixture against Farsley Celtic just as the 1985 season was getting under way.

But the introduction of the six should, in no way, be seen to dilute the efforts of the new generation of batsmen of the third decade who made a habit of lifting their aggregates for the a season beyond the 600 mark. After all, they still had to put bat to ball often and firmly and were led in no uncertain terms by Scalebor Park's admirable batsman Peter O'Brien who went through the 600 mark four times in the decade winning the league batting prize on four occasions, too.

The decade opened with a couple of familiar names on the trophies list in both 1976 and 1977. The wicket-keeping prize for the two seasons was collected by Roy Webster, who by then was a key member of the formidable Smiths Sports side, and the fastest fifty awards went to that big hitter from Esholt, Terry Dudley.

Tony Metcalfe.

Gentlemen and players. Esholt's captain, Brian Wall, centre, with the Spiveys, Arthur and Jim, studying form at the 1970 Pool Paper Mills final.

But the period opened with a new name on the title winners' list with Croma claiming the "B" Section title five points clear of Scalebor Park, who, in turn, were 22 points ahead of the rest of the field. However, **1976** was really all about the Smiths side whose players were touching the peak of their powers. They waltzed away with the double claiming the "A" Section prize by a massive margin of 13 points from second placed Oxford Place, their charge to the trophies ironically led by the former Oxford Place bowlers David Benn, who, to the batsmen of the Dales Council at the time was as quick as it gets, and Keith Robertshaw. When Benn went through the magical 100 wickets mark in league and cup games as Smiths beat Leeds Zingari with five games of the season still to go, the pair had claimed 165 scalps between them underlining their huge contribution to Smiths' big year.

Benn's barnstorming season eventually took him to 113 victims in all games, 94 of them in the quest for the league title at just 6.17 runs apiece, an average which gave him the league's bowling prize ahead of Pudsey Congs paceman Colin Oldfield who, in turn, also had a great season with 83 league victims at a cost of marginally over seven runs each.

Midway through the campaign, Oldfield looked to have done enough to lift Congs to their third successive cup success in the Pool Paper Mills final at Esholt when, with a fine display of tight bowling, he claimed 5-24 off 20 overs as Smiths struggled towards a 40 over total of 83-9. But the Rodley side stormed to a 31 run victory with their fearsome opening partnership of Benn (5-19 off 13.4 overs) and Robertshaw (4-23 of 13 overs) toppling Congs for just 52. With the first leg of their double in the bag, Smiths focused on the title, a target they hit with two games to spare. They became only the third side in Dales Council history to achieve the League and Cup double, an effort all the more notable because they lost their top all-rounder Kenny Booth with a broken arm midway through the campaign.

Their captain Roy Webster claimed an incredible 52 victims behind the stumps, 40 of them in the league while Lawrie Herbert, with 60 wickets at 6.01, demonstrated that Smith's had strength in depth, too, by taking the league-bowling prize for the second teams. But it was not a clean sweep for Smiths for Brian Anderson and Don Baker scored nearly 1,150 runs between them for Otley Town to take the top two slots in the "A" Division batting averages with Anderson also claiming the top all-rounder award.

Otley Town grabbed the limelight from Smiths in the next campaign. They claimed both the League title and the Second Teams title in **1977**. But the Smiths' 2nd wicket double act of Pearce and Metcalfe moved into rampant mood as May went out when they became the first pair to produce 200-plus runs in partnership in the league's history. Their new record stand of 227 was built on the back of 43 boundaries against Farnley Estate, Pearce helping himself to an unbeaten 158 to create a new League individual scoring high – 19 more runs than Keith Smith had amassed in 1974. Metcalfe was also unbeaten on 60, the unbroken stand halted when Pearce declared with Smith's on 232 for 1 but the Estate side hung on to claim a draw, losing seven wickets for 109.

There were a couple of new names on trophies, too. Kirkstall Forge in their first of just three seasons in the league took the B Section title while Oxford Place claimed their one and only Pool Paper Mills Cup triumph, Smiths Sports picking up the Cawthorne Cup. George Baines (Scalebor Park) topped the A Section batting list with the Smith's all-rounder Arnie Beech just pipping Colin Oldfield (Pudsey Congs) to the bowling prize by .33 of a run.

The **1978** season was an extraordinary one for both Ralph Middlebrook, the Pudsey Congs all-rounder, and Francis Quinn, Otley Town's wicket machine. Middlebrook was second in both the A Section's batting and bowling averages as he played a leading role in seeing Congs to the league title for the first time while Quinn, playing half the season in the second team then half in the first at Otley won the league's bowling prize with 35 wickets at 5.89 and went within a whisker of picking up the second team award finishing .64 of a run behind his team-mate Derek Hawley. "I remember our captain Billy Mason putting him in the seconds when he came back to us," said Hawley who picked up 73 wickets to take his prize while Quinn collected 35 scalps for each of the Otley sides. Neighbours Ben Rhydding claimed their first trophy as B Section champions while the Otley side carried off both the Cups.

Otley all but swept the board in **1979** taking the A Division title for both first and second team competitions and the Cawthorne Cup. But the Pool Paper Mills trophy was captured by Riddlesden in their first season in the league – and they went on to prove what efficient cup fighters they were for though they spent just four seasons in the Dales they picked up the Pool Paper Mills Cup three times.

Malcolm Franks, still a formidable performer, was top all-rounder in the league that season mainly on the strength of a bowling display, which saw him finish top of the bowling averages with 38 wickets at 8.47 runs apiece. Beech, another long serving all-rounder, had a similar season taking both awards in the second teams' competition and picking up all ten wickets for 25 against Olicanians on June 9 for good measure.

1980 was a watershed year for Smiths Sports, so long a major power in the Dales Council. They won the Division A title at both first and second team levels to mark the end of an era. They were told that the sports ground in Coal Hill Lane, Rodley, which had hosted cricket, football and tennis for many years was to become a residential development and so plans were put in motion for the Smiths side to merge with nearby soccer club Farsley Celtic.

A new ground alongside the soccer ground at Throstle Nest, Farsley, was levelled and seeded and left for a year to settle while Smiths started life anew as Farsley Celtic. It was fast bowler Kenny Booth who was the side's last player to make his mark as the league said farewell to Smiths by finishing second in the bowling averages with 60 wickets at 6.75 runs apiece to underpin his side's title winning effort. But Pearce did pass a personal milestone in that last year for Smith's when he lifted a six into the Coal Hill Lane pavilion in the May fixture with Scalebor Park to take his league runs tally beyond the 10,000 mark.

Meanwhile Park batsman O'Brien was also building a fine reputation as a most successful accumulator of runs. He had topped the league's batting average first in 1978 with 540 runs at 45.00, was second in 1979 with 600 runs at an average of almost 43, was top again in the season under review with 680 runs at 48.57, following that with another first place in 1981 with 613 runs at 51.08 and, after dropping to fifth place in 1982, won the batting prize for a fourth time in six seasons in 1983 with 633 runs at 45.21.

Before leaving 1980, however, it is worth noting there is the little matter of New Wortley's visit to High Eldwick on August 10. Eldwick and Gilstead's second eleven managed 110 on a damp wicket wondering whether it might be enough – it was by more than 100 with the Wortley side tumbling out for just six. Wilf Anderson led the demolition with six wickets for two runs from 12 overs, 10 of which were maidens and Andy Maude finished it off with three for none. Wortley held that particular unwanted record on their own until the opening day of June, 2002, when New Farnley, replying to a South Parade Baptist score of 42, also fell for six. This time around Steve Bedford picked up eight wickets for two runs from his seven overs, six of which were maidens

Eldwick's first team took the league title for the first time the following season with their second team finishing level at the top with Bramley in Section 1 of the 2nd XI's programme. The **1981** campaign was also marked by a new first wicket record set by the prolific Scalebor Park pair Baines and O'Brien who opened August with an unbroken partnership of 225 against neighbours Pool Paper Mills. Both of them hit centuries, the first time it had happened in the Dales. It was also a first (trophy year) for Olicanians who picked up the Cawthorne Cup.

Eldwick's second string picked up the Cawthorne Cup in **1982** – the club's one Cup success in its 10 year run in the Dales while neighbours Riddlesden made it three trophies in four seasons in the Pool Paper Mills Cup. Farsley Celtic celebrated their first season at their new ground by taking the league title while two wicketkeeping Wilkinsons topped the batting averages. In Division A it was Esholt's Geoff Wilkinson who led the way with a century among his 608 runs at an average of 35.76 while in Division B, PPM's Ken Wilkinson not only collected the batting prize but the league wicketkeeping prize, too, with 31 victims. The A Division top bowler was Keith Robertshaw whose medium pace swing bowling brought him 82 wickets at 7.74 for Wibsey. But perhaps the best afternoon's work came from Terry Fletcher whose 21 overs for Croma at New Farnley in Division A on July 3 cost him just 28 runs and earned him all ten wickets.

New Farnley were unstoppable in **1983** taking both the league title and the Pool Paper Mills Cup. Bowlers Barry Finch and Alan Swarbreck, sharing 116 league wickets, finished second and third in the league bowling list to play leading roles in the Farnley side's success. There was a new 10th wicket record partnership created, too, of 88 by Greg O'Hara and D. Sunderland for Eldwick and

Colin Oldfield.

Smiths Sports captain Roy Webster receives the PPM Cup in 1976 from league president Stanley Handford.

Gilstead against Farsley Celtic (whose second string picked up the Cawthorne Cup) while Eldwick's Stan Robinson topped the bowling averages and Tony Kingett turned in a 10 for 31 performance for the club against New Farnley.

The **1984** campaign brought a photo finish in the league with Esholt and Ben Rhydding finishing with identical records at the top well clear of Croma. Tony Winn took 58 wickets at an average of 8.48 to win the league bowling prize and spearhead Esholt's successful assault on the title though the batting of J. Clark, D. Sharples and N. Hatton did much for Ben Rhydding's search for glory. The procedure for deciding the title winners where sides finished with equal points, the handbook at the time indicated, was to divide the average runs per wicket FOR by the average runs per wicket AGAINST of the nose to nose finishing sides. A tight finale indeed!

Runs were the order of the day at Throstle Nest in early July when a new record aggregate high was achieved by Farsley Celtic (236 for 5 dec) and Leeds YMCA (241 for 8). When the clubs had met at YMCA on the opening day of the season Kenny Booth and Phil Spavin had put on 131 for Celtic to establish a new 5th wicket record. The 6th wicket record also went in 1984 with the Rodley pair Les Fussey and Glynn Brown sharing an unbroken stand of 141 against Adel in mid July. Ironically Fussey would later move on to the Adel club. Ingrow St Johns picked up their only trophy, too, in 1984 claiming the Pool Paper Mills Cup while Esholt made it something of a double campaign with their second string winning the Cawthorne Cup

Croma, winning 19 of their 22 games in Division A in 1985, finished just one point shy of 100 in taking their first senior title. P Wiggins, with 51 wickets at an average of 6.71 won the bowling prize to lead the way for them but runs from M. Ashworth and N. Hardy played an important role in Croma's success, too. It was a new league points record, their total of 99 a staggering 30 points more than second placed Eldwick and, perhaps more commendable, the record was achieved with an average age of Croma's players of 45.

In B Division it turned out to be a fine season for Peter Stebbings, the wicketkeeper-opening batsman of Lloyds Bank. He had one innings of 99 in his total of 668 runs which took him to second place in the B Division batting list while his 31 victims behind the stumps earned him the league's wicketkeeping prize. There was a 10 wicket haul for P. Bell (Ben Rhydding) in a second team game against Farsley Celtic in early July. His victims cost him 48 runs off 18 overs while Cup silverware this time around was claimed by Farsley Celtic and Meanwood Park Hospital.

It was, however, Ian Dobson who was the (six) hit of the campaign. Playing for Rodley, in their match against Farsley Celtic, he did Mick Knapton, (an all-rounder of no little skill who shared in a new league 8th wkt partnership for second elevens the following season), no favours in hitting him for 36 in a single over. Six successive sixes had never been managed before in the league nor since. But Knapton has broad shoulders for a diminutive man and can still bring out a wide smile when he is reminded about that afternoon which, after all, did provide the decade with a spectacular conclusion.

THE CHAMPIONS AND CUP WINNERS, DECADE BY DECADE

Division winners and their records and winners of the Cup competitions.............seasons 1976–1985

(Win 5pts, tie 2pts, draw 1pt with 2pts bonus pts for faster scoring in drawn games)

League	Winners	P.	W.	L.	Pts 1	Pts 3	Pts.	Year	Pool P M Cup	Cawthorne Cup
Sec. A	Smiths Sports	22	15	3	4	0	79	1976	Smiths Sports	Esholt
	Oxford Place	22	12	6	3	1	66			
	Pudsey Congs	22	12	6	3	1	66			
Sec. B	Croma	18	14	1	2	1	75			
	Scalebor Park	18	13	2	2	1	70			
	Pool Paper Mills	18	9	6	3	0	48			
2nd Teams	Otley Town	21	15	3	3	0	78			
	Smiths Sports	21	14	5	2	0	72			
	Esholt	21	13	5	2	1	70			
	Pudsey Congs	21	13	5	2	1	70			
Sec. A	Otley Town, 4pts-2ties	22	12	3	3	2	73	1977	Oxford Place	Smiths Sports
	Smith Sports	22	12	3	6	1	69			
	Pudsey Congs	22	11	5	3	3	67			
Sec. B	Kirkstall Forge	18	12	4	2	0	62			
	Olicanians	18	11	3	3	1	61			
	Ben Rhydding	18	11	5	2	0	57			
2nd Teams	Otley Town	18	12	2	4	0	64			
	Pudsey Congs	18	9	1	5	3	59			
	Ben Rhydding	18	10	6	2	0	52			

League	Winners	P.	W.	L.	D.	Pts.	Year	Pool P M Cup	Cawthorne Cup
Sec. A	Pudsey Congs	20	14	5	0	73	**1978**	Otley Town	Otley Town
	Scalebor Park	20	13	5	1	69			
	Otley Town	20	11	5	2	63			
Sec. B	Ben Rhydding	18	13	3	1	69			
	Pool Paper Mills	18	13	5	0	65			
	New Farnley	18	11	5	2	61			
2nd Teams	Otley Town	20	18	2	0	90			
	Ben Rhydding	20	13	5	2	67			
	Pudsey Congs	20	13	5	2	67			
Div. A	Otley Town	22	14	3	4	77	**1979**	Riddlesden	Otley Town
	Smiths Sports	22	13	4	3	74			
	Kirkstall Forge	22	12	8	2	62			
Div. B	Phoenix Park	26	19	3	4	99			
	New Farnley	26	18	5	3	93			
	Eldwick & Gilstead	26	17	4	4	92			
2nds. Div A	Otley Town	21	15	3	2	80			
	Smiths Sports	21	15	4	2	77			
	Ben Rhydding	21	13	4	1	75			
2nds. Div B	Morton, 2pts, 1tie.	20	12	5	2	64			
	Eldwick & Gilstead	20	11	5	0	59			
	Riddlesden	20	10	5	1	57			
Div. A	Smiths Sports	22	13	5	2	73	**1980**	New Farnley	Esholt
	New Farnley	22	13	5	0	69			
	Scalebor Park	22	9	6	3	58			

League	Winners	P.	W.	L.	D.	Pts.	Year	Pool P M Cup	Cawthorne Cup
Div. B	Bramley Sp. 2pts, 1tie	26	19	3	2	1	102			Olicanians
	Wibsey	26	15	6	3	2	84			
	Leeds YMCA	26	15	6	4	1	82			
2nds. Div A	Smiths Sports	22	17	1	3	1	91			
	Esholt	22	16	2	3	1	86			
	Ben Rhydding, 2pts, 1tie	22	10	7	3	1	58			
2nds. B Div	Pudsey St Law.	22	14	5	3	0	73			
	Pool Paper Mills	22	13	5	4	0	69			
	Civil Service	22	9	11	2	0	47			
Div. A	Eldwick and Gilstead	22	12	5	5	0	65	**1981**	Riddlesden	
	Croma	22	10	4	5	3	64			
	Wibsey	22	8	7	3	4	55			
Div. B Sec 1.	Leeds Zingari	21	11	3	3	4	70			
	Leeds YMCA	21	11	2	5	3	69			
	Pudsey St Law.	21	10	4	5	2	61			
Div. B Sec 2.	Lloyds Bank	20	10	1	5	4	67			
	Olicanians	20	7	11	2	0	37			
	Morton Banks	20	5	8	5	2	36			
2nds. Sec 1.	Bramley	21	15	4	2	0	77			
	Eldwick & Gilstead	21	15	4	2	0	77			
	Ben Rhydding	21	13	6	1	1	69			
2nds. Sec 2.	Pool Paper Mills	21	11	4	4	2	65			
	Morton Banks	21	11	6	4	0	59			
	Riddlesden	21	9	8	3	1	51			
2nds. Sec 3.	Leeds YMCA	20	8	10	2	0	42			
	Lloyds Bank	20	6	7	6	1	39			
	Ingrow St Johns	20	5	13	1	1	29			

League	Winners	P.	W.	L.	D.	Pts.	Year	Pool P M Cup	Cawthorne Cup
Div. A	Farsley Celtic	22	16	2	4	84	**1982**	Riddlesden	Eldwick & Gilstead
	Riddlesden	22	10	5	7	65			
	Esholt	22	11	6	5	64			
Div. B Sec 1.	Pool Paper Mills	22	13	4	5	74			
	Ingrow St Johns	22	14	6	2	72			
	Oxford Place	22	12	7	3	65			
Div. B Sec 2.	High Royds	22	12	4	6	72			
	Civil Service	22	12	7	3	65			
	New Wortley, 2pts, 1tie	22	11	8	3	59			
2nds. Sec 1.	Esholt	22	13	7	2	67			
	Ben Rhydding, 2pts, 1tie	22	12	7	3	66			
	Pool Paper Mills	22	10	8	4	58			
2nds. Sec 2.	Riddlesden	22	15	4	3	78			
	Farsley Celtic, 2pts, 1tie	22	13	2	7	77			
	New Farnley	22	10	5	7	61			
2nds. Sec 3.	Olicanians	22	10	8	4	56			
	Ingrow St Johns	22	9	8	5	50			
	Wortley Highfield, 2pts 1tie	22	7	11	4	40			
Div. A	New Farnley	22	12	3	7	71	**1983**	New Farnley	Farsley Celtic
	Eldwick & Gilstead	22	11	4	7	66			
	Esholt	22	9	5	8	55			
Div. B Sec 1	High Royds	21	14	1	6	76			
	Ben Rhydding	21	12	2	7	71			
	Olicanians	21	12	4	5	65			

League	Winners	P.	W.	L.	D.	Pts.	Year	Pool P M Cup	Cawthorne Cup
Div. B Sec 2	Adel	20	8	3	9	0	49			
	Nat West Bank	20	6	7	7	0	37			
	Wortley Highfield	20	6	8	6	0	36			
2nds. Sec 1.	Farsley Celtic	21	10	3	8	0	58			
	Ben Rhydding	21	9	5	5	2	56			
	Pool Paper Mills	21	7	5	7	2	48			
2nds. Sec 2.	Eldwick & Gilstead	21	9	2	8	2	59			
	Pudsey St Law. 2pts, 1tie	21	9	5	4	2	57			
	Olicanians	21	9	5	6	1	54			
2nds. Sec 3	Civil Service	20	8	3	9	0	49			
	New Wortley	20	7	6	6	1	44			
	Scalebor Park	20	5	7	6	2	37			
Div. A	Esholt	22	16	5	0	1	83	**1984**	Ingrow St Johns	Esholt
	Ben Rhydding	22	16	5	0	1	83			
	Croma	22	13	6	1	2	72			
Div. B Sec 1.	Olicanians	21	14	4	3	0	73			
	Leeds Zingari	21	12	5	0	4	72			
	Pudsey St Lawrence	21	13	4	3	1	71			
Div. B Sec 2.	Pudsey Congs	20	14	4	1	1	74			
	Meanwood Park Hospital	20	14	5	1	0	71			
	New Wortley, 2pts, 1tie	20	12	5	1	1	66			
2nds. Sec 1.	Farsley Celtic	21	16	3	2	0	82			
	Esholt	21	13	5	0	3	74			
	Ben Rhydding	21	14	6	0	1	73			
2nds. Sec 2.	Olicanians	21	18	3	0	0	90			
	New Farnley, 2pts, 1 tie	21	15	5	0	0	77			
	Rodley	21	9	10	1	1	49			

League	Winners	P.	W.	L.	D.	Pts.	Year	Pool P M Cup	Cawthorne Cup
2nds. Sec 3.	Ingrow St. Johns	20	10	9	0	1	53			Meanwood Park Hos.
	Scalebor Park	20	10	9	0	1	53			
	Meanwood Park Hospital	20	6	10	3	1	36			
Div. A	Croma.	22	19	1	1	1	99	1985	Farsley Celtic	
	Eldwick & Gilstead	22	12	5	3	2	69			
	Ingrow St Johns	22	11	7	2	2	63			
Div. B	Oxford Place	26	17	4	4	1	92			
	Adel	26	14	3	6	3	85			
	New Wortley	26	13	4	5	4	82			
2nds. Sec 1.	Olicanians	21	15	2	3	1	81			
	Ben Rhydding	21	12	4	3	2	69			
	Pool Paper Mills	21	10	5	3	3	62			
2nds. Sec 2.	Ingrow St Johns	20	12	6	2	0	62			
	Meanw'd PH # 1pt deducted	20	10	6	3	1	#55			
	New Wortley	20	7	6	6	1	44			

AN AVERAGE VIEW

Season by season leaders of the averages ~ the third decade, 1976–1985.

The Batsmen

* Denotes Not Out

League	Name/Club	Ins.	NO	H.Sc	Rns.	Av.
1976						
Sec. A	B. Anderson, Otley Town	20	1	113	617	32.47
	D. Baker, Otley Town	18	0	79	524	29.1
	M. Jackson, Pudsey Congs	13	3	59	284	28.4
Sec. B	R. Patrick, Scalebor P.	13	4	70*	337	37.44
	A. Thornton, Croma.	16	7	60*	317	35.2
	P. Newton Croma.	14	2	56	396	33
2nd. Teams	W. Smart, Pudsey Congs.	16	6	78*	324	32.4
	G. Bennett, Esholt	15	2	74*	268	20.69
	R. Bennett, Smiths Sports	17	1	57	312	19.5
1977						
Sec. A	G. Baines, Scalebor P.	17	2	87	509	33.93
	D. Pearce, Smiths Sports	17	3	153*	431	30.78
	J. Fletcher, Croma.	16	2	60	422	30.14
Sec. B	T. Drury, CEGB.	12	1	69	296	26.9
	B. Wilson, Ben Rhydding	17	0	90	407	23.94
	T. Rainford. Kirkstall Forge	16	4	39	287	23.91
2nd. Teams	C. Cawood, Pudsey Congs	12	4	59	224	28
	P. Brogan, Otley Town	13	4	74*	230	25.55
	R. Bennett, Smiths Sports	12	1	103	270	24.55

The Bowlers

Year	Name/Club	Ovs.	Mdn	Rns.	Wks.	Av.
1976						
	D. Benn, Smiths Sports	300	101	580	94	6.17
	C. Oldfield, Pudsey Congs.	275	79	584	83	7.04
	D. Jackson, Farnley Estate	114	25	330	38	8.65
	M. Cryer, PPM.	208	59	417	66	6.31
	T. Fletcher, Croma.	202	57	399	51	7.82
	J. Watson, Scalebor P.	163	41	359	40	8.98
	L. Herbert, Smiths Sports	146	45	361	60	6.01
	G. Bennett, Esholt	77	24	213	35	6.08
	D. Hawley, Esholt	184	62	354	58	6.1
1977						
	A. Beech, Smiths Sports	96	26	222	30	7.4
	C. Oldfield, Pudsey Congs.	257	83	534	69	7.73
	R. Middlebrook, Pudsey C.	104	37	248	31	8
	D. Ashton, Olicanians	189	59	370	64	5.78
	P. Chadwick, New Farnley	108	33	221	35	6.31
	S. Holmes, New Farnley	107	31	232	30	7.3
	M. Lockwood, Ben Rhydding	107	32	202	38	5.31
	G. Robinson, Pudsey Congs	123	36	263	43	6.11
	G. Lawson, New Farnley	207	74	398	53	7.59

Batting

League	Name/Club	Ins.	NO	H.Sc	Rns.	Av.
Sec. A	P. O'Brien, Scalebor P.	17	5	85*	540	45
	R. Middlebrook, Puds	17	3	107	561	40.07
	B. Rhodes, Smiths Sports	16	6	70	358	35.8
Sec. B	B. Wilson, Ben Rhydding	16	5	83*	470	42.73
	B. Martin, PPM	15	3	72	323	26.92
	J. Atkinson, Crompark	14	2	49*	303	25.25
2nd. Teams	R. Bolton, Otley Town	18	4	99*	478	34.14
	J. Slingsby, Ben Rhydding	14	4	38*	238	23.8
	T. Lazenby, Esholt	12	0	40	262	21.83
Div. A	D. Hunter, Leeds Zingari	15	7	82*	400	50
	P. O'Brien, Scalebor P.	17	3	79	600	42.86
	A. Danskin, Otley Town	18	4	101*	562	40.14
	O. White, Croma.	16	3	55*	459	35.31
	G. Baines, Scalebor P.	20	3	84	585	34.41
	B. Huby, PPM	19	4	92	504	33.6
Div. B	D. Spragg, Riddlesden	23	3	107	622	31.1
	C. Grinrod, Leeds YMCA	20	5	73	453	30.2
	M. Speight, Morton	13	2	63	298	27.9
2nd. Teams	B. Taylor, Otley Town	15	3	100*	305	25.42
	A. Beech, Smiths Sports	13	3	93	247	24.7
	R. Brogan, Otley Town	17	3	68	313	22.35

Bowling

Year	Name/Club	Ovs.	Mdn	Rns.	Wks.	Av.
1978	F. Quinn, Otley Town	122	40	206	35	5.89
	R. Middlebrook, Puds	126	47	272	36	7.5
	B. Newall, Pudsey Congs	100	28	280	35	7.76
	C. Bentley, PPM	185	61	381	59	6.46
	M. Parker, Ben Rhydding	141	38	291	43	6.77
	N. Hatton, Ben Rhydding	125	23	236	33	7.15
	D. Hawley, Otley Town	223	82	358	73	4.9
	F. Quinn, Otley Town	97	34	194	35	5.54
	G. Penwarden, Ben Rhyd.	89	25	207	33	6.27
1979	M. Franks, Esholt	117	28	322	38	8.47
	N. Hardy, Croma.	143	33	354	39	9.08
	F. Quinn, Otley Town	157	54	350	37	9.46
	W. Mason, Otley Town	169	56	357	39	9.62
	D. Benn, Smiths Sports	266	87	628	63	9.97
	B. Finch, Smiths Sports	149	41	342	34	10.05
	K. Ambridge, New Farnley	105	28	183	32	5.71
	P. Anderson, Riddlesden	144	48	219	35	6.28
	S. Robinson, Eldwick & Gils.	189	70	323	50	6.46
	A. Beech, Smiths Sports	153	45	348	64	5.44
	D. Hawley Otley Town	215	65	405	68	5.96
	S. Riddiough, Riddlesden	217	67	478	78	6.12

League	Name/Club	Ins.	NO	H.Sc	Rns.	Av.	Year	Name/Club	Ovs.	Mdn	Rns.	Wks.	Av.
Div. A	P. O'Brien, Scalebor P.	18	4	121*	680	48.57	**1980**	S. Robinson, Eldwick & Gil.	252	75	491	73	6.73
	J. Spragg, Riddlesden	17	2	112*	474	31.6		K. Booth, Smiths Sports	203	54	405	60	6.75
	D. Harris, Pheonix Park	15	3	57*	333	27.75		P. Anderson, Riddlesden	153	52	281	52	8.26
	A. Kingett, Eldwick & Gil.	16	2	77*	372	26.57		B. Finch, Smiths Sports	287	88	534	64	8.34
	S. Robinson, Eldwick & Gil.	14	3	61*	292	26.55		H. Rider, Oxford Place	161	40	347	40	8.68
	J. Clapham, Croma	17	2	64*	369	24.6		T. Fletcher, Croma	110	28	280	31	9.03
Div. B	J. Mortimer, Leeds YMCA	19	9	55*	350	35		K. Robertshaw, Wibsey	357	123	640	97	6.6
	J. Atkinson, Crompark	20	4	104*	454	28.38		T. Powell, Bramley Sports	104	31	235	34	6.91
	N. Thornton, Bramley Sp.	13	1	56	314	26.17		D. Walsh, Morton Banks	249	98	436	63	6.92
2nd. Teams	S. Rae, Ben Rhydding	15	1	52	356	25.43							
	W, Stott, Smiths Sports	16	5	50	239	21.73							
	N. Coward, Riddlesden	13	2	54*	222	20.18							
Div. A	P. O'Brien, Scalebor P.	19	7	106*	613	51.08	**1981**	A. Swarbreck, New Farnley	114	25	240	33	7.27
	T. Fletcher, Croma	15	6	73*	257	28.56		N. Thornton. Bramley	240	90	445	59	7.54
	G. Wilkinson, Esholt	15	1	54	366	26.14		K. Pinnion, Bramley	122	34	296	37	8
	K. Booth, Farsley Celtic	13	1	114	313	26.08		M. Haigh, Riddlesden	188	65	383	46	8.33
	G. Baines, Scalebor P.	18	1	101*	399	23.47		K. Booth Farsley Celtic	161	36	387	46	8.41
	J. Smith, Eldwick & Gilstead	14	4	46	234	23.4		P. Anderson, Riddlesden	170	56	349	41	8.51
Div. B.	J. Mortimer, Leeds YMCA	14	6	93	489	61.13		D. Hunter, Leeds Zingari	121	34	295	37	7.97
	P. Allinson, Adel	13	3	58	320	32		N. Batty, Morton Banks	121	32	314	38	8.26
	P.R. Fisher, Leeds YMCA	12	1	71*	327	29.72		A. Stevenson, Morton Banks	180	57	390	46	8.48

League	Name/Club	Ins.	NO	H.Sc	Rns.	Av.	Year	Name/Club	Ovs.	Mdn	Rns	Wks.	Av.
2nd. Teams													
	M. Wrigley, Ben Rhydding	13	1	115*	546	45.5		W. Anderson, Eldwick & Gil.	168	71	256	43	5.95
	W. Brace, Riddlesden	18	3	102*	533	35.53		C. Vorley, Bramley	199	62	313	52	6.02
	D. Waite, Leeds YMCA	17	0	95	472	27.76		M. Cryer, PPM	206	64	388	62	6.4
Div. A							**1982**						
	G. Wilkinson, Esholt	18	1	108	608	35.76		K. Robertshaw, Wibsey	329.4	110	635	82	7.74
	P. Anderson, Riddlesden	18	4	88	457	32.64		G. Royston, Riddlesden	302.1	107	615	73	8.42
	T. Dawson, Esholt	14	1	100	397	30.54		P. Anderson, Riddlesden	204.3	79	355	41	8.65
	D. Jones, Farsley Celtic	17	2	47	442	29.47		T. Fletcher, Croma.	158.4	43	412	43	9.58
	P. O'Brien, Scalebor P.	18	2	80	467	29.19		K. Booth, Farsley Celtic	250	76	646	66	9.79
	R. Burston, New Farnley	17	0	97	466	27.41		B. Finch, Farsley Celtic	298.2	77	716	72	9.94
Div. B.													
	K. Wilkinson PPM	20	5	63	484	32.27		R. Underwood, Lloyds Bank	110.3	36	219	31	7.06
	J. Barton, High Royds	18	4	85	428	30.57		R. Chew, Oxford Place	237.1	60	462	63	7.33
	N. Hatton, Ben Rhydding	19	4	85	430	28.67		D. Unwin, Ingrow St Johns	266	75	567	68	8.34
2nd. Teams													
	S. Riddlough, Riddlesden	12	1	123	428	38.91		G. Emmett, Riddlesden	102	34	201	35	5.74
	D. Naylor, Farsley Celtic	12	4	111*	267	33.38		A. Beech, Farsley Celtic	103.1	34	187	32	5.84
	W. Scott, Farsley Celtic	15	2	75*	404	31.08		I. Dobson, Bramley	127.2	26	298	43	6.92
Div. A.							**1983**						
	P. O'Brien, Scalebor P.	17	3	138*	633	45.21		S. Robinson, Eldwick & Gil.	153.1	51	304	38	8
	R. Bolton, PPM	12	1	113	391	35.54		B. Finch, New Farnley	182.3	65	377	47	8.02
	D. Unwin, Ingrow St Johns	12	1	92	332	30.18		A. Swarbreck, New Farnley	273	93	629	69	9.12
	D. Jones, Farsley Celtic	15	1	66	387	27.64		G. O'Hara, Eldwick & Gil.	170	68	346	37	9.35
	I. Mortimer, Leeds YMCA	18	5	92	357	27.46		N. Thornton, Rodley	183.4	62	441	42	10.5
	J. Smith, Eldwick & Gilstead	15	2	90	343	26.38		T. Fletcher, Croma.	138.1	26	370	35	10.57
Div. B.													
	C. Jones, Ben Rhydding	14	2	65	371	30.92		L. Herbert, Oxford Place	139.5	57	246	37	6.65
	M. Connolly, Lloyds Bank	16	4	52*	319	26.58		D. Noble, High Royds	91.1	29	211	30	7.03
	A. Plumb, Lloyds Bank	12	1	59*	256	22.27		P. Warburton, Pudsey St Law.	148	47	265	36	7.36

Batting

League	Name/Club	Ins.	NO	H.Sc	Rns.	Av.
2nd. Teams						
	R. Howley, Ingrow St Johns	13	5	53*	237	29.62
	R. Watson, Lloyds Bank	16	4	49	279	23.25
	J. Somers, Ben Rhydding	16	2	77	325	23.21
Div. A	P. Taylor, Scalebor P.	13	4	87*	461	51.22
	R. Elliston, Scalebor P.	20	4	105	589	36.81
	M. Ashworth, Croma.	21	4	69	508	29.88
	D. Unwin, Ingrow St Johns	20	0	92	588	29.4
	J. Clark, Ben Rhydding	13	1	112*	348	29
	D. Sharples, Ben Rhydding	16	4	71	340	28.33
Div. B	P. Bullock, Leeds Zingari	21	4	92*	623	36.65
	I. Cocking, Pudsey St Law.	17	7	64*	338	33.8
	P. Stebbings, Lloyds Bank	16	0	85	497	31.06
2nd. Teams						
	R. Hogarth, Olicanians	18	7	66	429	39
	M. Franks, Esholt	14	6	48	302	37.88
	N. Allitt, Pudsey St Law.	12	4	72	266	33.25
Div. A	J. Clark, Ben Rhydding	17	1	109*	596	37.25
	K. Booth, Farsley Celtic	17	3	111	442	31.57
	T. Houghton, Scalebor P.	15	4	98	335	30.45
	T. Burnley, Eldwick & Gilstead	14	1	95	335	25.76
	M. Ashworth, Croma.	20	3	80*	428	25.18
	G. Metcalfe, High Royds	20	3	60	426	25.06

Bowling

Year	Name/Club	Ovs.	Mdn	Rns.	Wks.	Av.
	J. Stephenson, New Farnley	122.5	52	235	38	6.18
	M. Christopher, Olican.	120.3	33	279	36	7.75
	A. Beech, Farsley Celtic	119.4	30	283	36	7.86
1984	A. Winn, Esholt	221.4	75	492	58	8.48
	D. Unwin, Ingrow St Johns	252.1	79	516	60	8.6
	J. Kinghorn, Scalebor P.	298.3	87	716	79	9.06
	P. Sutcliffe, Ben Rhydding	151.2	44	337	36	9.36
	S. Holmes, New Farnley	124.4	21	369	39	9.46
	T. Fletcher, Croma.	166.1	52	357	37	9.65
	G. Exley, New Wortley	130.5	40	277	45	6.16
	R. Middleton, Olicanians	297.4	109	490	64	7.66
	J. Coates, Olicanians	113	28	302	39	7.74
	R. Dewhurst, Olicanians	221.4	84	373	62	6.02
	M. Davis, Pudsey St Law.	181.1	63	319	46	6.94
	R. Newhouse, New Farnley	183.4	58	426	60	7.1
1985	P. Wiggins, Croma.	147.3	39	342	51	6.71
	N. Carroll, Ben Rhydding	126.3	38	280	39	7.18
	S. Worsnop, Pudsey St Law.	199.4	58	406	48	8.45
	G. Simpson, Pudsey St Law.	156.5	45	316	37	8.54
	K. Booth, Farsley Celtic	175.1	58	397	46	8.63
	M. Groves, Croma.	162	53	371	42	8.83

League	Name/Club	Ins.	NO	H.Sc	Rns.	Av.	Year	Name/Club	Ovs.	Mdn	Rns.	Wks.	Av.
Div. B	P. Allison, Adel	13	3	77*	535	53.5		P. Flint, Oxford Place	120.4	42	265	35	7.57
	P. Stebbings, Lloyds Bank	23	2	99	668	31.81		D. Hardcastle, Yorks Switch.	198.1	64	427	53	8.06
	K. Wilknson, PPM	19	0	73	550	28.95		M. Tinkler, Morton Banks	227.1	79	469	49	9.57
2nd. Teams	C. Bottomley, Ingrow St Johns	12	2	88	371	37.1		P. Bell, Ben Rhydding	113.1	43	192	39	4.92
	R. Driver, New Wortley	13	2	104*	391	35.56		R. Dewhurst, Olicanians	246.3	89	426	75	5.68
	J.B. Somers, Ben Rhydding	15	4	78*	322	29.27		S. Nelson, Olicanians	187.4	58	279	43	6.49

Award winners, Decade by decade, 1976–1985

Trophy winners of the league's miscellaneous awards over the years

Year	All-Round. A Div	All-Round. B Div	All-Round. 2nds	W-keeper	Fielder	U-18 Bat	U-18 Bowl	Fast 50
1976	B. Anderson Otley Town	R. Wallace Wil. & Math	G. Bennett Esholt	R. Webster Smiths Sp.	D. Thompson Farnley Est.	P. Heaton Esholt	A. Moss Pudsey S.L.	T. Dudley Esholt
1977	R. Middlebrook Pudsey Cong	T. Rainford Kirkstall Forge		R. Webster Smtihs Sp	D. Lewis Leeds YMCA	P. Brogan Otley Town	T. Lockwood Ben Rhydd.	T. Dudley Esholt & D.Holdsworth Phoenix P
1978	R. Middlebrook Pudsey Cong	A. Swarbreck New Farnley	J. Slingsby Ben Rhyding	P. Sidebottom	P. O'Brien Scalebor Park	R. Bolton Otley Town	G. Penwarden Ben Rhydding	D. Pearce Smiths Sports
1979	M. Franks Esholt	A. Swarbreck New Farnley	A. Beech Smiths Sp			R. Brogan Otley Town	S. Riddiough Riddlesden	D.Richardson Olicanians & P. Flint Oxford Place
1980	S. Robinson Eldwick & Gil.	J. Atkinson Crompark	N. Scott Morton Banks			M. Culley Pudsey St. L.	I. Beesting Pudsey St. L.	D. Boscow Leeds Zing
1981	K. Booth Farsley Celtic	J. Barker Lloyds Bank	J. Dobson Ben Rhydd.	P Stebbings Lloyds Bank	P. Lund Lloyds Bank	J. Dobson Ben Rhydd	J. Dobson Ben Rhydd.	D. Walker Ben Rhydd
1982	P. Anderson Riddlesden	J. Barton High Royds	J. Haider Riddlesden	K. Wilkinson Pool P.M.	S. Wilkinson New Wortley	J. Clark Ben Rhydd	C. Taylor Scalebor Park	J. Moody Scalebor Pk
1983	D. Unwin Ingrow St Johns	N. Hatton Ben Rhydd	R. Watson Lloyds Bank	J. Broklebank High Royds	S. Wilkinson New Wortley	T. Hatton Ben Rhydd	J. Clark Ben Rhydd.	F. Sparkes New Wortley
1984	D. Unwin Ingrow St Johns	R. Chew Oxford Place	J Dobson Rodley	G. Wilkinson Esholt	M. Griffin New Wortley	N. Allitt Pudsey St. L.	M. Harrison New Farnley	M. Hall Lloyds Bank
1985	K. Booth Farsley Celtic	P. Flint Oxford Place		P. Stebbings Lloyds Bank	S. Wilkinson New Wortley	C. Bottomley Ingrow St Johns	A. Dodds Sandmoor	P. Kitson Scalebor Park

AT THE DOUBLE......No 4.

The best place there is to play cricket

insists David Warner, cricket correspondent, Telegraph and Argus

NATURALLY, I jumped at the chance in 1975 of covering Yorkshire county cricket home and away for my newspaper, the Telegraph and Argus, and I am still reporting the ups and downs of the most famous cricket club in the world.

As well as writing on many thrilling matches at county level, I have also savoured some epic Test moments at Headingley, including Geoff Boycott's 100th century against Australia in 1977 and the heroics four years later of Ian Botham and Bob Willis as England pulled off one of the most amazing victories in Ashes history.

There was, however, a downside to taking on the job all those years ago – it effectively brought to an end my own playing career for Baildon Meths then in the Bradford Mutual SS League (but now a leading side in the Dales Council) and for Bradford Press whose games were "friendly" but always fiercely competitive. No matter how high the quality of cricket you are watching, nothing can compare with the enjoyment of playing the game oneself and I have also grown to appreciate that village green or minor league cricket has a charm of its own which county nor international cricket can never match.

My "halcyon" years with Baildon Meths, I suppose, were in the late 60s and early 70s when we climbed up through the divisions to become one of the best sides in the league although now "outsiders" were making their mark and fewer of the players were actively connected with the church. A Sunday School league it may have been, but there were still intense rivalries and no side did I enjoy beating more than our "friends" from Bolton Meths. I still remember clearly one game at Belmont (now Sandals School) when we had been dismissed for such a low score that a Bolton Meths batsman left early for a wedding, loudly making it known that his services would not be needed. The visitors still required a handful of runs with their last pair at the cease when a ball from fellow-journalist Steve Kendall found the edge and I held on to a diving slip catch. Sheer delight!

The same joy came from playing for Bradford Press – and never was the competition keener than when the author of this book was in the opposing Yorkshire Post team. Barry Foster and I are good friends and fairly close neighbours in Baildon but neither of us ever went to a cricket field without having one object in mind – and that was winning.

The Bradford Press team later broadened its intake and became the West Yorkshire Press CC with home matches being played at the Yorkshire Post's Glen Road ground at Headingley. If talent had matched enthusiasm in these teams we would have been world-beaters but that's how it generally is with local cricket throughout the Broad Acres – the best place there is to play the game.

David Warner, September, 2004

At the Double partner.............................Kenny Booth

"Kenny – I'm glad you were on my side"

EVERY once in a blue moon in cricket you come across a player who has it all. Good to be around and with talent to spare; a ferocious competitor yet compassionate when opponents deserved compassion; a player you are really glad is on your side.

The final thought of that first paragraph came from David Pearce in an appreciation in the programme for the game played in June, 1988, in aid of the Kenny Booth Memorial Fund. But I am sure that it had been a thought felt by every player fortunate enough to have shared their cricket with the great Smiths and Farsley Celtic all-rounder.

Fielding in the gully and at point for him I often felt I could hear the ball singing in an extremely high-pitched note as it fizzed down. Kenny Booth was not one of those fast bowlers with a run up from here to eternity, he used a few paces and got all his terrific speed with his back and arm – but he was really, really quick. He was also a firm striker of the ball when batting, a fast and big

David Warner.

Kenny Booth.

scorer when necessary and a stubborn defender when it was called for, he was a great fielder and, perhaps as important to his colleagues as all that, had one of the biggest smiles in the Dales Council. He has been sorely missed since leaving to join that great side in the sky at such a comparatively young age.

But he left his mark on Dales Council cricket - and sometimes on me when I faced him down the wicket before I went to join him at Smiths! Maybe the best way to remember him is to use some more of his former captain's programme notes for few people knew him better than the Smiths stalwart.

"A few years ago I had the privilege of presenting Kenny with an award when he reached 1,000 wickets in the Dales Council. When making the presentation I paid a personal tribute to my old mate and I make no apology for repeating what I said. Only seven words but they expressed exactly how I still feel about Kenny. Seven words which, I think, would be echoed by all his team-mates who played cricket with him and I believe any sportsman would have been proud to have them said about him, when said in all honesty, by one of his team-mates whether he was a cricketer, a footballer, a rugby player or whatever.

Kenny – I'm glad you were on my side." – David Pearce.

Earlier he had traced Booth's career with his usual attention to detail. It seems when he first joined the Smiths side in 1965 it was as a wicketkeeper. "All I want to say about that is that as a wicketkeeper he made a very fine bowler," Pearce wrote wryly. He helped to win four league championships and six cups – a major award every other season but on top of that he took the club bowling award seven times often in the face of strong opposition at Smiths, the league top all-rounder award twice and many trophies for outstanding individual performances.

In 1975 he went within a whisker of winning a county-wide competition for bowlers of all club sides and there was disappointment for him in the following season, too, when Smiths completed the league double. Part way through the campaign he was hit by a ball which broke his arm and so he missed both the cup final and the run-in to the title.

As a batsman his top score was 114 though in one match he accounted for 70 out of his side's 81 all out. But it was as a fast bowler that he really made his mark. He took a league record total of wickets of 1,107 and that would have climbed a good deal higher had his slips (and gully!) fielders held on to more fiery catches. But when you could not hang on to the ball that big grin was still there – he knew the batsman who had just escaped would not be free for very long.

Chapter Nine
1986 to 1995
The Fourth Decade: Double, double, toil and treble.

IT was soon clear in the fourth decade of life in the Dales Council that something had to be done about the decline in the numbers of clubs and teams in the league if comfortable survival was to be satisfactorily achieved.

The gradual rise in the size of the Dales during the previous decade began to tail off with clubs leaving to join higher profile leagues or disbanding. By the 1989 campaign the number of teams dipped back in to the 20's. With 22 clubs generating just 29 teams, the strength of the Dales was reduced to mid 1970s levels and it was in this atmosphere that Les Thompson took the helm.

The new president knew he had something of a developing crisis to deal with. "I could see what was happening and decided that the Dales Council must survive at all costs. It might have been a little bit selfish on my part but you see teams were leaving to go into what they saw as better leagues. So I took an active decision to lower our standards and take in clubs wanting to come to us," said Thompson.

"I had to argue my case at committee and there was opposition but I managed to get it through. I even had hopes at one stage that we might amalgamate with the Leeds League. Geographically it would have been a good move for the majority of our clubs but the Leeds League moved in a different direction so it did not happen. Yet we did start to grow once more."

By the end of the decade under review the number of clubs had reached 28, the highest number since 1982 and with 38 teams competing in four divisions, numbers were back in line with the best the league had enjoyed – and it was to grow even stronger in the years immediately following. Meanwhile, though, there was the day-to-day business of producing the goods on the field where Cookridge and Tong went about it at the double and New Farnley moved into treble mode.

There was some pretty fancy scoring, too. YMCA's Bill Davis pushed the boundaries further out in terms of the highest average, then Otley's Peter Lewis set a new top aggregate with 851 runs in 1991 before the final season of the decade brought a staggering effort from Michael Richmond. The New Rover opener achieved a phenomenal average by finishing well into the late nineties – and in the same campaign team-mate Richard Stevens more than matched him in wickets.

But it was Davis who was the star with Simon Stirling of High Royds pushing him hard as top dog for the season when the curtain went up on the decade. Davis topped the **1986** B Division averages with 63.58, hitting an unbeaten century in his 763 runs from 18 knocks. New Zealander Stirling, meanwhile, was doing his stuff in A Division helping to lift the High Royds side to the runners-up slot by taking the leading all-rounder prize for the campaign for finishing second to fellow Kiwi and team-mate Chris Cumberland in the batting list and topping the bowling averages with 60 wickets at 6.37 – and for good measure smashing the fastest 50 of the campaign in 31 minutes. He was at his most devastating in High Royds home game with Adel in mid June when he claimed nine wickets for just 10 runs. Yet it was Scalebor Park, led by George Baines with the bat and Chris Taylor with the ball, who ran away with the A Division title by 14 clear points, Taylor picking up an 8 for 13 return in their clash with Ben Rhydding in June.

In B Division, section one, Lloyds Bank finished champions in spite of Davis' heroics for YMCA. Already promoted, they went into the last game of the season at YMCA needing a draw to make sure of the title – but they had to manage without wicketkeeper and leading batsman Peter Stebbings. He was at his wife Jane's side as they waited for their first child to arrive so I played a dead bat to everything that was thrown down that afternoon and Lloyds took the championship finishing on the same number points as the YM side and the same number of victories - 62 and 10 – but with fewer defeats, three against five. Boring but effective.

Meanwood Park Hospital retained the Cawthorne Cup while the Pool Paper Mills trophy was won for the first time by Adel with C. Foord and P. Allinson setting up a new second wicket partnership record of 224 against Morton Banks in their first round tie, Foord creating a new individual high scoring record of 176.

Farsley Celtic won the PPM trophy for the second time in three years in **1987** with Pudsey Congs taking the Cawthorne Cup but it was Croma, led by the batting of M. Ashworth, who took the Division A title. Ashworth finished top of the averages on 46.90 but Celtic players featured among the other awards with Stuart Tempest picking up the second X1 all rounder trophy and the fastest 50 gong with a whirlwind knock of just 23 minutes. Their wicketkeeper N. Rider was top man in

Martin Connolly.

Peter Stebbings lets one go through to the 'keeper at Olicanians.

his profession and the ever reliable Arnie Beech was the league's leading wicket-taker with 79 victims in the second elevens competition.

The **1988** campaign was dominated by Eldwick and Gilstead batsmen as they charged towards the A Division crown. Roy Kilvington, John Smith and Kevin Tetley took the top three places in the A Division batting averages with Kilvington topping the list on 43.13 having hit 647 runs in his 20 visits to the wicket. Top all-rounder was the former Lloyds Bank captain Martin Connolly, who by this time had moved on to Horsforth, while S. Worsnop from Pudsey St Lawrence claimed the bowling prize with 33 wickets at seven runs apiece. Three bowlers turned in all-10 performances. In B Division A. Arslan (New Wortley) picked up a 10 for 23 return against Leeds Civil Service while P. Dwyer (Pudsey Congs) collected 10-22 at Sandmoor in a 2nd eleven fixture in late May and J. Emmett (Dunlop & Rankin) joined the all-10 club, too, in their last match of the season at home against Cookridge. He finished with 10-32 off 15 overs.

In addition, there was a new league highest fifth wicket partnership established when the Zingari pair Chris Cartmell and Paul Kirby put on 135 against Rodley at the beginning of July only to be topped two weeks later by M. Sowden and J. Batty of Thorite who shared a partnership of 155 against Horsforth. In the cup competitions the trophies were claimed by the two Pudsey clubs, St Lawrence and Congs.

St Lawrence batsman S. Camm took the top batting award in **1989** but it was the hard-hitting Les Fussey who collected the fastest 50 prize with a half century in an incredible 15 minutes. His Adel team-mates P. Shires and N. French had some moments of glory, too, when they were both unbeaten in a new league ninth wicket highest stand of 93 against Crompark in mid July. Leeds Civil Service took the A Division title for the first time and there was a first of a run of Pool Paper Mills Cup successes for Meanwood while Pudsey Congs completed a hat-trick of victories in the Cawthorne Cup. Among the top efforts that season, too, was a ten for ten wicket haul by J. Wilkes for Sandmoor against Cookridge in late May – the best return in the league by any bowler until Stewart Dobson's 2003 effort.

Cookridge led the way into the **1990s** at the double. They picked up the Pool Paper Mills Cup for the first time at the end of July then pipped Civil Service for the A Division title by winning more games after both clubs finished on 77 points. No prizes for guessing the winners of the Cawthorne Cup - Congs made it four in a row and for good measure completed a double of their own by taking the Second X1s title. Congs' A Division outfit grabbed a little of the limelight though as early as the second week of the season when they shared a new highest aggregate run scoring feast with Tong who managed 243 of the 483 hit that day.

Rob Guthrie scored 620 runs for Meanwood to take the batting prize while K. McGuinness who had done much to try and help Civil Service in their quest to retain the A Division title by taking 79 wickets at 8.32 runs apiece got some consolation by claiming the bowling number one spot. In B Division, the Arthington pair D. Samuel and A. Nicholls took the batting and bowling awards.

The **1991** season belonged to Lewis who set a new standard for run scoring in the Dales with 851 from 19 visits to the crease. His two undefeated innings enabled him to just get over the 50 point in the averages giving him figures that left the rest on the horizon. "He was from Melbourne and had turned up just too late to register for our Aire-Wharfe side so he played in our third team in the Dales. It was a one-off season, but what an impact he made," said Colin Bentley the Pool and Otley verteran. Simon Lindsay took 76 wickets at just over 10 runs apiece to be the league's leading wicket taker of the campaign but it was only good enough to place him fourth in the averages. It was good enough, though, to ensure New Farnley picked up the B Division title.

Ian Long topped the A Division bowling list with an average of 8.57, his 40 wickets playing a major role in Leeds Civil Service regaining the title. Pudsey Congs' second eleven were operating at the double again with league and cup successes – their Cawthorne Cup victory making it five in a row, an effort unmatched in the league's history. Meanwhile, newly promoted Castlehill claimed their first knock-out trophy when they won the Pool Paper Mills Cup. And to round off the campaign the highest aggregate number of runs in a day was pushed through the 500 mark by Adel and Cookridge who shared 517.

If there had been an Who Wants to be a Millionaire contest in **1992** it would not have been surprising if someone from the New Farnley club had won it for they won just about everything else that year. They submerged the rest of A Division taking the title by 25 clear points; their second eleven won their title by 11 points, they won both cup competitions to perform a double double and all the top prizes in the averages. Simon Lindsay took the top all-rounder title and the A Division batting award and was second to club-mate George Hepworth in the bowling list while John Baldwin and John Bentley picked up the second eleven batting and bowling trophies.

Top run scorer of the season was Whitehall's R. Brady who was a single shy of 700 finishing top of the B Division list with an average of 53.77. New Farnley took the Pool Paper Mills Cup again in **1993** but the Cawthorne Cup went back to Congs, for the sixth time in seven seasons, and their first team took the A Division title, too, by equalling New Farnley's record of the previous campaign of 111 points from 22 games. Paul Rainford hit 743 runs at 67.55 to establish a new highest season's batting average while T. Davis, the Pudsey St Lawrence bowler, was the league's top wicket taker with 88 victims – but it was not good enough to earn him the B Division bowling

Simon Lindsay.

John Baldwin.

prize. That went to D. Arundale of Thorite who returned an average of 5.84 as a result of taking 69 wickets. Arthington's Mark Pennington, who was fourth in the A Division batting list and fifth, one behind Matthew Hoggard (Pudsey Congs and later England), in the bowling averages was the league's top all-rounder. Meanwood's Rob Guthrie lifted the league's highest scoring mark to 163 with his unbeaten innings against Civil Service and also chipped in with the fastest 50 of the season, too.

Meanwood carried off the Pool Paper Mills Cup for the second time in **1994** but New Farnley managed a club double taking the Cawthorne Cup and the league title. They went through the 100 points mark to lift the A Division trophy with 103 points but Ilkley topped that in B Division setting up a new points record of 113 from 22 games. C. D'Arcy led the way for them taking the bowling prize with an average of 7.61. Nat West's Gary Edwards, with an average of marginally over 59, was top batsman of the season in A Division.

But it was **1995** that was to prove to be the blue ribbon season for batting averages, Edwards lifting his effort of the previous campaign to finish with an average of 68.40 in A Division with a new league top score of 166 not out among his 684 runs aggregate. But in B Division teenager Richmond set an altogether new benchmark. He was unbeaten eight times in his 14 trips to the wicket during which he accumulated 585 runs to leave him with an incredible average of 97.50, way, way higher than anything that had gone before or for that matter, since. Yet while the youngster from New Rover was setting his new record there was another marvellous display of batsmanship going on in Division B by veteran Reg Parker who defied his three score years and ten to score 815 runs for Adel in 19 innings to leave him with an average of 54.33 – good enough in many seasons to have won him the batting prize.

The campaign also provided a new third wicket highest partnership record when both Paul Slater and R. Webb hit centuries for Nat West against Arthington in early August in sharing a stand of 213. On the bowling front, Richmond's team-mate Richard Stevens missed out on his century of league wickets by one and had to settled for second place in the B Division averages, too, in the wake of Roger Kelso whose 80 wickets for Rodley came at an average of 7.70 – .14 of a run better than Stevens' return. There was also a notable bowling effort in C Division where Dean Simister finished top of the list with 92 wickets at 7.29 for Jarvis Porter who carried off the title with 109 points. New Rover, not surprisingly, were B Division champions but the team of the year was Tong who took the A Division title by 13 clear points after earlier lifting the Pool Paper Mills Cup for the first time. Meanwood, meanwhile, kept their hand in at winning cups by claiming the Cawthorne trophy.

THE CHAMPIONS AND CUP WINNERS, DECADE BY DECADE

Division winners and their records and winners of the Cup competitions............seasons 1986–1995

(Win 5pts, tie 2pts, draw 1pt with 2pts bonus pts for faster scoring)

League	Winners	P.	W.	L.	D.	Pts.	Year	Pool P M Cup	Cawthorne Cup
Div. A	Scalebor Park, 1 tie, 2pts.	22	14	2	5	81	1986	Adel	Meanwood Park Hos.
	High Royds, 1 tie, 2pts.	22	11	4	6	67			
	Eldwick & Gilstead	22	11	6	5	66			
Div. B Sec 1.	Lloyds Bank	21	10	3	8	62			
	Leeds YMCA	21	10	5	6	62			
	Crompark	21	10	7	4	54			
Div. B Sec 2.	Meanwood Park Hos.	20	12	3	5	67			
	Sandmoor, 1tie, 2pts.	20	8	5	6	54			
	Nat. West Bank	20	9	8	3	50			
2nds. Sec. A	Ben Rhydding	22	14	3	5	77			
	Pool Paper Mills	22	10	4	8	68			
	Ingrow St Johns	22	9	8	5	50			
2nds. Sec. B	Pudsey Congs	22	13	2	7	76			
	Eldwick & Gilstead	22	13	4	5	72			
	New Farnley	22	11	5	6	61			
Div. A	Croma.	20	12	2	6	68	1987	Farsley Celtic	Pudsey Congs
	Eldwick & Gilstead	20	11	4	5	62			
	Farsley Celtic	20	10	4	6	60			
Divi. B	Crompark	22	16	2	4	86			
	Pudsey Congs	22	14	3	5	79			
	Meanwood	22	14	4	4	76			

League	Winners	P.	W.	L.	D.	T.	Pts.	Year	Pool P M Cup	Cawthorne Cup
2nd Teams	Olicanians	22	16	2	3	1	86			
	Farsley Celtic	22	15	1	4	2	85			
	Pudsey Congs	22	12	2	3	5	78			
Div. A	Eldwick & Gilstead	22	15	3	2	2	83	**1988**	Pudsey St Lawrence	Pudsey Congs
	Leeds Zingari	22	13	3	3	3	77			
	Pudsey St. Lawrence	22	14	5	2	1	75			
Div. B	Leeds Civil Service	18	11	3	2	2	63			
	Sandmoor	18	9	4	4	1	52			
	Cookridge	18	8	5	3	2	49			
2nd. Teams	Pudsey Congs.	18	14	1	1	2	77			
	New Wortley	18	9	4	4	1	52			
	New Farnley	18	9	6	2	1	50			
Div. A	Leeds Civil Service	22	15	4	0	3	84	**1989**	Meanwood	Pudsey Congs
	New Farnley	22	16	5	0	1	82			
	Pudsey Congs	22	12	7	3	0	63			
Div. B	Otley	20	17	1	1	1	89			
	Tong	20	13	5	1	1	69			
	Whitehall	20	10	6	3	1	56			
2nd. Teams	Meanwood	18	13	5	0	0	65			
	Pudsey Congs	18	12	3	2	1	65			
	New Farnley	18	12	5	0	1	63			
Div. A	Cookridge	22	15	5	2	0	77	**1990**	Cookridge	Pudsey Congs
	Leeds Civil Service	22	13	3	3	3	77			
	Tong	22	11	7	3	1	61			
Div. B	Castlehill	20	14	4	1	1	74			
	Arthington	20	13	4	1	2	72			
	New Wortley	20	12	5	1	2	67			

League	Winners	P.	W.	L.	D.	T.	Pts.	Year	Pool P M Cup	Cawthorne Cup
2nd. Teams	Pudsey Congs	20	15	4	1	0	76			
	New Wortley	20	14	4	2	0	72			
	Pudsey St. Lawrence	20	12	7	1	0	61			
	(From 1991 season: Win 6pts, tie 3pts, draw 1pt plus 3 bonus pts for faster scoring)									
Div. A	Leeds Civil Service	22	12	3	4	3	91	**1991**	Castlehill	Pudsey Congs
	Thorite	22	12	4	4	2	84			
	Pudsey Congs	22	12	5	5	0	77			
Div. B	New Farnley	20	15	3	1	1	95			
	New Wortley, tie 3pts.	20	13	3	3	1	84			
	Crompark, tie 3pts.	20	11	3	3	3	83			
2nd. Teams	Pudsey Congs	20	17	1	1	1	107			
	Cookridge	20	14	1	2	3	98			
	New Farnley	20	9	6	2	3	68			
Div. A	New Farnley	22	16	0	3	3	111	**1992**	New Farnley	New Farnley
	Meanwood	22	13	4	4	1	86			
	Pudsey Congs	22	13	3	6	0	84			
Div B	Crompark, tie 3pts.	20	13	1	4	2	89			
	Whitehall	20	13	2	4	1	86			
	Pudsey St. Lawrence	20	9	5	4	2	66			
2nd. Teams	New Farnley	20	16	1	3	0	99			
	Pudsey Congs	20	13	1	5	1	87			
	Pudsey St. Lawrence	20	10	6	2	2	70			
Div. A	Pudsey Congs	22	15	1	5	1	111	**1993**	New Farnley	Pudsey Congs
	Otley	22	13	5	3	1	91			
	Arthington	22	11	6	3	2	77			

League	Winners	P.	W.	L.	D.	Pts.	Year	Pool P M Cup	Cawthorne Cup
Div. B	Thorite	22	17	2	3	111			
	Pudsey St Lawrence	22	15	5	2	95			
	Old Mods	22	13	5	4	88			
2nd. Teams	New Wortley	20	14	2	4	100			
	Pudsey Congs	20	16	1	3	99			
	Meanwood, tie, 3pts	20	12	4	4	84			
Div. A	New Farnley	22	13	2	7	103	**1994**	Meanwood	New Farnley
	Pudsey Congs	22	14	4	4	97			
	Nat. West Bank	22	12	4	6	84			
Div. B	Ilkley, tie, 3pts.	22	16	0	6	113			
	North Leeds	22	15	2	5	98			
	Rodley, tie, 3pts.	22	12	4	6	86			
2nd. Teams	Meanwood	20	15	3	2	95			
	New Wortley	20	15	3	2	92			
	Pudsey St. Lawrence	20	10	3	7	82			
Div. A	Tong	22	15	2	5	101	**1995**	Tong	Meanwood
	Nat. West Bank	22	13	5	4	88			
	Pudsey Congs	22	11	5	6	87			
Div.B	New Rover	22	15	1	6	105			
	Rodley	22	16	6	0	96			
	Adel	22	9	4	9	87			
Div. C	Jarvis Porter	22	16	2	4	109			
	Farnley Hill	22	15	5	2	95			
	Alwoodley	22	11	7	4	76			
2nd. Teams	Pudsey Congs	18	15	1	2	92			
	Crompark	18	14	2	2	89			
	Meanwood	18	10	5	3	69			

AN AVERAGE VIEW

Season by season leaders of the averages ~ the fourth decade, 1986–1995.

(Some statistical detail no longer used in later League handbooks)

The Batsmen

League	Name/Club	Ins.	NO	H.Sc	Rns.	Av.
Div. A	C. Cumberland, High Royds	16	5	118*	514	46.7
	S. Stirling, High Royds	12	0	92	439	36.6
	G. Baines, Scalebor Park	17	6	65*	390	35.5
	L. Fussey, Adel	13	4	53	295	32.8
	S Ross, Farsley Celtic	12	4	72*	243	30.4
	M. Ashworth, Croma.	16	2	83	364	26
Div. B	W. Davis, Leeds YMCA	18	6	103*	763	63.6
	K. Edwards, Leeds Zingari	18	3	105*	570	38
	N. Gledhill, Sandmoor	16	2	62	500	35.7
2nd. Teams	R. Hogarth, Olicanians	14	6	64*	389	48.6
	T. Morton, Pudsey Congs	13	2	107*	366	33.3
	R. Wolstenholme, Scalebor P	18	3	100*	449	29.9
Div. A	M. Ashworth, Croma.	14	4	88*	469	46.9
	J. Smith, Eldwick & Gilstead	15	1	130	546	39
	P. Stebbings, Lloyds Bank	14	1	80	460	35.4
	P. Stephenson, New Farnley	18	3	82	429	28.6
	T. Clapham, Coma.	16	2	55	373	26.6
	T. Lee, Eldwick & Gilstead	15	2	79*	325	25
Div. B	P. Bagley Meanwood Pk H.	14	3	104	418	38
	P. Guthrie, Meanwood	14	3	121	411	37.4
	P. Langley, Meanwood	18	2	111*	587	26.7

The Bowlers

Year	Name/Club	Ovs.	Mdn	Rns.	Wks.	Av.
1986	S. Stirling, High Royds	218	85	382	60	6.37
	C. Taylor, Scalebor P.	297	113	525	72	7.29
	K. Ambridge, New Farnley	125	31	352	41	8.58
	L. Fussey, Adel	154	46	364	42	8.67
	R. Addinall, Croma.	146	41	334	38	8.79
	D. Tricklebank, High Royds	197	52	547	51	10.72
	A. Sloan, Crompark	170	56	305	53	5.75
	P. Ruane, Meanwood Pk Hos.	257	68	514	57	9.01
	J. Wilks, Sandmoor	135	36	319	35	9.11
	M. Horner, Pudsey Congs	108	45	167	31	5.39
	A. Maude, Eldwick & Gil.	149	46	302	42	7.19
	C. Steele, Olicanians	187	57	374	51	7.33
1987	S. Worsnop, Pudsey St L.	146	54	283	35	8.85
	P. Blackwell, Olicanians	188	72	304	34	8.94
	R. Middleton, Olicanians	274	108	491	50	9.82
	P. Shires, Adel	236	65	546	53	10.3
	M. Harrison. New Farnley	189	69	457	41	11.51
	D. Sunderland, Eldwick & Gil.	213	69	514	46	11.17
	D. Reason, Pudsey Congs	126	45	249	37	6.73
	B. Newall, Pudsey Congs.	228	84	385	57	6.75
	A. Sloan, Crompark	268	83	468	69	6.78

Batting

League	Name/Club	Ins.	NO	H.Sc	Rns.	Av.
2nd. Teams						
	R. Waite, Leeds YMCA	12	1	77*	357	32.5
	F. Lodge, Pusdey St Law.	14	2	74*	376	31.3
	D. Smith, Farsley Celtic	13	4	54	254	28.2
Div. A	R. Kilvington, Eldwick & Gil.	20	5		647	43.1
	J. Smith, Eldwick & Gil.	18	3		608	40.5
	K. Tetley, Eldwick & Gil.	13	4		354	39.3
	M. Connolly, Horsforth	14	7		240	34.3
	N. Bulmer, New Farnley	16	3		307	31.3
	S. Gore, Leeds Zingari	20	2		516	28.7
Div. B	D. Bottomley, Nat. West Bk.	14	2		371	30.9
	P. Allinson, Leeds Civil Serv.	19	4		416	27.7
	P. Merrick, Leeds Civil Serv.	15	2		349	26.8
2nd. Teams	K. Hall, Pudsey Congs	13	2		384	34.9
	P. Taylor, Pudsey St. Law	15	5		330	33
	R. Dewhirst, Cookrdige	13	2		307	27.9
Div. A	S. Camm, Pudsey St. Law	17	4		530	40.8
	G. Sowden, Thorite	20	5		577	38.5
	I. Hanley, Civil Service	18	3		503	33.5
	R. Guthrie, Meanwood	21	3		576	32.6
	A. Perring, Cookridge	16	4		356	29.7
	C. Cartmell, Leeds Zingari	18	3		442	29.5
Div. B.	G. Chambers, New Wortley	20	2		489	27.2
	D. Rose, New Rover	18	3		332	22.1
	T. Henry, Otley	16	2		301	21.5

Bowling

Year	Name/Club	Ovs.	Mdn	Rns.	Wks.	Av.
	B. Moran, Olicanians	184	65	280	51	5.49
	A. Beech, Farlsey Celtic	271	110	497	79	6.29
	K. Hall, Pudsey Congs	252	111	400	54	7.4
1988	S. Worsnop, Pudsey St. L.	128	58	231	33	7
	M. Harrison, New Farnley	227	102	495	67	7.3
	D. Threlfall, Pudsey St. L.	131	50	326	41	7.95
	M. Dews, Meanwood	227	74	491	57	8.61
	D. Sunderland, Eldwick & Gil.	234	68	474	53	8.94
	D. Palmer, Thorite	147	45	347	37	9.38
	J. Wilkes, Sandmoor	232	63	565	74	7.63
	A. Arslan, New Wortley	196	75	353	46	7.67
	G. Simister, Leeds Civil Serv.	215	81	389	46	8.45
	P. Goodchild, Cookrdige	175	68	277	50	5.54
	M. Narey, Eldwick	101	40	201	31	6.48
	K. Hall, Pudsey Congs	163	77	244	34	7.18
1989	K. McGuinness, Civil Serv.	332	117	562	81	6.93
	S. Lindsay, New Farnley	330	101	605	82	7.37
	P. Shires, Adel	288	92	609	67	9.09
	D. Palmer, Thorite	193	53	391	38	10.28
	P. Slater, Nat. West Bank	182	38	481	46	10.45
	M. Harrison, New Farnley	250	70	657	61	10.77
	D. Smage, New Rover	244	86	492	77	6.38
	M. Woodhead, New Wortley	284	67	608	65	9.35
	J. Hunt, Otley	110	34	293	31	9.45

Batting

League	Name/Club	Ins.	NO	H.Sc	Rns.	Av.
2nd. Teams						
	R. Dewhirst, Cookridge	10	4		253	41.2
	M. Dews, Meanwood	13	1		353	29.4
	R. Lester, Pudsey Congs	14	3		283	25.7
Div. A	R. Guthrie, Meanwood	20	3		620	36.5
	M. Rankin, Tong	12	1		400	36.4
	D. Bottomley, Nat. West Bk.	16	3		451	34.7
	B. Dykes, Cookridge	18	3		441	29.4
	M. Edwards, Leeds Zingari	19	7		344	28.7
	S. Green, Pudsey St. Law.	15	5		271	27
Div. B	D. Samuel, Arthington	18	7		575	52.3
	M. Mills, Castlehill	15	5		449	44.9
	N. Belton, Old Mods.	17	2		539	35.9
2nd. Teams	J. Dickenson, New Farnley	13	3		431	43
	A. Hamilton, Meanwood	12	3		247	27.4
	C. Roberts, Castlehill	16	2		342	24.4
Div. A	P. Lewis, Otley	19	2		851	50.1
	J. Land, Cookridge	19	5		523	37.4
	G. Sowden, Thorite	15	5		373	37.3
	F. Stewart, Arthington	18	4		513	36.6
	M. Scaife, Thorite	19	1		524	29.1
	M. Hirst, Pudsey Congs	19	3		464	29
Div. B	R. Brady, Whitehall	14	3		538	48.9
	J. Jones, Crompark	14	3		334	30.4
	G. Chambers, New Wortley	15	3		346	28.8

Bowling

Year	Name/Club	Ovs.	Mdn	Rns.	Wks.	Av.
2nd. Teams						
	D. Reason, Pudsey Congs	125	49	210	30	7
	M. Horner, Pudsey Congs	103	28	254	32	7.93
	M. Dews, Meanwood	188	65	442	54	8.19
1990 **Div. A**	K. McGuinness, Leeds C.S.	355	129	658	79	8.32
	P. Slater, Nat. West Bank	140	38	359	39	9.21
	A. Perring, Cookridge	158	29	480	42	11.43
	M. Harrison, Thorite	250	53	647	54	11.98
	D. Palmer, Thorite	152	39	398	31	12.83
	A. Commery, Cookridge	235	47	765	59	12.97
Div. B	A. Nicholls, Arthington	189	58	463	53	8.74
	G. Edwards, Castlehill	199	66	421	46	9.15
	J. Henderson, Castlehill	206	66	485	52	9.32
2nd. Teams	D. Whittaker, Pudsey Congs	122	34	282	42	6.71
	R. Ackrill, New Farnley	172	56	364	47	7.74
	M. Horner, Pudsey Congs	133	28	341	40	8.62
1991 **Div. A**	I. Long, Leeds Civil Service	141	43	343	40	8.57
	M. Horner, Pudsey Congs	141	24	388	45	8.62
	M. Hodgson, Otley	144	53	284	31	9.16
	C. Oldfield, Pudsey Congs	241	69	614	65	9.45
	S. Saxton, Meanwood	180	46	472	47	10.04
	P. Shires, Adel	116	32	304	30	10.13
Div. B	D. Lambert, New Wortley	192	55	449	63	7.13
	M. Rushworth, New Wortley	198	58	471	48	9.81
	M. Reasbeck, Old Mods.	138	37	344	34	10.12

League	Name/Club	Ins.	NO	H.Sc	Rns.	Av.	Year	Name/Club	Ovs.	Mdn	Rns.	Wks.	Av.
2nd. Teams													
	P. Langley, Pudsey St. Law.	15	2		424	32.8		D. Reason, Pudsey Congs	161	56	333	56	5.94
	R. Benton, Cook. R'heads.	12	4		234	29.3		K. Hall, Pudsey Congs	196	64	411	48	8.56
	P. Hill, New Farnley	14	2		313	26.1		A. Perring, Cookrdige	155	49	344	40	8.6
Div. A	S. Lindsay, New Farnley	19	6		465	35.8	**1992**	G. Hepworth, New Farnley	117	22	291	42	6.93
	J. Ingham, Pudsey Congs	15	3		423	35.3		S. Lindsay, New Farnley	285	89	575	77	7.74
	D. Samuel, Arthington	13	3		282	28.2		M. Dews, Meanwood	203	54	450	57	7.89
	R. Guthrie, Meanwood	16			431	26.9		S. Saxton, Meanwood	210	46	485	57	8.57
	D. Breakwell, New Wortley	12			317	26.4		D. Dalby, Otley	296	88	741	72	10.3
	D. Bissett, Pudsey Congs	15	4		287	26.1		M. Rushworth, New Wortley	179	59	381	37	10.63
Div. B	R. Brady, Whitehall	16	3		699	53.8		C. Wright, Rodley	95	27	238	36	6.61
	P. Cooper, Crompark	16	6		486	48.6		T. Davis, Pudsey St Law.	150	45	427	51	8.37
	G. Edwards, Castlehill	14	4		468	46.8		J. Cassidy, Whitehall	214	64	476	51	9.33
2nd. Teams													
	J. Baldwin, New Farnley	12	3		223	24.8		J. Bentley, New Farnley	122	39	357	34	7.56
	P. Langley, Pudsey St. Law.	18	1		399	23.4		K. Dickens, Pudsey Congs	139	27	333	41	8.12
	S. Lynes, Pudsey Congs	13	1		277	23.1		J. Menzer, Meanwood	137	33	368	41	8.98
Div. A	P. Rainford, Whitehall	15	4		743	67.6	**1993**	D. Dalby, Otley	279	92	550	62	8.87
	R. Guthrie, Meanwood	18	3		551	36.7		B. Newall, Pudsey Congs	159	46	347	37	9.73
	P. Stephenson, New Farnley	21	4		615	36.2		M. Jones, Pudsey Congs	212	52	464	45	10.31
	M. Pennington, Arthington	19	4		532	35.5		M. Hoggard, Pudsey Congs	282	81	620	58	10.68
	P. Allinson, Pudsey Congs	18	2		552	34.5		M. Pennington, Arthington	308	96	610	55	11.09
	R. Webb, Nat West Bank	16	2		449	32.1		M. Dews, Meanwood	251	99	511	45	11.36
Div. B	K. Dickson, Pudsey St. Law.	16	5		608	55.3		A. Arundale, Thorite	208	72	403	69	5.84
	G. Sowden, Thorite	14	2		476	39.7		T. Davis, Pudsey St. Law.	332	70	586	88	6.66
	M. Richmond, New Rover	17	2		502	33.5		M. Harrison, Thorite	275	76	672	82	8.19

League	Name/Club	Ins.	NO	H.Sc	Rns.	Av.	Year	Name/Club	Ovs.	Mdn	Rns	Wks.	Av.
2nd. Teams													
	P. Langley, Pudsey St. Law	18	2		644	40.3		C. Oldfield, Pudsey Congs	85.3	24	166	30	5.53
	C. Haygreen, Cookridge	12	3		356	39.3		R. Stockdale, Castlehill	166	52	413	60	6.88
	C. Taylor, Pudsey St Law	16	5		417	37.9		B. Finch, New Wortley	249	91	446	56	7.96
Div. A	G. Edwards, Nat West					59.1	1994	M. Jones, Pudsey Congs					9.41
	K. Edwards, Pudsey Congs					47.3		J. Shires, Meanwood					9.5
	R. Mosley, New Farnley					41.6		S. Lindsey, New Farnley					10.05
	G. Sowden, Lawns Park					39.7		T. Davis, Pudsey St. Lawrence					10.22
	S. Lindsey, New Farnley					37.3		D. Lambert, New Wortley					10.95
	R. Guthrie, Meanwood					35.8		A. Simpson, New Farnley					10.96
Div. B	D. Rose, New Rover					46		C. D'Arcy, Ilkley					7.61
	A. Hull, St Chads					41.4		R. Kelso, Rodley					8.03
	D. Reynolds, Ilkley					38.3		M. Newberry, Ilkley					8.37
2nd. Teams	P. Langley, Pudsey St. Law					56.8		P. Dews, Meanwood					10.4
	M. Denney, Meanwood					41.5		B. Finch, New Wortley					10.7
	L. Young, Castlehill					35.4		K. Hall, Pudsey Congs					11.94
Div. A.	G. Edwards, Nat. West Bank	14	4		684	68.4	1995	A. Crake, Pudsey Congs			742	80	9.27
	R. Guthrie, Meanwood	17	1		776	48.5		J. Patrick, Nat. West Bank			692	71	9.75
	K. Dickson, Pudsey St Law	12	2		448	44.8		T. Davis, Pudsey St. Lawrence			499	46	10.84
	P. Slater, Nat. West Bank	17	5		516	43		N. Sleeman, New Wortley			349	31	11.25
	A. Crake, Pudsey Congs	19	7		458	38.2		J Henderson, Nat. West Bk.			682	58	11.76
	P. Kirby, Crompark	16	1		568	37.9		S. Benn, Lawnspark			816	68	12
Div. B.	M. Richmond, New Rover	14	8	90	585	97.5		R. Kelso, Rodley			616	80	7.7
	R. Parker, Adel	19	4		815	54.3		R. Stevens, New Rover			777	99	7.84
	D. Bultitude, Cookridge	12	1		515	46.8		S. Shires, Adel			520	46	11.3

League	Name/Club	Ins.	NO	H.Sc	Rns.	Av.
Div. C	K. Frankland, Jarvis Porter	20	4		623	38.9
	J. Metcalfe, Jarvis Porter	20	5		539	35.9
	S. Anderson, Farnley Hill	14	3		294	26.7
2nd. Teams						
	R. Kettlewell, Pudsey Congs	11	6		271	54.2
	C. Day, Meanwood	13	2		566	51.5
	G. Taylor, Pudsey Congs	13	5		285	35.6

Year	Name/Club	Ovs.	Mdn	Rns.	Wks.	Av.
Div. C	D. Simister, Jarvis Porter			671	92	7.29
	M. Newbound, Farnley Hill			505	62	8.14
	M. Walworth, Jarvis Porter			432	47	9.19
2nd. Teams						
	S. Wood, New Wortley			143	31	4.61
	B. Finch, Pudsey Congs			290	40	7.25
	M. Dews, Meanwood			345	43	8.02

Award winners, Decade by decade, 1986–1995

Trophy winners of the league's miscellaneous awards over the years

Year	All-Round. A Div	All-Round. B Div	All-Round. 2nds	W-keeper	Fielder	U-18 Bat	U-18 Bowl	Fast 50
1986	S. Stirling High Royds	K. Edwards Leeds Zingari	K.Lee Pool P.M.	G. Baines Scalebor Park	P Conway Pool P.M. & B. Green Farsley Celtic	A. Booth Farsley Celtic	R. Dewhirst Olicanians	S. Stirling High Royds
1987	R. Chew Oxford Place	K. Edwards Leeds Zingari	S. Tempest Farsley Celtic	N. Rider Farsley Celtic	P. Kirby Leeds Zingari		J. Grayson Leeds YMCA	S. Tempest Farsley Celtic
1988	M. Connolly Horsforth		K. Hall Pudsey Congs	J. Smith Eldwick & Gil	P. Kirby Leeds Zingari	A. Doidge Pudsey St. L.	D. Leng Pudsey St. L.	K. Page Sandmoor
1989	P. Stephenson New Farnley	M. Woodhead New Wortley	M. Dews Meanwood	C. Russell New Farnley	R. Owen New Wortley	C. Russell New Farnley	W. Hodgson Pudsey Congs	L. Fussey Adel
1990	K. Edwards Leeds Zingari	G. Edwards Castlehill		J. Land Cookridge	P. Jewey Rodley	P Smith New Wortley	J. Hawsworth Cookridge	K. Bradford Tong
1991	J. Shires Meanwood	J. Jones Crompark & S. Lindsay New Farnley	P. Hill New Farnley	D. Bissett New Wortley	J. Caines Cookridge	A. Eccles New Wortley	M. Pearson Old Mods.	M. Emmott Pudsey St. L.
1992	S. Lindsay New Farnley	G. Edwards Castlehill		A. Broadley Pudsey St. Law.	A. Duff Arthington	M. Dyson Meanwood		D Bissett Pudsey Congs

Year	All-Round. A Div	All-Round. B Div	All-Round. 2nds	W-keeper	Fielder	U-18 Bat	U-18 Bowl	Fast 50
1993	M. Pennington Arthington	M. Harrison Thorite	M. Woodhead New Wortley	K. Dickson Pudsey St. Law.	J. Nash Whitehall	C. Taylor Pudsey St. L.	S. Dammant Ilkley	R. Guthrie Meanwood
1994	S. Lindsay New Farnley	A. Hull St Chads		K. Dickson Pudsey St. Law.	L. Suddard Rodley	M.Duce Pudsey Congs		P. Whiteley New Farnley
1995	A. Crake Pudsey Congs	N. Bonnington Cookridge	S. Gautrey (C Div) Castlehill	M. Edwards Crompark	K. Henderson Nat.West Bank	M. Richmond New Rover		D. Fenton Castlehill

AT THE DOUBLE......No 5
In some ways it's the perfect life

believes Paul Dews, the Yorkshire Evening Post Chief Sports Writer and Meanwood all-rounder

IN some ways it's the perfect life – watching football all winter and combining playing and watching cricket over the summer. But believe me, it's not without it's headaches at times and the moral dilemmas I've faced over the years in balancing the day job and playing cricket are far too numerous to mention.

Covering Scunthorpe United at Wembley on a May Saturday in 1999 when I was captaining Meanwood in a big league game was just one of many times when the work had to come first. That's the trouble now you see. The football season starts in August and ends, well it doesn't really end anymore.

In between we have a couple of months of cricket and that means work as well although covering Yorkshire's title success in 2001 was a real honour and I would never grumble about my occupation. But over the years I've still been lucky enough to play more games than I miss despite the occasional dilemma.

My biggest headache came in the 2002 season when Yorkshire's Cheltenham & Gloucester Trophy semi-final tie against Surrey was re-arranged at 48 hours notice for the following Sunday. No problem, except that we were in the Pool Paper Mills Cup Final against Pudsey Congs. Now don't get me wrong, I would have loved to have seen Yorkshire win through to Lord's, but cup finals have always been special for me and I had booked the day off weeks in advance.

I played in my first cup final in 1989 as a 16-year-old when we beat New Farnley in a thriller and, along with Rob Guthrie and Graham Child, I've been lucky enough to play in every Meanwood final since. We beat NatWest in 1994, Rodley in 1997 and 1998, lost to Mount in 2000, beat Pudsey Congs in the 2002 final and Crompark the following year. On top of that, we've played in numerous semi-finals and the cup has always been a fairly happy hunting ground for Meanwood.

On a personal level, the 1997 final was my proudest moment when my seven-wicket return was enough to help us beat Rodley after we posted a score of barely 100 on a belter of a batting wicket. The following year I was privileged enough to watch Ron Guthrie hit an unbeaten 164 in what must be one of the greatest inning ever played in a cup final. League stalwart Mark Harrison also made 50 that day, playing an unfamiliar role as an opening bat.

That was probably the best Meanwood side I have ever played in and I was lucky enough to captain the side to the league and cup double that very season. Winning the league for the first time was a great achievement because we could justifiably claim to be the best team around.

Over the years we've played against some great players and some good sides. New Farnley are now among the front-runners in the Central Yorkshire League while some of the other, more competitive sides have also moved on. But it is pleasing that, at a time when some other leagues are in crisis, the Dales Council is still going strong. The standard may not be quite what it was – even though there are a handful of strong sides that could compete at a higher level – and the grounds aren't as they were, but it's a testament to the hard work of a lot of people that the league is still thriving.

Oh, and back to that heartfelt decision in 2002 when, for probably the only time, I put playing before working. There were no doubts about me missing out on the C&G Trophy final and playing in an end of season home game. London was the clear winner, along with the rest of the Meanwood lads of course! I'm sure it's true that you're longer retired and you should keep going as long as possible but, sadly, playing league cricket at our level simply doesn't put the bread on the table.

Paul Dews, September, 2003.

At the Double partner.......................Roy Webster

The top component in the team

YOU have to be a special kind of person to face a solid missile as large as an apple coming at you at the speed of not far short of a bullet from a distance of not much more than 22 yards time and time again. But in my book, wicketkeepers are special people – probably the most important component in a good cricket side.

That is why – together with his chirpy personality - so many teams, and bowlers of those teams in particular, loved having Roy Webster behind the stumps. His record in the Dales Council is

Paul Dews.

Roy Webster.

unmatched, as you will see from what follows. He was a terrific technician, tidy and very quick – all hugely important factors for the bowlers he supported.

All of them, to a player, will, I am sure, emphasise the confidence he gave them to pull out that little bit extra. He was a driving force, too, when he became captain of some of the teams he played in – right up to league side status.

There were times when you thought his stance, almost sideways on to the stumps, looked ungainly yet it served him well. He operated that way to accommodate knee injuries brought on from his footballing days but somehow it enabled him to see the missile that split second sooner and move that split-second faster.

And there were times when Smiths had what may be the fastest attack the Dales Council has ever encountered – when Kenny Booth was operating at one end and Dave Benn at the other in the late 70s – that you had to wonder how he even saw some of the deliveries never mind acted on them on the often really quick wicket at their Coal Hill Lane ground.

High on his list of achievements was the 1976 double season at Smiths. When club captain Kenny Booth broke his right arm after being hit by a ball Webster took over and led the side and maybe his proudest moment was when he was handed the Pool Paper Mills Cup by Dales Council president Stanley Handford at Esholt after a final in which Benn and swing bowler Keith Robertshaw saw Smiths home.

Smiths had been restricted to 83-9 in the 40 over contest by Pudsey Congs' incisive attack of Colin Oldfield and Ralph Middlebrook even though David Pearce had hit 33 in an opening stand of 43 with Colin Janney. But in a match dominated by the bowlers and some fine fielding, Webster guided Smiths to the cup with Benn (five for 19) and Robertshaw (four for 23) toppling Congs for 52 to sink their hopes of a third successive cup title.

That season Webster claimed a league record of 52 victims behind the stumps from 25 league and cup games including 40 in Smiths' league title success. It took him to 100 scalps in the space of two seasons in 49 league and cup games – a crucial sequence in his league career total of 511 victims accounted for in his 327 games. Build into that league wicketkeeping trophies in 1973, 1975, 1976, 1977, 1979, and 1980, seven league championships and three cupwinners trophies and nine appearances for the league side in a career which saw him play at Oxford Place until 1974, Smiths (Farsley Celtic) for eight seasons and Croma for six seasons and you have something of the man.

But if you need further evidence of what makes a great wicketkeeper tick, then think about this. In the first single wicket tournament held at Esholt in 1973 he kept wicket from 10-30am until 7-15pm – nearly nine hours on his own finishing it off by taking the catch which sealed the tournament for the winner Barry Searle. Some feat of concentration – but Webster's response when asked how it had been possible also answered why he was so good at his trade. "It was the most enjoyable day I ever had," he said simply. "It was a day that epitomised the Dales Council camaraderie of officials, umpires, players and family atmosphere. I shall never forget it."

Chapter Ten
1996 to 2004.
The fifth decade: Golden tons at the double

RUNS came in tons by the double in the run-up to the golden anniversary season of the Dales Council league. It was a period filled with new milestones - and the odd moments of misery. It was a decade when it became commonplace for clubs to muster more than a century of points in a season (once three teams in one division did it), when double hundreds came along fourfold, when one bowler had a mind-boggling spell of all ten wickets without conceding a run and when more than one club struggled to turn out 11 players on a regular basis, particularly if they were running more than one team.

But as cricket moved into a new century with hope and ambition at all levels, the Dales Council looked forward to reaching its own half-century and then settling down to go for 100 not out. It was a time when teams and players with Asian backgrounds came to the fore and many of the clubs in the league had good reason to thank the input of the largely new (for the Dales) brand of cricketers. They kept sides going and many turned in high-class performances, particularly over the turn of the century, when Mount proved to be the masters.

Nevertheless, the decade opened with familiar names leading the batting and bowling lists in Division A. The New Rover pair Michael Richmond and Richard Stevens took the **1996** honours, Richmond outscoring the field with 691 runs at an average of 62.81 and Stevens claiming 94 wickets at 8.53 runs each. Meanwhile four cricketers who have served the Dales well over the years also made their marks. Kevin Edwards, that formidable opponent with Pudsey Congs, hit over 600 runs in finishing third in the batting list - and his 30 wickets at 11.33 gave him ninth spot in the bowling averages making him the season's top all-rounder. Second leading wicket taker in A Division was Dennis Holmes, the Tong and former New Farnley all-rounder. His 80 wickets at 10.80 runs apiece earned him fifth place in the bowlers' table while the top two places in the B Division batting averages were claimed by the long-serving Adel pair Reg Parker and Les Fussey.

It was a big year for Rodley who took the A Division and Second Eleven titles while Jarvis Porter, backed by Dean Simister's 86 wickets at 7.60 runs each, romped to the B Division crown 12 points clear of Adel who themselves had accumulated 100 points. Nat West Bank provided yet another new name on the Pool Paper Mills Cup while Pudsey Congs added an old one to the list on the Cawthorne Cup but the cup performance of the season was claimed by a Crompark batsman – Paul Kirby setting up a new high scoring record with his unbeaten 183 against Otley in early May. Kirby's team-mate Ian Eccleshall kept the Crompark scorer busy, too, the following month in a league game at Castlehill when he turned in the remarkable bowling figures of 18.2 overs, 13 maidens, 8 runs, 9 wickets. Enough said.

Rodley, on a roll, retained their Division A champions tag in **1997** with Tong repeating their second place role again though this time Rodley's winning margin was stretched from two points to 15. Mount, making an immediate impact on the Dales, ran out champions of Division C in their first campaign by 24 clear points from fellow new boys Ramgarhia Sikh. Meanwood took the Pool Paper Mills trophy for the third time in nine seasons while Pudsey Congs picked up the Cawthorne trophy for an incredible eighth time in 11 campaigns. But the hero of the hour was Nat West's Paul Slater, top batsman with 774 runs and top all-rounder of the season - and the first Dales Council player to break the double hundred barrier.

Newly promoted Jarvis Porter fell victim to his big hitting as he went to his double ton in late August helping the Bank side to a new league highest score of 346 for three. Meanwhile the batsmen from one club were queuing up in the Division B averages, five from Whitehall in line behind Pudsey St Lawrence's D. Threllfall.

The **1998** season was one of those seasons of dripping Saturday afternoons of the kind they never seemed to get in the good old days, or so the story goes. But really, it was dogged by poor weather, particularly early on. In fact the weather was such an item that year that the league had to have a re-think on the matter of averages, which, in turn, opened the door for one stalwart of the Dales to return some startling figures.

When the league Management Committee discussed Fixture Secretary Steve Raistrick's report at their fifth meeting of that campaign on July 16 at Old Modernians clubhouse, the delegates, without any opposition, adopted a proposal to reduce the qualification figures needed for the end of season league batting and bowling averages to accommodate the difficulties the elements had already presented.

It had been decided from the outset back in the Spring of 1956 that individual prizes would depend on batsmen having gone to the crease at least 12 times (a minimum of 200 runs scored was added to that qualification later) and bowlers having claimed 30 or more wickets. League Rule 29 also included the rider that "in the event of exceptional weather conditions the Management Committee shall have the power to vary requirements" needed for the averages.

So in the minutes under review from their previous meeting, the league Management Committee's September get-together at Pudsey Congs ground got written confirmation of the new requirements for the 1998 averages. Minute 98.5.5 (iv) records "In view of the weather conditions early in the season it was proposed and agreed, nem con, that the qualifications for the averages be amended to be: A Division – batting 10 innings/200 runs; bowling 30 wickets. B, C, D Divisions – 8 innings/175 runs; 25 wickets."

It was almost inevitable then that something extraordinary would evolve from such a move but as they say, records are there to be broken. And while there is a case for acknowledging that the final averages for 1998 had a manufactured look about them in some instances, rules are rules. One offshoot of it all though was an all but unbeatable place in Dales Council's records for the worthy Mick Wright, the Rodley spinner who has probably played in more Dales Council games than any other player since his debut in the league in the late fifties. Using flight and accuracy in a way that had deceived many batsmen for more than the previous three decades, the bowler who has given so much to the league and the Bramley/Rodley clubs over the years picked up 25 victims for a miserly 71 runs. The effort left him with the all-time record bowling average of just 2.84 runs per victim. It was a one off season, maybe, and perhaps it is hard to put his effort at the top of the list against bowlers who, over the years, collected more wickets in order to qualify for the averages — but it is in the record book now and no-one can argue about that.

The weather, of course, was not all bad and proof of that came in another minute in secretary Alan Wardle's report at that July meeting. It noted that Tong (266/9) and Adel (267/9) had set a new league aggregate record with Adel's Reg Parker, then aged 71, contributing 68. That kind of run output deserved its share of sunshine as did the new highest score in an innings of 377 for five mounted by Mount against Arthington that season. Among the other notable efforts was a fluent hundred collected by Tony Clegg in late July.

Clegg was best known as a footballer — as a central defender he became a popular player in the 1980s with both Bradford City and York City before having a spell in Sweden. A back injury and then a broken ankle curtailed his Soccer career but at 32 he was enjoying his cricket with Esholt and maybe never more so than when he smacked his maiden century that July day at Farsley. Esholt were chasing 175 and his huge contribution to their three wicket success was 105 before falling to a boundary catch after hitting 12 fours and four sixes. "I've left it a bit late in my sporting career to start getting hundreds but it's a great thrill nevertheless," he smiled.

But maybe the most extraordinary performance of the campaign came in Division D down by the River Aire at Baildon on that same afternoon. Cookridge found Shipley Prov's wily Don Pattison far too tricky to control, the medium pace bowler sweeping them away with eight wickets at a cost of just a single run, capturing five victims in one over. He was in his 50th year at the time; amazingly he had not started playing cricket until 17 years earlier after finishing his football career in the local Sunday league. "It was moving a little in the air but basically I just bowled straight and the wickets came," he said. In his sixth over he picked up four in four deliveries, missed out with the fifth ball before then grabbing another wicket with the last delivery of the over finally finishing with an analysis of 6.3 overs, 4 maidens, 1 run, 8 wickets, seven of his victims being bowled.

It was a double season for Meanwood who retained the PPM Cup then took the A Division title for the first time with Tong once more the bridesmaids. Meanwood's key batsmen were Gary

Neil Kettle.

Mount's captain Yusuf Kayat handed the Cawthorne Cup by league fixture secretary Steve Raistrick in 2001.

Don Pattison.

Walton who topped the A Division averages on 45.10 and Rob Guthrie who was third in the list. But the top average of the campaign was claimed by D. S. Ryatt of Ramgarhia Sikh in B Division with 70.00 which included a new highest individual score for the division of 157 taken off Horsforth's bowling in mid July. Just over a month later with A. S. Ryatt, he set up a new third wicket highest partnership, too, the pair taking 220 off Farnley Hill's attack.

Mount followed up their C Division title of the previous season with the B Division crown while Mount B claimed a double by taking the C Division and Cawthorne Cup trophies. As the millennium was drawing to a close the newcomers from Batley, who at this point were playing their home games out in the middle of Pontefract Racecourse, were establishing themselves as one of the strongest forces in the league and in **1999** they did the double carrying off both the PPM Cup and the A Division title for the first time with Mount Pleasant finishing top of B Division and Mount B retaining the Cawthorne Cup.

It was a big year, too, for Kala Khan of New Wortley who won the league batting prize with an average of 49.38 after hitting 790 runs. But when it came to high scoring no-one matched Jonathan Collier of Motivators. In their home game with Shipley Prov on May 1 he thrashed an unbeaten 253 to set a highest score record for the league and at the same time create a new highest third wicket partnership record of 262 with Terry Bowler who a week earlier had starred with the ball taking nine for 31 at Pudsey Congs.

What had been a new achievement for Mount in 1999 was carried out all over again to welcome the new millennium when they completed an unprecedented double double by taking the league and cup titles once more. Mount B made it a hat-trick of wins in the Cawthorne Cup, too, in **2000** to underline the strength of the Batley side while at league level the Dales Council took the Bradford Area Cup for the second time.

On the individual front performances reached a high standard also with the 200 mark being breached for a third time when Neil Kettle, the Rodley wicketkeeper/batsman, set a new A Division record with his unbeaten 206 against New Wortley in late June. The innings helped him claim the A Division batting prize with an average of 45.69 but he was not the only big achiever that season for the club who play by the Leeds and Liverpool canal. In their home game with Castlehill on September 2 Simon Dickens took all ten wickets for 32 in a 10 over spell.

It was one of several impressive performances with the ball that year for Gary Child (Meanwood), Mark Burton (Skeltons Wood) and Nicky Lawson (Crompark) all turned in nine wicket efforts with Lawson's spell at Pudsey St Lawrence on July 8 particularly noteworthy for he badly split the end of the middle finger of his bowling hand going for a run out off his own third over. He had picked up five wickets by then but, bleeding badly, bowled another 3.2 overs to finish with nine for 30.

In a tight struggle for the title, New Wortley pipped Meanwood for the A Division crown on the most wins rule after both clubs finished on 97 points in **2001** to complete the double having already claimed the Pool Paper Mills Cup. Meanwhile, in B Division Baildon Meths were creating a new points record for the league in taking the title with 114, thirteen points clear of fellow centurions New Farnley. The Baildon side had two formidable performers in particular in a great team effort.

Their veteran opening batsman Don Butterfield, who on his day has been a hard to play medium pace bowler, clocked up 678 runs with a best score of 90 not out to top the B Division averages on 52.15. But it was the bowling of Mohammed Nawaz, 19, that really caught the eye. Not since Gloss Sample had had such a remarkable season in the birth campaign of the league in 1956 had any bowler managed to go through the 100 league wickets in a season mark. Now, Nawaz had earned himself a place in the record book alongside the great Green Lane all-rounder.

"It was my first season in English cricket after coming over from Pakistan where I played a bit so I was particularly pleased to pick up so many wickets so quickly. A friend had pointed me towards the Baildon club and I remember all the lads knew when the 100th wicket came and there was a terrific roar from them when I made it," said the opening bowler.

He hit top gear in early August when he tore into Farsley's batting to grab nine for 23 finishing the campaign just 10 wickets shy of Sample's all-time record of 111 but with nearly twice as many wickets as any other bowler in the division. His 101 victims claimed at 7.35 gave him the bowling prize while in the other divisions only Paul Dews of Meanwood in A Division, New Wortley all-rounder Fred Smith in C Division and Shipley Prov's Don Pattison in D Division managed to get into the 60s in the wicket count.

Top run scorer was New Wortley's Akhlaq Ahmed. Besides smashing a rapid century in the cup final he was the only batsman to hit 800-plus league runs. But while his average of 44.83 did much for his side's cause in taking the championship, it was Meanwood's Rob Guthrie who finished at the top of the A Division's batting list with an average of 52.69, his 685 aggregate including an unbeaten 125 in a new opening partnership record for the league of 233 with fellow century maker Mark Lone. The pair collected their runs against Crompark in early May.

A week later the Crompark club was on the end of another top performance, too, when their C Division side took on Wibsey Park Chapel. Swing bowler Andy Hirst finished with 10.3 overs, 4 maidens, 16 runs and nine wickets but no-one could have argued if he had not been satisfied with

Left: Akhlaq Ahmed salutes his century in the PPM final of 2001.
Right: Matthew Hoggard, left, just before going on tour to India with England, presents New Wortley double winners' captain Martin Knowles with the Jack Shuttleworth Cup at the league's annual dinner in October, 2001.

that haul for Crompark had managed to field only 10 men. "It was just one of those things," he said philosophically. "I might not have got that last one had Crompark had a full team. But I can tell you it felt strange to be on that hat-trick in the first over." It was as near to grabbing the magical all ten as it gets without being able to add it to his bowler's cv but he was just glad to be bowling again after being out of action with a double hernia and hamstring problems.

It was not all downhill without brakes though at Crompark for just before the season ended their D Division side wicketkeeper/batsman Andy Halliday grabbed seven catches in their victory over Hawksworth to get into the record book and point the club towards new horizons. The only club to have played in the league since it was formed suddenly found another gear and turned the **2002** season into their finest hour. They not only finished champions in both B Division and D Division, their D Division side losing fewer matches than any other side in the league's four divisions, but their second string also reached the Cawthorne Cup final only to lose out in the penultimate over to a Baildon Meths side whose victory brought to an end the stranglehold Mount B had had on the trophy after winning it in the four preceding seasons.

The season brought any number of eight-for performances, even I managed one of them, but the best of the pack was achieved by Steve Bedford whose eight victims for South Parade Baptists against New Farnley on June 1 cost him just two runs as the Farnley outfit crumbled to just six all out – equalling the record low score of 22 years earlier managed by New Wortley. John Butterfield of Baildon Meths took the league-batting prize with an average of 44.30 while New Wortley's Kala Khan, with 75 wickets at an average of 7.38, was top of the bowling list. New Wortley also had the league's top wicket taker of the season in John Blackburn in B Division who claimed 81 scalps while in D Division Nicky Lawson, with 47 wickets, and yours truly shared 123 wickets in Crompark's title success.

New Wortley retained their league title and pushed out the boundaries of run accumulation in cup competition with a 40 over record total of 428-6 against Esholt in early May. But their big rivals Meanwood were back in business, too, in the cup going on to pick up the Pool Paper Mills trophy for the third time in six seasons – and the following July they made it four in seven seasons.

The **2003** season was marked by the third success for the league side in the Bradford Area Cup in late August but, in particular, by the record breakers who gave Shipley Providence a particularly tough time through the middle three months of a most testing campaign.

First the Shipley side conceded the A Division's highest individual score and along the way a new second wicket highest stand in mid June against New Farnley when New Zealand born Nick Oram hit 208 while sharing in a partnership of 239 with John Baldwin. Then in early August Meanwood's all-rounder Stewart Dobson tore into them to take all ten wickets for four runs – the four being taken off him before he claimed his first victim – only to be followed up on August 23 by the free scoring Mount side who hit them for a new league record team score of 398 for three which included an unbeaten innings of 165 from H. Javed in an unbroken 202 stand with N. Khan (108no). Even by early May the little club, overlooked across the River Aire by the famous Salt village, had found times too difficult to put out two sides and withdrew their second eleven from D Division – but to their credit, they soldiered on in A Section with their weakened resources.

Dobson's ten-wicket haul was the start of a memorable weekend for Meanwood who retained the

Pool Paper Mills Cup the following afternoon in some comfort against Crompark. Bob Guthrie, described by League Fixture Secretary Steve Raistrick when he handed the opener his man of the match award as "the man who really likes Cup finals" followed up his century of the previous final with an unbeaten 82 in Meanwood's nine-wicket success.

But if the senior cup final had been something of an anti climax, the Cawthorne final a fortnight earlier had been a real nail-biter with New Wortley grabbing victory with one delivery to spare after Pudsey Congs had had one hand on the trophy with their score of 150 for nine. All-rounder Blackburn's well judged 43 tipped the balance leaving former league president and New Wortley veteran Les Thompson congratulating both sides. "I've seen many, many finals but this has been one of the best," he said as he presented the cup to Phil Worsnop, the New Wortley captain.

In the league Baildon Meths led the way for much of the season but had to wait until the final day to confirm their first league championship title. They pipped Meanwood by two points with champions of the previous two campaigns, New Wortley, a distance behind in third place. Castlehill and Churwell were comfortable winners of B and C Divisions, Churwell picking up their first piece of Dales silverware with Ian Dawson taking the C Division batting prize with an average of 38.50. The side's batting strength was emphasised by them claiming five spots out of the first 11 in the division's batting list, which included, poignantly and pointedly, the name of Keith Duckett in 14th position. The popular Crompark batsman, who had led the club's D Division side to the brink of a double in the previous season, tragically died a little over a month after the season ended.

Oram, from Christchurch, took the A Division batting prize with an average of 62.50 from the 750 runs he accumulated but Dobson had to settle for third place in the bowling list behind Nigel Stubbs of Adel and New Wortley's Khan. He was the league's top wicket-taker, however, on 65 wickets from 241 overs with Dominic Allen (South Parade Baptists) second with 63 wickets from 287 overs in Division B and yours truly third with 54 wickets from 269 overs for Crompark in Division C.

New Wortley's Cawthorne Cup winning captain 2003, Phil Worsnop, right, with man of match John Blackburn.

Nicky Lawson.

Iain Clark.

Gary Walton, Meanwood's captain, shows off the PPM Cup after leading his side to success in the 2003 final.

Above: Crompark's president and a committeeman since 1958, Robert Kibble, left, and secretary Bob Pritchard, officers of the only club in the league that has played in every season since the formation of the Dales Council.

Steve Bedford was top batsman in Division B with an average of 51.00. The South Parade Baptists' all-rounder finishing second to Keith Mardsen (Pudsey St Lawrence) in the division's bowling averages in an exceptional season of all-round performances in all divisions. John Whitney (Rodley) was top bowler in Division C with the Meanwood pair Graham Child and Matthew Ross accounting for the batting and bowling prizes in D Division, Child's new second teams record average of 78.60 the league's highest average for the season and Ross's average of 4.72 the league's lowest with Child's aggregate of 786 making him the league's top run scorer, too. Amongst the other award winners in that special season, too, was Crompark's first team captain Steve Thompson – not for batting though he had hit over 300 runs in every campaign since joining the club in the early 90s, but as the top wicketkeeper.

The **2004** campaign saw new club faces while others were lost. Bramley Beacon Sports whose ancestors included the successful Smith Sports sides called it a day as did Farsley but Halifax Direct and Burley Park signed on to keep the number of clubs involved static at 25. The season, however, got off to a major setback for three clubs in particular and their plight had a knock-on effect for the rest of the Dales sides they faced. Churwell, New Farnley and Farnley Hill lost their home in Farnley Park from the second week of the season onwards when a mini village of travelling caravans moved in. There had to be a clean-up operation and so the three clubs were forced to play their home games across Leeds at Soldiers Field, Roundhay.

The same problem then hit New Wortley but eventually cricket returned to normal and July arrived with one of the league's longest standing records falling - the Derek Ellsworth-H Wild (Bramley Sp) second elevens fourth wicket highest partnership of 170, which had stood for 42 years, was claimed by Ghopal Makwana and B Suryavansi who shared an unbeaten 199 stand as Leeds Sikh hit 317-3 (three shy of Meanwood's record high for second elevens of three years earlier) against Shipley Prov. Prov replied with 261-8 to play their part in a new highest aggregate score in second eleven games of 578. But with the opening of the league's 50th year under a month away, unbeaten Kirkstall Educational achieved the most striking record of the campaign by setting a new points total for a season of 122, dropping just 10 points on their way to the B Division title and winning 19 of their 22 games.

After just missing out 12 months earlier, Pudsey Congs had claimed the Cawthorne Cup beating Rodley by two wickets in July. Then Mount had denied Meanwood a hat-trick of PPM Cup successes winning in the last over of the final by five wickets with Qasim Raja hitting 90 to earn the man of the match award. Rodley claimed their third A Division title in nine seasons and Halifax Direct celebrated their first season in the league by becoming C Division champions. The top batting award was taken by New Farnley's Tim Oram, brother of our 2003 record breaker Nick, with an average of 52.50 with Stuart Liddell (Rodley) winning the top bowling honours with 66 A Division wickets at an average of 7.74.

THE CHAMPIONS AND CUP WINNERS, DECADE BY DECADE

Division winners and their records and winners for the fifth decade, 1996–2004

(Win 6pts, tie 3pts, draw 1pt with 3 bonus pts for faster scoring)

League	Winners	P.	W.	L.	D.	Pts.	Year	Pool P M Cup	Cawthorne Cup
Div. A	Rodley	22	15	2	2	104	**1996**	Nat. West Bank	Pudsey Congs
	Tong	22	15	1	4	102			
	Nat. West Bank	22	13	4	3	89			
Div. B	Jarvis Porter	22	18	3	0	112			
	Adel	22	13	2	5	100			
	Whitehall	22	11	4	6	91			
Div. C	Cookridge	22	12	6	3	79			
	Castlehill	22	12	9	1	76			
	Old Modernians	22	11	5	1	75			
2nd. Teams									
Div. A	Rodley	18	15	1	1	95			
	Pudsey Congs	18	12	4	2	80			
	Crompark	18	10	5	3	72			
Div. A	Rodley	22	14	1	6	94	**1997**	Meanwood	Pudsey Congs
	Tong	22	11	4	5	79			
	New Rover	22	11	4	5	79			
Div. B	Whitehall, tie, 3pts.	22	13	1	4	100			
	Castlehill, tie, 3pts.	22	10	5	2	75			
	Pudsey St. Law, tie, 3pts.	22	10	8	2	72			
Div. C	Mount	18	12	1	3	86			
	Ramgarhia Sikh	18	9	4	1	62			
	Farsley	18	7	4	1	52			

League	Winners	P.	W.	L.	D.	Pts.	Year	Pool P M Cup	Cawthorne Cup
2nd. Teams	Pudsey Congs	22	16	3	0	99			Mount B
	Meanwood	22	13	3	2	90			
	Skeltons Wood, tie, 3pts.	22	11	5	0	74			
Div. A	Meanwood	20	16	1	1	102	**1998**	Meanwood	
	Tong	20	13	4	0	81			
	Nat. West Bank	20	11	3	2	78			
Div. B	Mount	18	14	1	2	93			
	Farnley Hill	18	11	5	0	68			
	Ramgarhia Sikh	18	9	4	3	68			
Div. C	Mount	18	11	3	2	76			
	Shipley Providence	18	12	4	0	74			
	Farsley Celtic	18	9	5	2	64			
Div. D	Rodley	16	13	2	1	82			
	Meanwood	16	10	5	0	61			
	Shipley Providence	16	9	3	0	58			
Div. A	Mount	22	14	2	4	102	**1999**	Mount	Mount B
	Meanwood	22	13	3	3	93			
	Adel	22	14	5	0	87			
Div. B	Mount Pleasant	22	15	3	3	103			
	Baildon Meths.	22	14	3	3	98			
	Crompark, tie, 3pts.	22	12	4	2	86			
Div. C	Carr Manor	20	18	1	1	112			
	Skeltons Wood	20	14	3	2	93			
	Motivators	20	14	6	0	84			

League	Winners	P.	W.	L.	D.	Pts.	Year	Pool P M Cup	Cawthorne Cup
Div. D	New Wortley	21	17	3	1	103			
	Skeltons Wood	21	10	6	5	74			
	Cookridge	21	10	8	3	66			
Div. A	Mount	22	10	3	9	87	**2000**	Mount	Mount B
	New Wortley	22	11	7	4	73			
	Crompark	22	11	8	3	69			
Div. B	Farsley Celtic	22	16	2	4	103			
	Carr Manor	22	14	4	4	88			
	Shipley Providence	22	13	2	7	88			
Div. C	Pudsey Congs	22	14	2	6	93			
	New Farnley	22	12	4	6	84			
	Baildon Meths	22	12	6	4	79			
Div. D	Crompark	20	12	4	4	76			
	Cookridge	20	10	4	6	75			
	Carr Manor	20	12	6	2	74			
Div. A	New Wortley	22	15	3	4	97	**2001**	New Wortley	Mount B
	Meanwood	22	14	4	4	97			
	Mount Pleasant	22	13	3	6	96			
Div. B	Baildon Meths	22	19	3	0	114			
	New Farnley	22	16	4	1	101			
	Pudsey Congs	22	12	8	2	74			
Div. C	New Wortley	20	13	3	2	88			
	Wibsey Park Chapel	20	12	4	3	79			
	Baildon Meths	20	9	7	2	64			

League	Winners	P.	W.	L.	D.	Pts.	Year	Pool P M Cup	Cawthorne Cup
Div. D	New Farnley	21	12	6	2	78			
	Shipley Providence	21	11	6	2	76			
	Wibsey Park Chapel	21	10	6	4	68			
Div. A	New Wortley	22	16	4	1	101	**2002**	Meanwood	Baildon Meths B
	Rodley	22	14	5	2	93			
	Baildon Meths	22	13	3	3	93			
Div. B	Crompark	22	16	4	1	101			
	Baildon Meths	22	12	6	2	82			
	Mount	22	10	6	3	75			
Div. C	Whitehall	22	18	3	0	109			
	Hawkesworth	22	16	3	2	105			
	South Parade Baptists	22	16	4	1	101			
Div. D	Crompark	22	13	2	3	94			
	Ramgarhia Sikh	22	12	8	0	74			
	Pudsey St. Lawrence	22	9	6	1	64			

(A new points scoring system was introduced for the start of 2003)
(Win 6pts, tie 3pts, drawn fixtures: 1pt., 2pts., 4pts., or 5pts.)

League	Winners	P.	W.	L.	5	4	2	1	Pts.	Year	Pool P M Cup	Cawthorne Cup
Div. A	Baildon Meths	22	16	2	1	1	1	1	108	**2003**	Meanwood	New Wortley
	Meanwood	22	16	3	0	2	1	0	106			
	New Wortley	22	13	8	0	0	1	0	80			
Div. B	Castlehill	20	15	4	1	0	0	0	95			
	South Parade Baptists	20	12	4	1	3	0	0	89			
	Whitehall	20	11	5	1	1	2	0	79			
Div. C	Churwell	21	13	5	0	0	3	0	84			
	Esholt	21	12	5	0	0	2	2	78			
	Rodley	21	10	6	2	1	2	0	78			

League	Winners	P.	W.	L.	5	4	2	1	Pts.	Year	Pool P M Cup	Cawthorne Cup
Div. D	Meanwood	20	13	3	1	2	1	0	93			
	New Farnley	20	13	3	0	1	2	1	87			
	Pudsey St. Lawrence	20	9	8	0	0	1	2	58			Pudsey Cong
										2004		
Div. A	Rodley , 1 tie 3 pts.	22	14	1	2	2	2	0	109		Mount	
	Baildon Meth	22	16	4	0	1	1	0	102			
	New Farnley	22	11	3	2	3	2	1	93			
Div. B	Kirkstall Ed	22	19	0	1	0	1	1	122			
	Burley Park	22	15	4	1	0	2	0	99			
	New Wortley	22	13	5	1	0	2	1	88			
Div. C	Halifax Direct	22	14	2	2	0	3	1	101			
	Pudsey Cong	22	12	3	3	0	3	1	94			
	Cookridge	22	10	6	2	2	2	0	82			

AN AVERAGE VIEW

Season by season leaders of the averages ~ the fifth decade, 1996–2004.

League	Name/Club (The Batsmen)	Ins.	NO	H.Sc	Rns.	Av.	Year	Name/Club (The Bowlers)	Ovs.	Mdn	Rns.	Wks.	Av.
Div. A	M. Richmond, New Rover	16	5		691	62.81	**1996**	R. Stevens, New Rover			802	94	8.53
	K. Dickson, Pudsey St. Law	19	7		653	54.41		M. Allison, Rodley			431	47	9.17
	K. Edwards, Pudsey Congs	19	4		617	41.13		S. Dickens, Rodley			414	43	9.62
	P. Hudson, Tong	19	5		546	39		R. Kelso, Rodley			718	73	9.83
	R. Griggs, Lawns Park	13	3		325	32.5		D. Holmes, Tong			864	80	10.8
	J. Shires, Meanwood	20	3		548	32.23		B. Newall, Pudsey Congs			601	55	10.92
Div. B	R. Parker, Adel	17	5		522	43.5		S. Shires, Adel			508	77	6.59
	L. Fussey, Adel	14	6		299	37.37		D. Simister, Jarvis Porter			654	86	7.6
	A. Stoddart, Whitehall	22	4		600	33.33		D. Nash, Whitehall			562	58	9.68
Div. C	C. Yewdall, Hawksworth	22	4		660	36.66		S. Gautrey, Castlehill			480	49	9.79
	N. Bonnington, Cookrdige	19	3		487	30.43		M. Reasbeck, Old Mods.			361	33	10.93
	T. Hales, Alwoodley	18	5		379	29.15		S. Shah, Cookridge			630	56	11.25
2nd. Teams	G. Redshaw, Cookridge	13	5		381	47.62		B. Finch, Pudsey Congs			443	70	6.32
	M. Poucher, Crompark	10	3		275	39.28		K. Schmitz, Crompark			287	38	7.55
	D. Child, Meanwood	15	2		456	38		P. Dyson, Meanwood			270	35	7.71
Div. A	P. Slater, Nat. West Bank	17	3	200	774	55.28	**1997**	S. Brown, Rodley			256	33	7.76
	M. Richmond, New Rover	17	4	81*	600	46.15		J. Patrick, Nat. West Bank			287	35	8.2
	G. Child, Meanwood	13	5	57*	349	43.63		R. Kelso, Rodley			544	57	9.54
	S. Phillips, Tong	13	2	123*	432	39.27		R. Stevens, New Rover			589	56	10.52
	D. Holmes, Tong	16	5	70	369	33.55		J. Henderson, Nat. West Bank			356	32	11.12
	P. Rakusen, New Rover	13	3	88	327	32.7		S. Shires, Adel			381	34	11.2
Div. B	D. Threllfall, Pudsey St. Law	19	5	68*	576	41.14		D. Crozier, Whitehall			232	30	7.73
	A. Mandreker, Whitehall	16	4	136	487	40.58		D. Fenton, Castlehill			332	40	8.3
	D. Crozier, Whitehall	12	5	67*	279	39.86		S. Smith, Cookridge			545	53	10.28

Batting Averages

League	Name/Club	Ins.	NO	H.Sc	Rns.	Av.	Year
Div. C	A. S. Ryatt, Ramg. Sikh	11	2	58*	305	33.88	
	L. Brook, Farsley	10	2	76*	256	32	
	M. B. Loonat, Mount	11	0	73	317	28.81	
2nd. Teams							
	R. Brady Whitehall	17	4	144	730	56.15	
	C. Day, Meanwood	16	2	93	600	42.86	
	N. Griffiths, Pudsey Congs	10	2	59	286	33.5	1998
Div. A	G. Walton, Meanwood	13	3	164	451	45.1	
	D. Holmes, Tong	11	3	119	331	41.38	
	R. Guhtrie, Meanwood	17	4	131	456	35.08	
	G. Bottomley, Tong	17	4	67*	392	30.15	
	D. Rule, Tong	12	0	83	345	28.75	
	J. Metcalfe, Rodley	16	4	102*	337	28.08	
Div. B	D. S. Ryatt, Ramgarhia Sikh	9	0	157	630	70	
	B. Meredith, Arthington	17	4	103*	566	43.54	
	M. Seedat, Mount	17	1	129	693	43.31	
Div. C	J. Batty, Carr Manor	14	3	75	536	51.18	
	I. Rajah, Mount	13	8	49*	230	46	
	S. Tempest, Farsley Celtic	10	1	74	344	38.22	
Div. D	F. Smith, New Wortley	11	1	119*	407	40.7	
	C. Day, Meanwood	13	1	137	352	29.33	
	A. Cohen, Meanwood	10	0	143	281	28.1	
Div. A	K. Khan, New Wortley	20	4	109	790	49.38	1999
	C. Higgs, Tong	13	5	78	356	44.5	
	S. Shaw, Meanwood	15	2	103*	508	39.08	
	N.A. Loonat, Mount	19	1	99	663	36.83	
	M. Dyson, Meanwood	16	3	81	464	35.69	
	M. Hobson, New Wortley	15	4	88	356	32.36	

Bowling Averages

Name/Club	Ovs.	Mdn	Rns.	Wks.	Av.
J. Bharj, Ramgarhia Sikh			281	36	7.8
S. Karolia, Mount			353	40	8.82
M. Wilson, Green Lane			339	31	10.93
R. Taylor, Crompark			217	32	6.78
P. Dyson, Meanwood			274	36	7.61
R. Rainford, Skeltons Wood			355	46	7.72
S. Brown, Rodley			203	31	6.55
M. Harrison. Meanwood			222	30	7.4
D. Rule, Tong			338	37	9.14
B. Welch, Meanwood			552	60	9.2
M. Allinson, Rodley			363	39	9.31
J. Patrick, Nat. West Bank			484	47	10.3
I. Lee, Cookridge			204	28	7.28
Y. Akudi, Mount			378	51	7.41
M. Newbound, Farnley Hill			445	49	9.08
D. Belcher, Shipley Prov.			497	71	7
M. Yousef, Carr Manor			330	38	8.68
M. Wildsmith, Baildon Meths			265	29	9.14
M. Wright, Rodley			71	25	2.84
A. Medd, Rodley			335	57	5.88
D. Pattison, Shipley Prov.			368	61	6.03
J. Henderson, Nat. West Bank			363	39	9.31
C. Henry, Adel			586	61	9.6
N. Chambers, New Wortley			314	31	10.13
M. Harrison, Meanwood			564	55	10.25
P. Slater, Nat. West Bank			438	41	10.68
D. Rule, Tong			424	38	11.16

League	Name/Club	Ins.	NO	H.Sc	Rns.	Av.	Year	Name/Club	Ovs.	Mdn	Rns.	Wks.	Av.
Div. B	A. Mandrekar, Whitehall	16	4	123	605	50.42		R. Taylor, Crompark			534	82	6.51
	N. Rajah, Mount Pleasant	13	2	122	478	43.45		S. Mace, Whitehall			241	30	8.03
	C. Walker, Old Mods.	12	4	78*	328	41		M. Ravat, Mount Pleasant			282	35	8.06
Div. C	J. Batty, Carr Manor	19	6	81	710	54.62		R. Rainford, Skeltons Wood			282	46	6.13
	D. Storey, Carr Manor	12	3	73*	317	35.22		K. Duckworth, Skeltons Wood			522	75	6.96
	Y. Rawat, Mount	11	0	67	371	33.73		D. Thomas, Baildon Meths			276	39	7.07
Div. D	R. Brady, Whitehall	16	0	103	566	35.38		R. McKenzie, Cookridge			362	37	9.78
	J. Farrar, Crompark	13	6	55*	206	29.43		D. Field, Skeltons Wood			732	74	9.89
	S. Haw, Whitehall	11	2	53	244	27.11		D. Gunn, New Wortley			508	50	10.16
Div. A	N. Kettle, Rodley	15	2	206*	594	45.69	2000	D. Fenton, Castlehill			338	36	9.38
	G. Walton, Meanwood	12	5	103*	318	45.43		K. Akudi, Mount			431	45	9.57
	J. Kendal, Adel	13	3	80*	404	40.4		G. Child, Meanwood			362	35	10.34
	M. Seedat, Mount	19	3	127*	601	37.56		R. Taylor, Crompark			735	71	10.35
	S. Kayat, Mount	15	1	89	472	33.71		S. Gautrey, Castlehill			356	32	11.12
	K. Khan, New Wortley	16	1	144	494	32.93		R. Kelso, Rodley			481	43	11.18
Div. B	P. Blackburn, Pudsey St L.	12	3	118	339	37.66		R. Rainford, Skeltons Wood			260	46	5.65
	J. Batty, Carr Manor	19	6	55	373	28.69		S. Tempest, Farsley Celtic			355	61	5.82
	W. Springer, Motivators	15	2	63	392	26.13		M. Duckworth, Pudsey St Law			278	40	6.95
Div. C	J. Hodson, Rodley	10	2	75*	429	53.63		M. Burton, Skeltons Wood			624	72	8.66
	R. Owen, Nw Wortley	12	3	56*	293	32.55		D. Nash, Whitehall			693	74	9.36
	M. Edwards, Pudsey Congs	19	5	63	420	30		D. Pattison, Shipley Prov.			582	60	9.7
Div. D	T. Hanley, Wibsey P.C. Ac.	12	5	99*	277	39.57		P. Waring, Carr Manor			279	42	6.64
	M. Seed, New Farnley	15	4	78*	371	33.73		R. Ackrill, New Farnley			298	39	7.64
	A. Halliday, Crompark	12	0	116	361	30.08		J. Whitney, Carr Manor			347	44	7.88
Div. A	R. Guthrie, Meanwood	17	4	125*	685	52.69	2001	Y. Akudi, Mount Pleasant				44	7.98
	A. Ahmed, New Wortley	21	3	112*	807	44.83		M. Pathan, Mount				49	10.26
	G. Walton, Meanwood	17	7	87*	440	44		G. Child, Meanwood				35	10.6

League	Name/Club	Ins.	NO	H.Sc	Rns.	Av.	Year	Name/Club	Ovs.	Mdn	Rns.	Wks.	Av.
	N. Lorgat, Mount	15	5	80	372	37.2		S. Shires, Adel				30	11.7
	M. Seedat, Mount Pleasant	18	4	72	520	37.14		P. Dews, Meanwood				69	12
	A. Khaliq, Mount Pleasant	17	2	109	539	35.93		S. Tempest, Farsley Celtic				41	12.09
Div. B	D. Butterfield, Baildon Meths	19	6	90*	678	52.15		M. Nawaz, Baildon Meths				101	7.35
	C. Glover, Skeltons Wood	12	3	100*	371	41.22		D. Bottomley, New Farnley				49	7.5
	J. Petty, Farsley	13	3	80*	364	36.4		D. Sanderson, New Farnley				56	7.73
Div. C	F. Smith, New Wortley	16	7	102*	339	37.67		A. Hirst, Wibsey Park Chapel				46	8.36
	C. Yewdall, Hawksworth	19	4	89*	532	34.87		M. Linley, Rodley				34	8.76
	R. Owen, New Wortley	16	1	63	452	30.13		A. Walker, Wibsey Park Chapel				34	8.88
Div. D	C. Simons, Wibsey Pk. Ch.	16	6	73	399	39.92		D. Pattison, Shipley Prov.				64	7.77
	M. Seed, New Farnley	17	1	65	450	28.13		B. Ali, Pudsey St Lawrence				31	7.8
	P. Hiley, Baildon Meths	15	1	56	375	26.79		M. Duckworth, Pudsey St Law.				46	8.9
Div. A	J. Butterfield, Baildon Meths	17	4	84*	576	44.3	2002	K. Khan, New Wortley			554	75	7.38
	A. Ahmed, New Wortley	19	4	135*	649	43.26		M. Allinson, Rodley			411	35	11.74
	M. Scaife, Bramley Sp. Bcn.	15	1	95	533	38.07		S. Dickens, Rodley			590	48	12.29
	R. Guthrie, Meanwood	16	4	84	411	34.25		S. Shaw, Meanwood			432	35	12.34
	T. Smith, Adel	13	3	53	325	32.5		N. Lorgat, Mount			497	40	12.43
	G. Ryatt, Leeds Sikh	18	1	87	548	32.23		P. Dews, Meanwood			704	56	12.57
Div. B	L. Walsh, Farnley Hill	15	3	104	472	39.33		R. Bott, Pudsey St. Lawrence			283	41	6.9
	C. Field, Garforth	15	6	62*	324	36		J. Blackburn, New Wortley			573	81	7.07
	S. Lee, Pudsey St. Law.	13	4	65*	288	32		M. Gummerson, Garforth			267	34	7.85
Div. C	Z. Jaffary, Whitehall	20	8	74	495	41.25		T. Townsend, Hawksworth			350	50	7
	C. Yewdall, Hawksworth	20	4	63*	600	37.5		P. Whincup, S. Parade Bap.			373	51	7.31
	M. Denney, Meanwood	13	2	65*	361	36.1		M. Woodhead, Rodley			356	45	7.91

League	Name/Club	Ins.	NO	H.Sc	Rns.	Av.	Year	Name/Club	Ovs.	Mdn	Rns.	Wks.	Av.
Div. D	B. Ali, Pudsey St. Lawrence	13	3	69*	343	34.3		N. Lawson, Crompark			395	47	8.4
	A. Halliday, Crompark	21	3	94	564	31.33		B. Foster, Crompark	302	88	718	76	9.45
	B. Bryan, Baildon Meths	12	1	85	339	30.82		M. Senior, New Farnley			332	34	9.76
Div. A	N. Oram, N. Farnley	17	5	208	750	62.5	**2003**	N. Stubbs, Adel				36	9.33
	I. Mahmood, Baildon Meth	18	7	105	570	51.82		K. Khan, New Wortley				52	9.98
	K. Edwards, Pudsey Congs	14	2	120	524	43.66		S. Dobson, Meanwood	241	69	697	65	10.72
	M Hobson, Rodley	16	2	111	561	40.07		M. Nawaz, Baildon Meths				48	11.02
	M. Pearson, Pudsey Congs	12	2	92	378	37.8		J. Monkhouse, Meanwood				34	11.03
	R. Kayat, Mount	18	5	57	490	37.69		M. Zubar, Meanwood				30	11.43
Div. B	S. Bedford, South Par. Bap.	19	10	74	459	51		K. Marsden, Pudsey St. L				36	8.69
	D. Fenton, Castlehill	18	3	146	701	46.73		S. Bedford, S. Parade Bap.				33	9.09
	T. Dasgupta, Hawksworth	13	3	84*	396	39.6		D. Allen, South Parade Bap.	287	80	748	63	11.87
Div. C	I. Dawson, Churwell	13	3	90*	385	38.5		J. Whitney, Rodley				31	9.26
	I. Lee, Cookridge.	13	1	85	393	32.75		S. Mahmood, Kirkstall Ed.				30	10.17
	A. Barker, Esholt	15	2	89*	401	30.85		N. Cooper, Esholt				43	10.21
Div. D	G. Child, Meanwood	14	4	139	786	78.6		M. Ross, Meanwood				36	4.72
	M. Seed, New Farnley	14	3	86*	453	41.18		M. Duckworth, Pud. St L.				30	10.67
	R. Smirthwaite, Wibsey P.C.	14	4	64*	384	38.4		A. Green, Old Mods.				34	10.7

2004

Batting

League	Name/Club	Ins.	NO	H.Sc	Rns.	Av.
Div. A	T. Oram, N Farnley	17	5		630	52.50
	C. Bradbury, Rodley	16	5		525	47.73
	I. Mahmood, Baildon Meth	17	4		584	44.92
	R. Guthrie, Meanwood	14	6		335	41.88
	M. Lone, Meanwood	18	2		605	37.81
	G. Lewsley, Pud Congs	13	4		329	36.55
Div. B	A. Butt, Burley Park	16	4		574	47.83
	R. Bott, Pudsey S L	15	6		316	35.11
	A. Latif, Burley Park	14	4		349	34.90
Div. C.	S. Raistrick, Pudsey C	18	5		521	40.07
	G. Makwana, Leeds Sikh	14	6		297	37.13
	A. Hailliday, Crompark	17	4		471	36.23

Bowling

Name/Club	Ovs.	Mdn	Rns.	Wks.	Av.
S. Liddell, Rodley			511	66	7.74
S. Jeffrey, Crompark			335	34	9.85
M. Allinson, Rodley			402	39	10.31
S. Dickens, Rodley			401	35	11.46
S. Bedford, S Parade B.			781	62	12.39
T. Oram, N Farnley			715	57	12.54
S. Levitt, Kirkstall Ed			302	46	6.57
S. Brooke, Baildon Meth			311	39	7.97
K. Marsden, Pudsey S L			560	64	8.75
D. Cunningham, N Farn.			404	43	9.39
R. Mackenzie, Cookridge			354	37	9.57
A. Green, Halifax Direct			647	67	9.65

Award winners, Decade by decade, 1996-2004

Trophy winners of the league's miscellaneous awards over the years

Year	A Div	B Div	All - Rounders C. Div	D. Div (2nd X1s)	U-18	W-keeper	Fielder	U-18 Field	U-18 Bat	U-18 Bowl	Fast 50
1996	K. Edwards Pudsey Con	A. Stoddart Whitehall		R. Jarvis Pud. St L	R. Jarvis Pud. St L	J. Metcalfe Jarvis P	J. Hobbs Whitehall		M. Poucher Crompark	R. Jarvis Pud. St L	M. Button Ilkley
1997	P. Slater Nat. West	D. Crozier Whitehall		N. Griffiths Pudsey Con		M. Krause Pud. St L	A. Mandrekar Whitehall		L. Brook Farsley	A. Dutton Horsforth	J.Hainsworth New Wort.
1998	D. Rule Tong	S. Karolia Mount	I. Kayat & I. Rajah Mount	F. Smith New Wort.		D. Collins Old Mods & M. Kahalid Mount	S. Avery Baildon M.		P. Clayton Horsforth	S. Ahmed Baildon M.	S. Kayat Mount & A. D-Masters Adel
1999	K. Khan New Wort.	C. McLaren Ship. Prov.	T. Bowler Motivators	F. Smith New Wort.	J. Petty Farsley	A. Khalid Mount	W. Charles Baildon M.				J. Hainsworth New Wort.
2000	C. Neale Adel	W. Springer Motivators	J. Hainsworth New Wort.	J. Whitney Carr Man. & G. Forster Wib. PC Ac.	A. Amir Farsley	A. Khalid Mount & N. Kettle Rodley	W. Charles Baildon M.				M. Seedat Mount
2001	A. Ahmed New Wort.	R. Bott Pud. S Law	F. Smith New Wort.	C Simmonds Wib. PC.	G. Makwana Ram. Sikh	D. Collins Old Mods	W. Charles Baildon M.	S. Kirk New Wort.			G.Makwana Ram. Sikh & S.Mammaniat Mt. Pleasant

Year	All - Rounders				U-18	W-keeper	Fielder	U-18 Field	U-18 Bat	U-18 Bowl	Fast 50
	A Div	B Div	C. Div	D. Div (2nd X1s)							
2002	S. Dickens Rodley	F. Smith New Wort.	Z. Jaffary Whitehall	B. Ali Pud. St L	G. Makwana Leeds Sikh	J. Dolamore Adel	S. Fenton Wib. PC	S. Clapham O. Mods & P. Hiley Baildon M			M. Dyson Meanwood
2003	N.Oram N. Farnley	S. Bedford Sth. Par. B.	A. Barker Esholt	C Wheelh'se N. Farnley		S Thompson Crompark	P. Hiley Baildon M	G Jackson Pudsey C	M. Walsh Wibsey PC	M. Ross Meanwood	I. Hussain Whitehall
2004											

AT THE DOUBLE......No 6

Investing in cricket's future

By David Markham, for over three decades the Soccer writer on the Telegraph and Argus and leading commentator on local cricket affairs

I HAD some sympathy with a caller who phoned in to a programme when they were discussing the state of English cricket. The caller from the Midlands rightly pointed out that cricket is not confined to the England team and, while it may be difficult for the London based media to grasp, cricket is still strong in the leagues where the game plays a big part in the life of local communities. He went on to refer to other areas like the North East and Lancashire where cricket is also strong, but surprisingly he did not mention Yorkshire where the game is probably at its strongest.

The strength of all sport lies in the grass roots. Cricket's strength in Yorkshire lies in the competitive league structure that leads to the county side and beyond. For instance, there was pride in the Bradford League when Anthony McGrath, who has played all his cricketing life for either Bankfoot or East Bierley, was appointed Yorkshire captain. Other Yorkshire captains in recent years, Phil Carrick (who as a schoolboy played the odd game or so in the Dales Council) and David Bairstow also started and finished their senior careers in the Bradford League.

The Dales Council have also enjoyed a proud record in providing players for first class cricket, the latest being Yorkshire pace bowler Matthew Hoggard who began playing in the league for Pudsey Congs and is now part of the England Test and one day teams. Essex and former

David Markham.

Paul Slater.

Yorkshire all-rounder James Middlebrook began his senior cricket in Pudsey Congs' Dales Council team while, at the other end of Pudsey, Worcestershire all-rounder David Leatherdale, Sussex and former Yorkshire left arm pace bowler Paul Hutchison and Yorkshire opener Chris Taylor all began in the Dales Council with St Lawrence.

Congs and St Lawrence have run third and fourth teams in the Dales Council for many years and they have proved to be the ideal way of giving young players the chance of senior cricket and a step into the Bradford League for the more talented youngsters. Also the league president, Yorkshire's cricket chairman and former player, Geoff Cope first played senior cricket at Leeds Zingari in the Dales.

The league, of course, is not all about producing first class cricketers. It is all about enjoying cricket in a competitive setting and that is precisely what the Dales Council have been about throughout its proud history. Long may that remain so, but changes in the last 50 years have shown we all have to work extra hard so that league cricket can survive and prosper in the face of competition from other sports and the many leisure choices our youngsters enjoy.

The decline of cricket in state schools has led to the growth of junior cricket, which is a healthy development, and there is competitive cricket on offer at many clubs from under-11 through to under-17s. In other words, clubs now produce their own players, but all this costs money. The ECB receive considerable income through TV contracts and the distribution of this money to the counties goes a long way towards keeping first class cricket going, but league cricket also needs financial help to keep the grass roots of the game in a healthy state.

Some clubs I know – notably Buttershaw St Paul's and Saltaire – have done well with lottery grants, but there are so many other deserving cases of clubs who desperately need to upgrade their facilities like pavilions, ground equipment and practice areas. What better sporting investment could there be than in helping cricket clubs, who give so much to all ages in their communities but particularly young people, to survive and prosper?

David Markham, September, 2003.

At the Double partner......................Paul Slater

An overthrow into the record book

THE league was in its 41st season when the individual 200 barrier mark was broken for the first time and though it has been passed on three further occasions since no-one can take away Paul Slater's moment as "the first batsman there."

In fact, it was a record-breaking day not only for Slater but for his team, NatWest, as well. Both the Bank side and their opponents Jarvis Porter found themselves free on Saturday, August 23, 1997, so it was mutually agreed, with the league's permission, that the A Division fixture which had been postponed three weeks earlier when NatWest's ground had been double booked could go ahead. "The council had let the ground for an Asian event unaware that we had a Sunday fixture," the

Nat West secretary explained at the time so maybe it was written that records should go as a result, who knows?

Yet in the event the match was played on the Bradford University ground nearby. It was a much larger playing area and on the face of it harder to hit a big score. But to counter this Jarvis Porter turned up with just eight players and the Bank invested heavily in run-scoring hitting 346 for 3 with JP responding with 111. "We knew there was no point in going beyond 250 except for records but we wanted to wipe an unwanted record we held from the record book," said David Smith the Nat West treasurer.

Ten years earlier Meanwood had hit the Bank's bowlers for 329 for 4 to lift the highest score in an innings by six from Smiths Sports. "We'd been near to wiping it out three seasons before when Gary Edwards and Mark Mills hit centuries against Tong. Oddly enough that was in late August, too. But on that occasion we ran out of overs at 322 for 4," said Smith.

"But this time it was all about Paul Slater. Gary held the individual highest score with his unbeaten 166 against New Wortley hit a couple of seasons earlier for us but now we all wanted Paul to go on and top that once he got near the record. He is such a good batsman technically and I believe one of the best the league has produced," said Smith.

Slater's rich vein of runs continued the following Saturday against the powerful New Rover side when he got into three figures again. But the landmark 200 was the high point catching the imagination of the whole league and leading to a special presentation at the annual league dinner three months later by the then president Les Thompson. The glass tankard received by the 28-year-old recorded that the 2hr 44 min knock included 25 fours and five sixes.

Smith was convinced Slater was out that day trying to lift the Bank's total to the 350 mark from the penultimate delivery of their innings. But Slater, a photo lab technician lost his wicket more to a tired shot than going for a big hit. "I had got to 200 with two deliveries to go then tried to square cut a slow ball and it flew to first slip," he said. Result was an end to the mammoth knock brought about by the Scanlon brothers, caught Dennis bowled Sean.

John Patrick, with 40, Dave Bean, 38, and Jason Stubbs, 50 no, had been the supporting cast for Slater who started his career as a fast bowler and never in his wildest dreams thought he would hit a double hundred. "Gary held the record for the top individual score and there's no way I could be a better batsman than him. But when I got to 150 that day his 166 was in the back of my mind and the lads were shouting support as each run got me nearer the record.

"Some might say it's not a true record because they had only eight players but it was on a big playing area and it's in the book now. I was lucky to reach 200 though for on 198 I was dropped going for a really silly sweep – it went up in the air screwing off towards point. Their keeper tried to get there but couldn't but the worst moment had come when I was on 192," he said.

"We went for a single and if the ball had hit the stumps I was gone but it went for a four overthrow and suddenly I was on 197. I should have been out but luck was with me. Then when I got to 200 it was just a terrific relief."

Chapter Eleven
OUT and about with the Umpires

THEY say old cricketers never die they simply fade away....or do they become umpires? Certainly it has to be one of the more popular routes into the umpires' union but whichever way umpires become umpires they all have a common bond – they all love the game and in a lifetime of writing about sport I have seldom come across one who did not relish the chance to talk cricket.

Dickie Bird, maybe the most famous of them all and one of my most regular callers when I was on the sports writers' circuit full time, would usually let me know if something extraordinary was about to happen to him like standing in a special Test or completing a career milestone. And at Dales Council level I could count on some special stories when umpires turned up in numbers to support their colleagues at big games like cup finals. They like to promenade and expand on their magical moments in the Dales.

Who is to say whether most of their tales are true or not – but of course, they insist they are. Like the one about the umpire who came from the north of the county who, captains believed, had an obsession about catching the 7-30pm bus from Pool to get home in time for the tele on Saturday evenings and so encouraged loud appeals once the clock ticked beyond 6-30pm. And the one about the official who was partial to four or five pints before going out to take a match and who was known while officiating to "water the wicket when nature called".

A team to reckon with – some of the Dales Council's best known umpires at the turn of the millennium, l to r: Colin White (the umpires' association secretary), Bernard Greaves, Peter Rafton, Andrew McLaughlan, Brian Brown, Gerry Dove, Mick Lockwood, president, Mick Price, chairman, and Dennis Thompson.

Then there is the tale about the umpire who was always using a concealed radio while standing at square leg. Early in one match he had sentenced a wicketkeeper to an lbw decision but then found himself stumped when the same wicketkeeper later called upon him to give a stumping decision just when the Test match he was listening to arrived at a critical point. Another story concerned an official who, when confronted by an angry batsman he had just given out caught behind and who vehemently maintained the ball had come off his pads, calmly instructed his "victim" to tell the scorer on his way to the dressing room that the decision was lbw.

But maybe the most bizarre anecdote is the one about one umpire who was rumoured to have suddenly died. Colleagues in the umpires' fraternity not unnaturally immediately took up a collection in his memory but were amazed later in the day when they found him at his usual job behind the bar at a local hostelry. Yet they were even more astounded when he actually claimed the money they had collected for him. Tall tales, maybe. But not the one about the little old lady with the umbrella - that one can be substantiated.

It involved Jack Toothill, one of the Dales Council's best-known officials during the league's first three decades, and Nelly Webster, mother of the league's most celebrated wicketkeeper Roy Webster. On this particular occasion Nelly, then in her late 70s and tiny being just 4ft 8ins tall, was watching her son's side batting and was furious when Toothill gave their last man out caught when the fielder had stepped over the boundary line after he had taken the catch.

"It was in the rules that when a catch was made good that a fielder could step over the boundary line with the ball but my mum would have none of it," recalled Webster. "When Jack came off she confronted him waving her umbrella and pointing out the boundary line had been crossed. Jack, trying to avoid being prodded to the floor and even worse, explained the rule as it stood while players gathered round and laughingly encouraged the little old lady to 'run him through'.

"It was hilarious at the time but Jack took it all in good heart and no matter where he went on holiday from then onwards he always sent my mum a postcard. After looking warily around, his first words to me every time he turned up to umpire one of our games would be 'which direction

Peter Langley, left, and Keith Dibb, the umpires in charge at the 2001 PPM Cup final.

Cyril Chapman, whose service as a player, umpire and administrator in the Dales provided a strong part of the league's backbone.

will the attack come from today?'," said Webster.

Toothill's name did not appear among the 18 umpires listed in the initial Dales Council handbook in 1956 but he was there from the following season onwards and played a key role in the founding and development of the umpires association. When he left the area to move to Cleveland two decades ago there was a special ceremony to mark his contribution to the league held at Esholt cricket club. He had held a position as one of the umpires' association officers continuously for 25 years and even before that had been a committee member for the association. He took on the role of secretary in 1960, a position he held for the next 20 years combining it over the last eight years with the job of treasurer, too. Then in 1981 he was made president and held the office for four years.

The Dales Council was in its third campaign in 1958 when the Dales Council Umpires Association was really up and running with officers, rules and a motto "WITHOUT FEAR OR FAVOUR". In the first two seasons there had been a simple list of names and addresses, 18 in 1956 and 22 in 1957. By 1958 that had developed into a 34 strong list with sitting Dales Council League president Kenneth Hodgson installed as the umpires' president as well, George Baxter made chairman, C. J. E. Sladen appointed secretary and Harry Benson chosen as the treasurer. The committee comprised of Messrs. Baxter, Benson, Sladen, Toothill, Arthur Howe, C. Sedman, and J. Yeadon with H. Sugden the association's vice-president and G. W. Oddy taking on the job of auditor, a role he kept until 1985.

The rules stated that the "objects of the Association are to remain an independent body, to create friendship amongst members and to improve through discussions the efficiency of all umpires." The annual subscription was fixed at 5s, 25p today, rising to 6s the following season and at the new umpires' association first annual meeting at the White Cross Hotel at Guiseley on 18 February, 1959, Baxter spoke glowingly of a "very successful first season as an Association."

The 1959 season saw the association with its own cricket X1 with Eddie Laurie, who later became the association's chairman for a year, elected as captain. Laurie was instrumental in getting Yorkshire opener Bryan Stott to address the umpires on a couple occasions when the county opener talked about things like a throwing controversy in Australia, the county's championship winning season and how popular the choice of Vic Wilson as captain had been.

But at the September meeting of the umpires association in 1965 Laurie, who had been with the league since its inception, announced he was giving up umpiring because he felt there was far too much grumbling about decisions during the past season. It would have been interesting to have been a fly on the wall when that kind of thing has come up over the years at umpires' meetings. On-the-field indiscipline has to be an important issue for umpires if and when it comes up while another important theme they have to address is the ongoing search for new faces to take up the calling. But it has been evident over the years just how much the association's members have enjoyed their time in the middle, a point demonstrated by the association's enviable record of loyalty by its members.

Over the five decades there have been several officers who have served the association over a run of years like J. L. Metcalfe (president from 1962 to 1968); W. Marshall (president from 1969 to 1979); Les Bulmer (president from 1985 to 1990); Walt Scott (president from 1991 to 1995 and secretary in 1986); George Baxter (chairman from 1958 to 1961, treasurer from 1970 to 1972 and president in 1980); Tom Cartwright (chairman from 1964 to 1971); Arthur Bullock (chairman from 1972 to 1978); Jack Dibb (chairman from 1981 to 1984); Brian Wrigglesworth (chairman from 1996 to1999); Charles Sharman (secretary and treasurer from 1981 to 1987); John Collins (secretary from 1988 to 1994); Bill Beckett (secretary from 1995 to 2000 and treasurer from 1988 until now) and Dennis Marsden (who was the first appointments secretary, holding the office for two seasons before taking in on again in 1995 this time for a four year run).

Sitting officers besides Beckett are Mick Lockwood (president since 2000); Michael Price (chairman since 2000); Colin White (secretary since 2001) and Ray Keeling (who took over as appointments secretary the same year). The general committee is made up of the president, chairman, secretary and treasurer plus Harry Rider, Brian Brown, Stan Stafford, Brian Wrigglesworth and Peter Langley while there are four hon. Life members in Ernie Robinson, John Jackson, Charles Sharman and Bernard Varley.

The association had vice presidents from 1958 until 1964 with Sugden in office the first two years before teaming up with Cyril Chapman in the role in 1960. In 1961 Hodgson joined them to give the office a three-way option and for the final three campaigns the office was in existence it was jointly held by Hodgson and Chapman, a stalwart of the Dales Council, who was also secretary at Ross Mills when the league was formed and had close links with the sides at Rodley for more than 40 years. Throughout he was always closely involved with the Umpires' Association and from 1996 until his death in 1999 was the association's president.

One of my former colleagues at Yorkshire Post newspapers John Morgan has long held a close affinity to the Dales Council, too, and for many years has been one of the chief speakers at the league's annual dinner. Awards for Young Cricketer of the Year and the Umpires' Award are both in his name and in 1993 Chapman became the fifth winner of the trophy first won by John Collins in 1989.

Drifting down the list of long serving officers you will find the name of Sharman and midway through his stint in the dual role of secretary and treasurer back in1984, he apparently raised a few smiles with his annual report at the annual meeting in December of that year when he made the point: "It must be said that, after 1983, this year has given us the kind of weather we always wish for. The standard of cricket and sportsmanship has been like the curate's egg – good in parts but with some real stinky bits."

Seemingly, soon after he took on the role of secretary he ended up apologising for the loss of some minutes which had been destroyed. Minutes of the November meeting of the umpires in 1982 reveal that the documents in question had been in the boot of his car when it had been hit by a coach. "The secretary had not been able to recover them before going to hospital and when he had managed to force his way into the boot the petrol from the broken fuel tank had ruined them," the umpires' association records revealed.

One of the more unusual names to be found amongst the 100s who over the years have been on the association's lists is that of Fortune as in John Fortune Jackson who was umpiring four years before the Dales started but then did the rest of his 27 years in the middle for the newly formed league - along the way taking two cup finals before being installed as a life member of the association. A family connection with the Klondyke Gold rush of the late 1890s up in the northern reaches of Canada inspired the Fortune name though his son Mervyn, who has himself played many years in the Dales chiefly with Crompark, insists that the only Fortune he has known has been his dad.

"He recalls one game in particular he took at the Farnley Estate ground on the far side of Otley," said Merv. "It seems a police car turned up to take away his fellow umpire – you see the man's wife was having a baby and he was needed at St James's Hospital in Leeds. He came back later in the afternoon though and partnered my dad saying 'I'll stay on and do the rest of the match if you'll drop me off at the hospital afterwards' and, of course, that's what happened."

A further unusual addition to the umpires list was that of one Miss S. Foster. Susan, my elder daughter, was a sixth former at Salt Grammar School, Baildon, back in the early 1980s but already steeped in cricket. She had watched her first big match at Park Avenue from her carrycot but as a six-month-old toddler had not appreciated the finer points of Australian Brian Booth's unbeaten 193.

Yet the taste for the game was soon apparent and in the years that followed she played, scored and finally umpired in local cricket. In fact, at 16 she was the first female to be accepted by the Dales Council for their umpires list taking her first games officially at 17. At the time she was believed to be the first teenage girl to officiate in league cricket on a regular basis in the county and so there was the usual publicity which goes with such territory.

But it was good for her in her new role and the league benefited along the way from the additional publicity exposure. Within a couple of years she was taking the record with her into the Bradford League where, despite being just 5ft 1ins tall and seven stone, she handled county and big reputation players with the same confidence she had displayed in her years in the Dales – even to the point of warning one high profile giant of a fast bowler in her first outing in the senior league.

The youngest at 16 – and first female – umpire on the Dales Council's umpires list, Susan Foster, is these days on the committee of her village team at Car Colston, Nottinghamshire. Here she is chatting with Richie Benaud who had just opened the club's new pavilion.

One of a band of dedicated scorers in the league, Margaret Foster, centre, has kept the figures straight in the Dales in each of the last five decades.

JOHN MORGAN'S UMPIRES AWARD

1989: J. Collins.
1990: B. Wrigglesworth
1991: K. Quine
1992: W. Beckett
1993: C. Chapman
1994: M. Reubens
1995: J. Jackson
1996: S. Stafford
1997: D. Marsden
1998: B. Tearle
1999: W. Beckett
2000: K. Dibb
2001: P. Langley
2002: G. Tarbatt
2003: K. Dibb
2004:

LES BULMER TROPHY

1991: New Wortley 2nds.
1992: Pudsey St. Law. 2nds.
1993: Cookridge
1994: Whitehall
1995: Rodley 2nds.
1996: New Wortley
1997: Castlehill
1998: New Wortley
1999: Cookridge B.
2000: Baildon Meths. C.
2001: Rodley.
2002: Old Mods.
2003: Baildon Meths 2nds
2004:

Past winners of the Bulmer award, Baildon Meths celebrate victory after a close finish in the 2002 Cawthorne Cup final.

UMPIRES' ASSOCIATION SPORTSMANSHIP TROPHY

1983: New Wortley. 1984: Leeds Zingari. 1985: Pudsey S.L. 2nds. 1986: Croma.
1987: Thorite. 1988: Thorite. 1989: New Farnley 2nds. 1990: Otley.
1991: Pudsey Congs. 1992: Esholt. 1993: New Wortley. 1994: Otley T.
1995: Rodley. 1996: Lawns Park. 1997: Farsley. 1998: Carr M.
1999: Baildon Meths. 2000: Esholt. 2001: Wibsey Park Chapel. 2002: Whitehall
2003: S. Parade Bap. 2004:

JOHN MORGAN'S YOUNG CRICKETER OF THE YEAR AWARD

1989: W. Hodgson, Pudsey Congs
1991: G. Lee, Pudsey St Lawrence.
1993: C. Taylor, Pudsey St Law &
       M. Hoggard, Pudsey Congs
1995: M. Richmond, New Rover
1997: A. Dutton, Horsforth.
1999: S. Kirk, New Wortley
2001: G. Makwana, Ram Sikh
2003: J. Mallinson Pudsey Congs

1990: P. Smith, New Wortley.
1992: D. Bowers, Cookridge.

1994: M. Duce, Pudsey Congs
1996: R. Jarvis, Pudsey St Law.
1998: P. Clayton, Horsforth.
2000: A. Amir, Farsley
2002: S. Clapham, Old Mods.
2004:

Unsung heroes and heroines of local cricket

There is more to league cricket than the cricketers, the umpires, the groundsmen and the band of helpers who make the teas. Each individual has a vital role to play and the Dales Council readily acknowledges as much and there is no depth to the thanks the league puts forward to all who make cricket happen — but there is one company of enthusiasts who maybe deserve special thanks for without scorers, competition is a non starter. There are a number of scorers in the Dales who have been keeping track of games for many years but few have had the problems faced by one Crompark scorer around two decades ago. At one of their games played at Five Lane Ends - on a matting wicket, too - there were no fewer than six Coopers in the Crompark side. Mark, Kevin, Richard and Matthew from one family and Phil and Matthew from another. Just imagine sorting that lot out should a rush of wickets fall, it must have been a day when even Cooperman, or should that be Superman, might have struggled. It certainly was a day someone really had to know the score.

Chapter Twelve
THE CLUBS:
The original 18 sides of 1956.

The Clubs feature will take a sometimes brief, sometimes longer look at all the clubs involved in the Dales Council league over the last half-century. The feature, obviously, covers a lot of ground – and grounds – and therefore to avoid it dominating any one part of the Dales Council story the decision was taken to split it up into four chapters spread throughout the second half of the book. The chapters will cover the original 18 clubs which formed the league in the winter of 1955-1956; then the clubs elected to the league in the years from 1957 to 1974; then covering the period 1975 to 1988 and finally, the clubs elected from 1989 onwards. The first list runs in the order clubs appeared in the league's original handbook in 1956 but thereafter clubs appear according to the years in which they joined the Dales Council.

1. BUTTERFIELD SPORTS. (1956-1958. Best position, 9th in Div A, 1956).

Butterfield Sports played in the opening three seasons of the new Dales Council league without making a big impact. Their best position was ninth place achieved in the first campaign, winning seven out of their 21 games. There were still 18 teams in the league in 1957 when Butterfields dropped to 15th place in the final table and along with Otley Mills (13th), Thackley (14th), Netherfield Sports (16th) and Otley Wesley (17th) they dropped down into the newly formed Section B division for 1958 (Newlands, who finished at the foot of the table in 1957 spent just the one season in the Dales Council). In their final campaign in 1958, Butterfields finished seventh in Section B's 10-team division.

They played at Fyfe Lane, Charlestown, Baildon, and at the time most teams travelled there by bus – the number 53, 55, 68 and 65 West Yorkshire. But the ground has long since disappeared beneath a housing estate though I know of one resident at least in Fyfe Crescent who often looks longingly through his lounge window across the road to where he used to play cricket and yearns for the old pitch.

Butterfields had two players who appeared in league averages in their three-year spell in the league. In 1957 G. Hopwood finished 13th in the bowling averages with 35 wickets at 8.26 runs apiece and J. Allison was fourth in the Section B batting averages with a top score of 60 in an aggregate of 315 runs at an average of 28.64 in their final campaign. Butterfields posted the first 8th wicket highest partnership record of 52 against International Harvesters in 1956. Then with a stand of 73 by D. Craig and J. Walker against Otley Wesley, they claimed the 7th wicket record in 1957. The record stood until the 1962 season when the Esholt pair Ernest Barker and Malcolm Franks shared an unbeaten partnership of 89 against English Electric - but by then Butterfields were already a memory.

2. CROMPARK. (1956 onwards. League champions 1957. B Section winners 1967, 1974, 1987, 1992, 2002. D Section winners 2000 and 2002).

Crompark hold the unique place in the history of the Dales Council as the only club to maintain unbroken membership in the league throughout the whole of its first 50 years in business. During their unbroken run the club has endured many ups and downs, played at four different grounds, achieved a fair share of honours in the lower divisions and though they have never managed to win either of the two cup competitions, they were finalists in both the Pool Paper Mills Cup and the Cawthorne Cup early in the new millennium. But to find their top moment as a team you have to go back to the second season of the Dales – 1957. It was then that they won their one and only league title and in the same season Crompark players topped both the league batting and bowling averages. As a club, however, maybe their finest season was relatively recently for in 2002 they carried off both the B and D Division titles besides reaching the Cawthorne Cup final only to miss out on their first cup triumph in a tight finish with one of the closest neighbours Baildon Meths. Captain of the cup side and the D Division champions that season was the much missed Keith Duckett, who, less than nine months later became very seriously ill yet played on for his side to make an important contribution in the fight to avoid relegation.

Back in the mid fifties, Crompark's giant of an opening bowler Geoff Milner made an immediate impact on the league by becoming the first player to win the bowling averages. In 1956 he managed 32 wickets at five runs each to snatch the prize from Gordon (Gloss) Sample whose average was 5.45 but whose 111 league wickets in that opening campaign has never been topped. In 1957, however, Milner confirmed his status by winning the league bowling prize again and Derek Pinder won the batting prize with an average of 57.7, his aggregate number of runs of 520 including an unbeaten 111. The pair led the charge to the Crompark's only league title, achieved by winning 17 and drawing two of their 21 fixtures. It was also the season in which Crompark found a long lasting place in the record book, too, at the expense of their neighbours Netherfield who they toppled for ten early on in the campaign – still the lowest score in an innings in the league by an A Division outfit.

The Crompark players who carried off the D Division title in 2002 and missed out on the double by a whisker in the final of the Cawthorne Cup.
Back row l to r. A. Halliday, Mark Cooper, N. Lawson, P. Clark, R. Pritchard, M. Shaw, J. Farrar.
Front row: B. Foster, W. Duckett, Matthew Cooper, K. Duckett, S. Whyte, scorer, Stephanie Robinson.

Over the years there have been many notable performances for Crompark with one afternoon in 2003 particularly memorable for one of the club's senior players and one of their youngsters. It was when the club's C Division side faced Cookridge in early July and hit 208 for 7. Keith Ellis, then 43, claimed his first century by going to the landmark off the penultimate delivery of the allotted 45 overs with a single. The innings then allowed Crompark to make the most of Iain Clark's legbreaks, the 16-year-old bowling through to claim nine for 84 in his longest bowling stint to that point of 20.5 overs as Cookridge were toppled for 141. But Crompark's major spot in the league's individual records section is held by Paul Kirby who smashed his way to the highest individual score in the cup competitions when he finished unbeaten on 183 against Otley in May, 1996.

At present Crompark play at the oval in the grounds of the former High Royds Hospital at Guiseley. But when the league started Crompark played at Back Lane in the village moving nearer the firm after which the club is named to play at the sloping ground at Netherfield Road in the 1968 season. In the eighties the club moved to Shaw House Middle School, Five Lane Ends, Idle, before transferring back to Guiseley at High Royds for the 1991 campaign.

3. DAVID BROWN TRACTORS (1956).

Although they played in the Dales for just the first season of the new league's life, David Brown Tractors made an impact finishing fourth in the table winning 11 of their 21 games. They set up the first ninth wicket record stand of 36 in their match with Wilson & Mathiesons in July and had two of their attack, R. Lowis (third with 32 wickets at 5.9 runs apiece) and L. Newall (11th with 32 wickets at 7.65) in the bowling averages. They played at the Canal Bank ground, Rodley, the home of many Dales sides over the years.

4. ENGLISH ELECTRIC (1956-1963. 2nd X1 Section winners 1960 and 1962, 2nd X1 Cup winners 1961 and 1962).

English Electric spent eight seasons in the Dales Council with a top position of third in Section A in 1959. But they followed that by finishing on the foot of the table in 1960 even though their second team managed the club's first trophy in that same season by winning the second teams division with 18 victories and a draw in their 20 games. They took the first 2nd X1's Cup (now the Cawthorne Cup) in 1961 before completing Second Eleven's first league and cup double in 1962. The club had

Geoff Wilkinson, keeping the pitch right, keeping behind the stumps, keeping the runs flowing. It is all in a day's work for him at Esholt.

Lifetime friends at Esholt, big John Taylor and Malcolm Franks.

Francis Quinn

started life in the Dales by finishing 13th behind the league's first champions Green Lane in 1956 and bowed out in fourth place in 1963 by which time the Dales had reverted to a single division of 17 teams.

Among their notable individual performances were the nine wickets for 10 runs effort in 1957 by H. Johnson while two seasons later J. Illingworth and D. Carter created a league ninth wicket record of 76 against Green Lane. H. Grice was their only player to appear in the league averages in the first season of the Dales, finishing 10th in the bowling list with 32 wickets at 7.53. In 1958 J Evans carried off the leading wicketkeeping award and P. Renton won the league's second teams bowling averages while D. Harkness was the league's leading bowler in the following campaign with 32 wickets at 5.94. E. Hodgson was the leading batsman in Section B in 1961 with C. Moores finishing top bowler in the Second Teams competition and Hodgson then topped the batting averages in the First Elevens competition in 1962. The club played at Phoenix Park, Thornbury, their old home now part of the car park at a multi-cinema complex.

5. ESHOLT (1956–1984 and 1986 onwards. League champions 1959, 1962, 1965, 1967, 1984. D. Section winners 1982. Cawthorne Cup 1976, 1980, 1984).

The home of the league's founder Jack Shuttleworth, Esholt has played in every season but one since the Dales was formed. Five times league champions, they have yet to win the Pool Paper Mills Cup though they did reach the final in 1970. The club now runs teams in the Bradford League with their third team competing in the Dales, appropriately many thought, winning promotion from the C Division in 2003 under the leadership of Malcolm Franks who was celebrating his 50 years association with the club.

Over the years many stars have appeared in games at the club's picturesque ground on the banks of the River Aire not least actors of television's Emmerdale at the time when the soap's home was a few hundred yards down Esholt Lane. Former Yorkshire and Nottinghamshire batsman Ashley Metcalfe who started his cricket life as a junior at the club aged eight, opened his benefit year 23 years later with a New Year's Day match involving Yorkshire's best players of the time at Esholt and nowadays some of the top league players in the country can be seen in Bradford League fixtures there. But while some of Esholt's Dales Council games are still played at the venue, the third team generally use a school ground at West Lane, Baildon for the home fixtures these days.

The club was founded in 1895 moving into the Airedale and Wharfedale Second Class League. They also had two short spells in the Bradford League in their early years but spent from 1929 until joining the Dales Council 27 seasons later in the Wharfedale League. They picked up their first of five Dales championship titles in the new league's fourth campaign, their fifth success coinciding with their second team's cup victory in 1984. By then the development of the ground was on its way. In 1970 Esholt had agreed with Airebronians Rugby Union Club and Bradford Council to take over the use of three derelict cottages at the ground and convert them into a clubhouse. Aided by grants, donations and much hard work, the premises were officially opened by former Yorkshire and England captain Brian Close in 1979 and in 1980, the present scoreboard, built in memory of Ralph Shuttleworth, was introduced.

Esholt left the Dales for a year in 1984 and went into the Leeds League reaching a high point in 1991 by lifting the Hepworth Cup before moving on again and back into the Bradford League. Meanwhile they had rejoined the Dales Council by way of their third eleven in 1986.

Ralph Shuttleworth, brother of Jack and himself a leading figure in the formation of the Dales Council, was one of the league's most prominent players in its formative years figuring in two league partnership records in 1957 among his achievements — 130 for the first wicket with S. Dalby and 190 for the fourth wicket with Malcolm Franks, a record which, with Gloss Sample's 111 league wickets of a year earlier, would outlast all others in the league's progress. Franks defied the years to keep on scoring runs and taking wickets in the Dales into the new millennium along the way in 1962 sharing in another league record stand with the late Ernest Barker — 89 for the seventh wicket. The record was one of three partnership records held at the same time by the hard-hitting batsman Barker who had shared in the top eighth wicket stand of 88 with Terry Dudley in 1959 and would help John Spivey to create a new 10th wicket record partnership of 83 in 1966, an unprecedented league treble achievement by the now much missed Barker. Esholt's hall of fame list is too long to mention everyone but room should be found here for one of the league's most accomplished wicketkeeper-batsmen Geoff Wilkinson and Les Heaton, a league vice president, former Esholt captain and opening batsman and captain of the first Dales side to win the Bradford Area Cup in 1967.

6.   GREEN LANE (1956-1961 and 1990-1997). League champions 1956, 1958, 1960 and 1961. Second Teams winners: 1959. Pool Paper Mills Cup winners 1957, 1959 and 1960).

In just six seasons Green Lane set the standard for the fledgling league. The first Dales Council champions in 1956, first cup winners the following year and first double winners in 1960, they picked up an incredible eight trophies in their short stay in the Dales besides introducing the league to its first star in all rounder Gloss Sample and a record breaking batsman in Malcolm Dibb.

They galloped to the initial title with 17 victories and two draws in 21 games in 1956 with Sample grabbing the still unbeaten record bag of 111 league wickets besides finishing sixth in the league's batting averages. The first Dales campaign also saw Green Lane's second eleven finish second to Wilson and Mathiesons in the second teams division. In 1959 Dibb hit 716 runs at an average of 42.1 to set a new high watermark at the crease and win the A Section batting prize while after going near in the first three seasons, Green Lane's second string finally finished champions of the second teams division.

Green Lane had a third team in the Dales for eight seasons from 1990 playing at Horsforth, Pudsey and Otley without finding much success this time around. The club was originally formed in 1919 to provide recreational activities for employees of Green Lane Dyeworks and played for 16 seasons in the Yorkshire Council where they were joint champions in 1930. They were founder members of the Airedale and Wharfedale Senior League in 1936 and included former Yorkshire and England wicketkeeper Don Brennan in their ranks. Disbanded during the Second World War, the club became one of the 18 founder member clubs in the Dales Council before being re-elected to the Aire-Wharfe in 1961. The club went through its most traumatic time in 1973 when they lost their Green Lane ground to building developments and they had to move to the Bradford University ground at Woodhall, Calverley, before being permanently re-housed at Nunroyd Park, Guiseley, where as part of the Aireborough Nunroyd Sports Association they have magnificent new premises.

The club held the official opening of their new pavilion on September 1, 2002, with a match between Green Lane and the Airedale and Wharfedale League President's X1 when the Yorkshire chief and Dales Council president Geoff Cope did the honours.

7.   JAMES IVES SPORTS (1956-1968).

Neighbours but unlike Green Lane never among the trophies, Ives Sports played at New Scarboro', Yeadon, around half a mile from their high flying contemporaries. Their ground was also eventually used for housing, too, but they had 13 seasons in the Dales Council and had their best run in the three seasons from 1963 when they finished second, second and third in the table - each time one place behind the strong Otley Mills side. Bowler Peter Forkin was their first player to appear in the league averages finishing fifth with 57 wickets at 6.35 runs apiece in 1956.

8. NETHERFIELD SPORTS (1956–1965).

Netherfield Sports made an inauspicious start to life in the Dales Council finishing 17th out of 18 in the first elevens' table and bottom of the second elevens division in the opening season in 1956. In 1957 it was third from bottom for the first team and a repeat showing by the seconds. However, the seconds had a star – P. Robertson winning the league's bowling averages with 36 wickets at five runs each, a performance which included an 8-20 return and a 7-17 effort. But the 1957 campaign also saw their first team shot out for just 10 by Crompark – still the lowest score in an innings for a first eleven and they were also on the end of a five wickets in seven deliveries (inc. the hat-trick) performance by Gerald Hardaker of Smiths. They then had a run in the newly formed B Section until 1962 when the Dales reverted to just one first teams division and one for second teams again. It was a season that opened with a bang for the side that had struggled so consistently for their second team, helped by a six for five return by N Jackson, toppled Otley Wesley for just seven runs. But the club could not build on that, the first eleven managing just a single victory to finish on the foot of the table with the seconds ending just below mid-table. They were 12th in the 17 team-strong Dales Council league of 1963 but when the B Section was re-introduced in the following campaign they had their moment of glory gaining promotion behind Otley Wesley in a tight finish with Turner Sports. In their final campaign they finished in the highest league position of fourth. But early on in that campaign, on FA Cup final day, May 1, 1965, when Leeds United were meeting Liverpool at Wembley, they were shot out for eight when they managed to field just eight players against Esholt. They played at Netherfield Road, Guiseley.

Green Lane's ground these days with its modern new pavilion around half a mile from where the league's first champions put down the standards for the Dales.

9. **OTLEY MILLS (1956-1968). GROVE HILL (1969-1973). OTLEY TOWN (1974-1979). OTLEY TOWN (1993-1997). League champions: 1963, 1964, 1966, 1970, 1974, 1977 and 1979. B Section winners: 1958,1968 and 1972. D Section winners: 1976, 1977, 1978 and 1979. Pool Paper Mills Cup winners: 1966, 1971and 1978. Cawthorne Cup winners: 1964, 1968, 1973, 1974, 1978 and 1979.**

The record of the Otley side in the Dales Council from the league's first year in business speaks for itself – members of every team venturing into the Wharfe valley in the 60s and the 70s knew they had a game on their hands at both first and second eleven level. At times the two outfits were invincible.

Town began life as Otley Mills in 1922 and for 55 years played at Grove Hill Park, now engulfed by the Otley ring road. Back then the property was owned by the Duncan family who were directors of William Ackroyd, proprietors of Otley Woollen Mills. A war memorial to the 14 Mills employees who gave their lives during the 1914-18 conflict was unveiled at the opening of the park in May, 1922, and the first match – against Major H. S. Duncan's X1 – followed. Mills then spent their early years in the Wharfedale League along with a number of the other clubs that would form the Dales Council.

The park, also used for bowling and tennis, was purchased by the local council in 1968 when Mills changed their name to Grove Hill but following the decision to put the ring road through the park in the early 70s the club decided to amalgamate with Otley Town FC. The move took place in 1974 when the lengthy process of creating a new playing area at the Old Show Grounds on the Pool Road got under way. Three years on the job was completed and the half century plus tenancy at

The Otley Mills league championship winning side of 1963 showing off the first of a run of cups to go the club's way over the next decade. Back row l to r. Stan Handford, president, B. Bolton, M. Horst, B. Farrington, F. Rose, W. Mason, K. Gawtry, R. Bradley, Susan Handford, scorer. Front row: D. Hawley, S. Reyner, B. Gawtry, J. Hamer (capt), W. Imeson, G. Ives, R. Siddall.

Grove Hill was given up — and three years later the club joined the Leeds League, returning to the Dales with a 3rd X1 in the mid 90s, the side folding after four and half seasons.

But in those initial 24 seasons in the Dales, their impact had been immense. They picked up a staggering 23 trophies — and added the Umpires Association Sportsmanship Trophy in 1994 when their third team joined the Dales. They put their success down to having a settled player base — but they had their outstanding individual performers. In league and cup games their opener Don Baker hit 5,029 runs in the decade from 1969; Francis Quinn took 501 wickets from 1968 to 1979; Bill Mason, the club captain for 10 years, collected 961 wickets between 1957 and 1979; Derek Hawley picked up over 1,100 wickets from 1959 to 1979 (at the time a league record) while wicketkeeper — and later well-known umpire - Gordon Ives claimed 202 victims from 1960 to 1979. Backing their efforts was Stanley Handford, the club secretary for 21 years besides a stint of five years as president of the league not to mention Hawley's long service behind the scenes — as club president for 10 years, treasurer for 38 years and league treasurer for seven years. "Undoubtedly, amongst the reasons we had so much success in the 50s to 80s was that we had so many players who were happy to stay and play with one club. You don't often get that these days," commented Hawley.

10. OTLEY WESLEY   (1956-1966. B Section winners: 1964).

It was a bit of a trek to Otley Wesley's ground on Wharfe Meadows Park by the river Wharfe though well worth the effort of walking through the park, around the tennis courts and up through a wooded area usually hauling no end of cricket equipment. But the club did not pull up many trees during their 11 seasons in the Dales. Yet though they finished bottom of the table in the league's first season with just three wins in their 21 fixtures J. Towers did find his way into the league handbook records with a six for seven including the hat-trick in mid May.

In 1957 they managed the second bottom place and things did not get much better until the 1964 campaign when they were comfortable winners of B Section with 13 victories and four draws in their 21 match programme with both Jack Danskin and Barry Jenkins finding places in the league batting averages and Norman Lightfoot taking third place with 57 wickets at 7.4 runs apiece in the bowling list. Back in the A Section in 1965, Wesley finished in a handy mid-table slot with Francis Quinn, who would move on to Otley Mills, playing a key role. He had figured in the league averages for them a number of times in the previous five seasons but now topped the league averages with 47 wickets at six runs apiece, nearly half of his overs being maidens. Wesley, however, finished at the bottom of A Section in the following season and called it a day in the Dales.

11. POOL PAPER MILLS (1956-1986. B. Section winners: 1982. Pool Paper Mills Cup winners: 1958).

Pool Paper Mills was formed in August, 1947, with league experience gained initially in the Wharfedale League. The firm behind the club's fortunes had been established in 1886 by the Whiteley family, the company buying the Cartref estate soon after the Second World War to create a new cricket pitch, bowling green and tennis courts for the benefit of mill employees. It was a particularly dry summer when the work was being carried out and water had to be pumped from the nearby Wharfe to help proceedings. The league has PPM and the Whiteley family to thank for the senior knockout competition trophy, the Pool Paper Mills Cup, and the D Section's Holmes Whiteley Trophy. Appropriately, after Green Lane's success in its first year in 1957, it was the Mills side that picked up the PPM Cup next time around. But their only other trophy win in their three decades in the Dales turned out to be the B Section title in 1982.

Kenny Wilkinson was their first captain in the Dales in 1956 and he underlined his importance to the side by winning both the club batting and bowling awards and taking the first hat-trick in the league's history in that first season. His four sons have also played for the club and in 1990, by which time the club had moved into the Leeds League, his grandsons were selected, too. The Whiteley family have always had close links with the club, several of them as playing members including Peter Whiteley, who went on to play for the county, and his brother Richard. Their father John was the league's second president — in office for 10 years from 1964.

Mills finished 12th in the Dales in the first season with John Otty claiming fourth place in the league batting averages. In their second team Malcolm Throp had a five for seven return in July and Keith Butterill finished with six for 10 just over a month later. May 16, 1959, saw the Mills side hit 281 for 7 dec. against Ives Sports as their share of 447 runs on the day – a league record aggregate score which was to stand until 1984. The 1961 Section A batting prize was won by Bernard Bolton who included an unbeaten 124 innings in his 532 aggregate for an average of 48.36 and he was second in the following campaign, again with over 500 runs. The B Section batting award was claimed by Norman Smallwood in 1965 who repeated the feat in the following season and in 1968, too. M Cryer, a regular in the bowling averages, finally won the B Section prize in 1976 with 66 wickets at 6.31 and in the B Section title winning season six years later the league batting prize was picked up by K Wilkinson who was following in his father's footsteps.

12. ROSS MILLS (1956-1960)

The forerunner of the clubs from the Rodley area to play on the side of the Leeds and Liverpool Canal in the village, Ross Mills played in the Dales for the league's opening five seasons. They finished in 10th place in the first season with Bob Binks

The Pool Paper Mills PPM Cup winning side of 1958.

and Les Elliott finding places in the league bowling averages. Mills also created the first seventh wicket highest partnership that season – 61 scored against Otley Wesley on 26 May. But the club's major milestone was set up by Sidney Newton a week earlier when he hit an unbeaten 107 against Butterfield Sports to claim the Dales Council first century.

The mill was situated further up the canal towards Bramley and that was where you could usually find Cyril Chapman, player, club secretary and for many years a solid servant of cricket in the valley and of the league both as official and umpire. His side finished in fifth spot in 1957 – the season when G. Jackson had an eight for 11 return and Green Lane's Gloss Sample claimed the first all 10 haul against them. But fifth spot proved to be as good as it got for Mills.

13. SMITH'S SPORTS (1956-1961 and 1965-1980). FARSLEY CELTIC (1981-1987 and 1998-2001). BRAMLEY SPORTS BEACON (2002-2003). League champions: 1971, 1976, 1980, 1982. B. Section winners: 2000. D Division winners: 1980, 1983, 1984. Pool Papers Mills Cup: 1967, 1969, 1973, 1976, 1985, 1987. Cawthorne Cup winners: 1977, 1983.

In the 70s and 80s the Smith's Sports sides were as powerful as it got in the Dales Council. They had some formidable players like David Pearce, Kenny Booth, Roy Webster and Dave Benn who commanded respect wherever they played. But right from season one when Archie Carrick finished as the league's top batsman in a side that finished fifth in the table they made their mark. In the following campaign all-rounder Gerald Hardaker grabbed nine wickets for eight runs against Otley Mills and with Eddie Gill he set up the highest league partnership for the third wicket of 102 against Otley Wesley while in the B

Farsley Celtic's league champions of 1982.
Back row l to r. P. Spavin, D. Jones, C. Taylor, G. Clifton, D. Pearce, B. Finch.
Front row. B. Hughes, R. Webster, K. Brattley, capt., C. Janney, K. Booth. Umpire: W. Scott.

Section promotion campaign of 1959 Terry Thorpe and Bill Dacre topped the bowling averages. Paceman Hardaker's most incisive spell brought him five wickets in seven deliveries which included the hat-trick while Dacre, a gentle giant of a man, once picked up six wickets for three runs. But it was not until the late 60s and early 70s under the disciplined captaincy of Pearce that Smith's really took off.

The club had disbanded in 1961 to be re-formed by Pearce three years later. They joined the Bradford Central League with Carrick's son Phil, destined to be captain of Yorkshire, making his league debut at Adwalton. But Smith's finished at the foot of the table and again turned to the Dales Council where fortunes changed dramatically. Cups and league titles started to flow under Pearce's guidance and by the mid 70s when Booth and Webster led the side to the double they were established as one of the Dales Council's premier outfits.

After a third title win in 1980 the club had to leave their home just above the factory in Coal Hill Lane, Rodley, to make way for a housing development ironically named Cricketers Green. One of the finest wickets the league has known was lost but after examining their options they moved to Farsley where Celtic Football Club had tip land available on which a new cricket ground was built. As Farsley Celtic now, Pearce's warriors continued to collect the trophies and were champions in 1982 and Cupwinners in 1985 and 1987 when they felt it was time to try their luck in the Leeds League.

The Dales years had seen Booth, who tragically did not live to play in the Leeds League, pick up 1,104 wickets including an all bowled four wickets in four deliveries. Arnie Beech collected over 1,000 wickets with his swinging seamers including a 10 for 25 feat and Pearce finished on 11,809 runs. Benn and Webster had a magical season when Smith's achieved the league and cup double in 1976, Benn claiming 94 league scalps which together with cup wickets left him with a record total in all games of 113 wickets while wicketkeeper Webster hit the record books with 52 victims.

Celtic returned to the Dales with a side in 1998 and picked up the B Section title with 103 points in 2000 with Stuart Tempest, son of Geoffrey Tempest the former Ross Mills and later a top performer in the Bradford League, getting through 355 overs to finish second in the league averages with 61 wickets at 5.82 apiece. But after one more season under the Celtic banner they became Bramley Sports Beacon for two seasons before calling it a day.

14. THACKLEY (1956-1958).

Thackley lasted three seasons in the Dales finishing 15th in the 18 strong table in 1956 with batsman F. Wood and bowler C. Jude squeezing into the league averages. They moved up a slot in 1957 but finished in the newly formed B Section for their final campaign in fourth place. They played at North Hall, Ainsbury Avenue, near Thackley corner.

15. TONG PARK (1956-1958).

Another three-season stopover, this time for a club you will find not far from the main Otley Road at Baildon. The Tong Park club is blessed with one of the most beautiful settings for a cricket ground in the county — and to a Yorkshireman that means as good as it gets anywhere in the world. The view from the approach track 200 or so feet above a secluded valley takes in a cricket arena bounded by a lake, woodlands and grazing land: it is breathtaking. The club dates back to 1880 and in the early part of the 1900s played in the Bradford League. At one cup tie against Windhill in 1914 an amazing 3,000 spectators turned up to provide gate takings of £27 to underline the times in more ways than one. After the Great War they moved into the Aire/Wharfe section of the Yorkshire Council, disbanding in 1942 and rejoining the Council in 1950 before being accepted in the Airedale and Wharfedale League in 1958. In the meantime they had entered a team in the Dales Council, their secretary at the time Kenneth Hodgson becoming the first president of the new league.

They finished third, 11th and bottom in their three years in the Dales with W. Metcalfe (batting) and R. Patch (bowling) getting into the first league averages. Hodgson had captained the second eleven when just 19 in the mid 20s and in one match in 1926 claimed nine wickets for none as Addingham were flattened for four. The story goes that Addingham requested that they should bat again – with Hodgson not bowling. Tong Park agreed and this time Addingham managed 11 so they were allowed to combine their totals – and still were still beaten by 10 wickets.

16. LAISTERDYKE (1956–1959).

Laisterdyke, who played at Broad Lane in the village, finished in sixth place in the league's opening campaign with three batsmen, J. Hartley, K. Bolton and R Coope dominating the middle of the league's batting averages and scoring more than 700 runs between them. The highlight of the club's first campaign though was the league's first, first-wicket highest partnership - an unbeaten stand of 110 against English Electric at the end of June. In their remaining three seasons in the Dales they never quite matched their opening season's effort though their 10th wicket pair B. Yorke and T. Forthrop did share an unbeaten stand of 33 against the Pool side in 1957 to claim the highest partnership record for the last two at the crease.

17. INTERNATIONAL HARVESTERS (1956-1962. Pool Paper Mills Cup winners: 1961).

Finishing 16th out of 18 clubs in the opening season of the league was not perhaps what Harvesters had hoped for but Norman Hartley, who along with B. Tate, figured in the league bowling averages, did enjoy one special moment – he took four wickets in four deliveries against Ives Sports on July 28. He followed that up by taking 80 wickets in 1957 to spearhead Harvesters' surge towards the top – they eventually finished in second place behind Crompark – with Hartley also finishing in second place in the bowling averages, his huge haul costing him just 5.82 runs per wicket. H. Patchett pitched in with 61 wickets at 8.8, too, the pair of them getting through almost 500 overs between them.

Harvesters finished runners-up again in 1958 this time with Hartley taking 57 wickets to finish ninth in the league averages which were topped by Harvesters' S. Farquason with 65 wickets at 5.63 runs apiece, a return which included one effort of nine for 20. He was second in the bowling list in the following campaign with 77 victims while Hartley was fourth with 57 scalps – and second again in 1960, this time picking up 73 wickets. Astonishingly Harvesters finished second again in 1961, this time with J. Bartle winning the bowling prize for them and A. Walker taking second place in the league batting list. In their final season in the Dales they were agonisingly close again – this time finishing third.

18. WILSON & MATHIESONS (1956-1972 & 1974-1976. B. Sections winners: 1966, 1971. D. Section winners: 1956, 1957, 1958. Pool Paper Mills Cup winners: 1963, 1964, 1965).

From the off Wilson & Mathiesons were up with the best in the Dales Council and it is fair to say that as a team they were the leaders in the art of hat-tricks. They were the first club to achieve a hat-trick of title wins in the league with their second team topping what was then named the Second Elevens competition (but which has now been re-designated as D Division) in the first three seasons. Then they picked up the senior cup competition trophy in the three successive campaigns from 1963.

They played about the length of a cricket ball throw from where the old Rodley railway station was situated and for a time you could get to their ground by train. In that first season they were the team hard on the heels of the powerful Green Lane side, finishing second to the first champions in the senior competition and just beating them to the second team's trophy.

In Billy Russell and Peter Seaman they had a couple of the league's top all-rounders with Russell far outscoring everyone in that special opening season by hitting 476 runs to finished second in the batting averages. With George Harris he set the league's first highest partnership for the second wicket when the pair hit 146 against Butterfields and with his trademark collar up and sleeves rolled down he also finished sixth in the bowling list (his 80 wickets second only to Gloss Sample's record breaking 111 haul) grabbing eight for nine when W&M met Sample's Green Lane in the run-in for the title. Seaman topped the league's Second Team batting average highlighting his season with an unbeaten 104 against Otley Wesley in the penultimate game while on the opening day of the campaign his team-mate Jimmy Lawrence had opened and hit what was to be his top score of the season of 64 before being last man out against Esholt.

Len Greenhall topped the second team batting averages when W&M's seconds went to the title again in 1957 with Russell again second in the senior division and 19th in the bowling list, the 62 wickets he claimed with his quick stuff the fourth highest haul of that second campaign. Jeff Walton made it a hat-trick of successes for the seconds in the batting averages in 1958 as the team made it three titles in a row, too. In mid July he managed an unbeaten century while George Adams hit 65 not out in an unbroken second wicket stand of 158 as W&M went to 204 for one against International Harvesters. The 1959 campaign was one to forget, however, with both teams finishing at the bottom of their respective divisions. But Peter Hargreaves did have a game to cherish when he claimed all 10 wickets for 36 runs to find a place in the record book.

Keith Cowgill had a great all-round campaign finishing second in the league batting averages and 11th in the bowling list when W&M next figured on the trophy list – in 1963 when they picked up the first of their hat-trick of wins in the Pool Paper Mills Cup. But the bowling performance of the league's five decades came in 1966. It was the year W&M claimed their first B Section title and leading the way for them was Eddie Fox who claimed the divisional bowling prize with 63 wickets at an average of 3.71, an average that has never been bettered under the 30 wicket qualification rule. Jimmy Lawrence was fourth in the league batting averages and won the bowling prize when W&M dropped out of the Dales in 1972 but though the club returned to the Dales for three seasons from 1974 they could not recapture their earlier days.

AT THE DOUBLE......No 7.

When my hero Len Hutton was my chauffeur

By John Morgan, the former Racing Correspondent of the Yorkshire Evening Post and for many years now one of Yorkshire's top sports writers and a much loved friend of the Dales Council.

IT took the violation of the hallowed square at Headingley cricket ground for this reporter to meet his idol. For years my deep admiration of Len Hutton simmered from a distance with little chance of interviewing the greatest of Yorkshire-born batsmen.

Long before the "Free George Davis" campaign resulted in the desecration of the world famous Test pitch a few fleeting words from the maestro was my treasured achievement. And it cost money.

Do you remember "Madge's Bar" in the Headingley grandstand? She was a buxom, motherly character – popular and professional. She dispensed pints of liquid sunshine with a happy greeting and speed which quickly eased the plight of her parched customers. But Madge and her helpers were overwhelmed on one occasion when play finished early and customers fairly thronged the cramped premises.

I was on the front row and one of the first to be served with orders from the back of the queue filtering down through me to Madge. We passed pints in chain gang fashion to the latecomers. Suddenly a recognisable voice from the rear of the pack murmured: "Young man, you seem to have a little influence with the bar staff!"

John Morgan.

Len Hutton.

It was Len – my hero –and I nodded agreement of the fact that I was one of Madge's favoured patrons. Len was in the company of Denis Compton – thereby giving the lie to popular general conception that they didn't see eye to eye – and Godfrey Evans, the bewhiskered retired England wicketkeeper. Len continued: "Would it be possible for you to get me three gin and tonics with ice and lemon please?"

How could I refuse the request of the cricket icon? It was not long before the drinks were passed to the sporting pensioners and a muffled "well done lad" reached me as Madge totted up the financial damage. "That will be thirty bob if I have a half" smiled the number one barmaid and I turned for Len's contribution to the expensive round. The trio had disappeared and it was left to this skint journalist to scrape the amount together and settle the bill.

There was only one way I could recover the unexpected financial outlay. Expenses were submitted to the Yorkshire Evening Post editor with the claim: "Drinks for Len Hutton and company at the Headingley Test etc." Of course the amount was challenged because Hutton, Compton and Evans did not appear in any stories written by me and the explanation that I was lining the cricketing colossus up for an exclusive tale was accepted. It never saw the light of day.

Rodley's wicketkeeper/batsman Neil Kettle in action for the league side at Adel, 2001.

A few years later my brief was to extract quotes from notable folk visiting the scene of the cricket carnage perpetrated by those who crusaded for the release from prison of the London-born George Davis. The crease was butchered with gaping holes slashed in the turf. Oil and tar destroyed the surface. It was a sight that brought tears to the eyes of scandalised cricket lovers.

Len appeared on the scene with Rugby League hero Arthur Clues and Aussie cricketer Chappell. They did not speak. Their faces mirrored anger, anguish and disgust.

Sir Len – as he was then – broke the silence. He turned to me and murmured: "I saw Don Bradman hit centuries here." He did not mention the fact that he had also played many a memorable innings on this pitch. His immediate thoughts were for Don who enjoyed the adulation of all who claim that the game of cricket was fashioned in Heaven.

The opportunity to achieve the outstanding ambition of an interview with him finally arrived. He was usually a man of few words but opinion and castigation of those responsible for the ugly demonstration flowed from the great man.

We were joined by the Yorkshire TV producer David Lowen and we mentioned to Sir Len that we had reason to visit Pudsey St Lawrence CC that night. The intention was to travel by taxi but he insisted on driving us to the ground where he embarked on his illustrious career. It was the ultimate thrill – being chauffeured by a man we had worshipped from afar.

When we arrived Sir Len declined the invitation to join us in the pavilion bar. He explained that Lady Dorothy was waiting for him and it was more than likely that he would be extremely late had he entered the premises. I was on the point of mentioning the debt incurred in Madge's bar but refrained from recalling the incident. After all he did not charge us for the drive.

Years later the annual Horserace Writers' Association Lunch was held at the Royal Lancaster Hotel, London. Naturally we had done the wine justice and after the formalities, speeches and presentation, seasoned troupers – like yours truly – decided to spend the evening at a pub renowned for its celebrity clientele. The Irish singer Rose Marie is a regular and so is John Inman of "Are You Being Served" notoriety.

After an hour or two in their company we opted for a taxi ride to another bar. The driver was introduced to us and the blood ran cold when he revealed his identity as "George Davis". This meeting coincided with the news from Headingley that a move from the traditional home to Wakefield was in the pipeline and that members would be asked to vote on the proposition.

George was irate. He posed for pictures – taken by my pal Paul Mallinson - and he said: "Tell all them Yorkies to leave the ground as it is. Don't even think about leaving. That club and Test match arena mean a lot to me."

He added: "Mind you, if the worse comes to the worst and the decision is made to quit Headingley you can always take the pitch with you. I'll get some of my pals to dig it up for you." We didn't laugh. I wrote the story but unfortunately did not have the photos to go with the headlines. Paul Mallinson shot 24 pictures of George but failed to wind the film on and all 24 images were on one snap!

This year – as we look forward to the celebration of the anniversary of the Dales Council Cricket League in two years' time – commemorates the season when Len Hutton hit a record 364 in a Test against Australia at The Oval. Sixty-five years have elapsed since that feat and now we are launching a 364 Club at Headingley. There will be no membership fee. Simply buy the tie and wear it with the pride we all have in the Dales Council League neckwear.

Cricket is a grand game isn't it? We have so many, many memories.

John Morgan, September, 2003.

At the double partner..............Neil Kettle.

Kettle steams to new record with press-ups

THE first double hundred of the new millennium came at the half way point in season 2000 and, fittingly perhaps in view of their success in the league in the run up to the new century, it came from a Rodley player.

Wicket-keeper batsman Neil Kettle had previously never managed to get beyond the 70s when he opened against New Wortley on June 24, 2000, but by the time he had smashed his way to 150 he was celebrating with press-ups at the wicket and he managed a lap of honour round the pitch when the 200 mark was achieved. "I was trying to keep loose when I did the press-ups but when I got to the double ton I just went berserk. The highest knock I'd had before had been an unbeaten 77 two seasons earlier," said Kettle.

He had cracked 158 of what finished as the A Division new record individual score of 206 not out in boundaries (17 fours and 15 sixes) and rounded off his afternoon by collecting two stumpings and three catches even though he opted not to keep for the first 10 overs of Wortley's innings. Rodley, with the help of a six for 48 effort from captain Roger Kelso, completed a 182 run victory by dismissing the Wortley side for 96.

"It was a day I shall never forget though it never crossed my mind about going for Paul's (Slater) record until I was around 160. It was the first time I had opened that season, it was not my regular slot in the batting order," said the Northamptonshire-born Kettle who has cricket in his blood. His father Mike opened the bowling for Northants in the 1960s and his godfather Peter Willey, who also played for Northants, was a regular for England before becoming internationally famous all over again as an umpire. "My mum rang my dad to tell him about the knock I'd managed and he did not believe her at first," smiled the Rodley record-breaker whose good fortune continued on his big day for that was when he first met his new girlfriend while celebrating in Bradford.

Chapter 13
THE CLUBS:
Sides joining The Dales from 1957 - 1974.

19. NEWLANDS (1957).

Newlands arrived and departed in 1957. One of a number of sides to have used the ground by the Leeds and Liverpool Canal at Rodley, they made little impact finishing bottom the first teams' division with 17 defeats in their 21 games and falling to the power of Gloss Sample who took eight wickets for just 10 runs when they met Green Lane.

20. LEEDS ZINGARI (1957–1990. B. Section winners: 1981; Cawthorne Cup winners: 1966 & 1972).

The starting point of the Leeds Zingari club can be traced back to 1933 and over the years there have been many fine cricketers who have represented them, like our president Geoff Cope who went on to play for England after getting his first

The combined Rodley/Meanwood (champions) sides on parade for Mick Wright's testimonial game in September, 1998 to mark his 40 years with the Rodley club.

taste of league cricket with the experienced travelling cricketers. But they made a modest start in the Dales fielding a team in the Second Teams division in 1957 to finish the campaign in third place with Ernest Smelt claiming fourth place in the division's bowling averages. Their first taste of glory came via the bat of Norman England who topped B Section batting averages in 1959 with 524 runs at 34.9 and in the following season, when they finished second in Section B, Smelt won the division's batting prize and John Sharpe was the division's top bowler. Sharpe gave the club a real lift early in their first season in the top division when he claimed all ten wickets in Zingari's clash with Smiths Sports on May 13, 1961, finishing with 10 for 23, including the hat-trick, off 19 overs but Zingari ended the campaign at the foot of the table. The first of their two successes in the Cawthorne Cup came in 1966 and third place in B Section in 1967 was enough to earn a spot back in the top division but they struggled and two campaigns later settled back into B Section. In fact, in their first match of the 1968 season they could muster only nine men and were routed by Francis Quinn who took 5-1 as they fell for just five against Otley Mills. But Brian Newall topped B Section bowling averages in 1972 when they picked up the Cawthorne trophy for the final time and their third position in the table earned them promotion. A run of mid-table performances came to an end in 1980 with relegation but the season earlier had been special for David Hunter who had topped the league batting list with an average of 50.00.

Zingari bounced straight back to the A Division as champions in 1981 with Hunter this time carrying off the B. Section bowling prize but it was back to the B Section for the 1984 campaign when Peter Bullock's batting earned him the division's batting prize and played a major role in another promotion season. Keith Edwards was usually somewhere to be found in

The Rodley ground next to the Leeds and Liverpool canal.

the league averages as Zingari's chequered career continued with two more seasons back in the B Division before promotion and a climb to the heady heights of second place in Division A in 1988, a campaign which saw Chris Cartmell and Paul Kirby hoist a new league fifth wicket record partnership of 135 against Rodley in early July. That was as good as it got for them and after yet another mid-table finish in 1989 followed by the penultimate position in Division A 12 months later, Zingari said farewell to the Dales.

21. BRAMLEY SPORTS (1958–1980), BRAMLEY (1981–1982), RODLEY (1983 onwards). (League champions: 1973, 1996, 1997, 2004. B Section winners: 1959, 1961, 1980. D Section winners: 1961, 1981, 1996, 1998. Pool Paper Mills Cup winners: 1970).

The Bramley side, under its various names, has been a valued member of the Dales community from the early days of the league's existence. The club has not enjoyed much success over the years in cup cricket, their single trophy being their 1970 Pool Paper Mills success over Esholt with five defeats in other finals, but they have always been a force to reckon with in the league, especially on their home patch just over the canal at Rodley. Formed in 1957 from the remains of the former Wharfedale League side Bramley Moriah, they made their debut in the Dales in 1958 finishing at the foot of Section B. The only way was up as they say and in the following campaign they finished top of the division with four of their batsmen in the top nine of the division's batting averages including one of two Cyril Chapmans at the club who was seventh with an average of 22.13. Two seasons later Bramley achieved a double with their first team taking the B Section title and their second finishing top of the Second Teams division. Throughout these and the ongoing years, the second Cyril Chapman (he was known as C.C. Chapman) was a key figure for the club as a player, captain, secretary, treasurer and groundsman and after putting away his bat he became a highly respected umpire and life member of the league. Derek Elsworth, another former captain of the club who hit five centuries for them in the 60s, also went on to become a Dales umpire.

But maybe the best-known player the club has had through its ranks was Keith Smith. Before going on to a higher grade of cricket in the Bradford League, the star of the early 70s with a swashbuckling style with both bat and ball, took award after award including the A Section batting prize when Bramley swept to their first league championship in 1973. But they then had to wait until the mid 1990s for their next league championship title. In their first season back in the top flight in 1996, Dean Carter's side, which had a strong bowling line-up, took the title and underlined their success by retaining the championship next time around. The Division B title in 1980 had been the only first team success in the interim years but the Second X1 were champions in 1981 besides matching the First X1 in the 90's with titles 1996 and 1998.

Club president Michael Wright first played for them as a 16-year-old in 1959 and has played every season since, picking up the D Division Bowling award in 1998 with his record breaking return of 25 wickets at just 2.84 runs apiece. A testimonial match that same year saw past and present Rodley players take on the reigning champions Meanwood to mark his 40th season with the club. He has also been honoured with life membership of the league.

In 2000 wicketkeeper Neil Kettle smashed the A Division's highest score when making an unbeaten double century against New Wortley while two of the club's bowlers have achieved the feat of all 10 wickets in an innings – Tony Imeson (10-16 against Reuben Gaunts in 1963) and Simon Dickens (10-32 against Castlehill in 2000). Roger Kelso went within a seam's width of matching them, too, in 1991 when the accurate left-arm bowler took the first nine wickets against Green Lane only to find they were a man short that day. But if he was unfortunate, spare a thought for former Rodley bowler Mick Knapton who when facing his old club while playing for Farsley Celtic in 1985 was smashed for six sixes in one over by Ian Dobson – the only time the Dales has seen the like.

22. ILLINGWORTH ST MARY'S (1958-1961).

Illingworth, who joined the Dales with Bramley Sports and finished one notch above them at the foot of the table in Section B in their first campaign in 1958, played at The Ainleys, Whitehall Road, Illingworth. In their four season run in the league they never managed to finish in the top half of Section B though S. Firth finished third in the division's batting averages in 1959, his 310 aggregate including an innings of 92, and G. Foulds took the division's wicketkeeping award 12 months earlier.

23. REUBEN GAUNTS   (1958-1968. pool Paper Mills Cup winners: 1962. Cawthorne Cup winners: 1967).

Reuben Gaunts, whose ground was at Throstle Nest, Farsley (next to Farsley Celtic's football ground), were promotion winners in their first season, elevated with the 1958 champions Otley Mills with T. W. Hudson capturing the divisional bowling award after taking 76 wickets for just 4.41 runs apiece and J. Holdsworth finishing in the runners-up slot in the batting averages. He re-produced the effort in the A Section in the following campaign scoring 489 runs at an average of 30.55 while Hudson again topped the 70 mark in wickets. Hudson then hit the record book in 1960 claiming nine wickets for eight runs against International Harvesters but it was 1962 before the team got their hands on silverware — the Pool Paper Mills Cup. Though they finished fourth from bottom in the 10-team A Section in 1965 they were relegated under the rule that said any club running two teams, the first eleven shall be in the A Section which kept Smiths Sports and Bramley Sports up even though they finished the season below Gaunts. It did, however, enable Gaunts to play in the Cawthorne Cup or B Section Cup as it was then for a couple of seasons and in 1967 they won the trophy and, ironically, promotion from a fourth placed position in the final placings after Crompark and Otley Mills, who both had first elevens in A Section, and Zingari. But the 1968 campaign, when they finished on the foot of Section A, was their last in the Dales.

24. SOWERBY BRIDGE (1958-1960. B Section winners: 1960).

One of the outposts of the Dales, Sowerby Bridge played at Walton Street in the township. They played in B Section throughout their three year run in the league finishing on a high note in 1960 as champions of the division with D. Foster their leading batsman hitting 346 runs to finish sixth in the averages.

25. TURNER SPORTS. (1961-1970).

Turner Sports' ground was on Swinnow Lane, Bramley, now one of all too many cricket grounds in the Dales used for light industry or housing. John Fenton, captain at Turners at the time, recalls one game at home in the early part of the decade when an unusual approach had to be employed. Netherfield, apparently, decided to dig in when faced with a useful score from Turners so Fenton used rarely seen tactics. "The two Bullocks, father and son, were umpiring that day and when it was clear Netherfield had no intention of going for the runs I asked them to inform the Netherfield batsmen that I was going to bowl an over of under-arm deliveries," he said. "Well I gave the batsman six very high full tosses and each ball was shown the full face of the bat and dropped at the batsman's toes. Sad to say the affair ended in a tame draw but at least we tried something that bit different." There was no such indifference to his bowling years later when he had joined Bramley Sports.

In 1976 he achieved the league's first recorded five wicket plus a century in the same match feat when he took 5-28 and hit an unbeaten 101 at Pudsey Congs to lead the side to a 55 run victory.

But when it came to all-rounders, Turners had, arguably, the prince of the pack for in those mid-60s days they provided the launching pad for Keith Smith whose exploits with bat and ball were to become the talk of the league and beyond. He first figured in the league averages when he finished fourth in the batting list in Section B in 1964 and sixth in the bowling list before playing a leading role in the club's promotion in the following campaign. Second in the league batting averages in Turners' first season in the top flight in 1966, he won the league batting award for the first time in 1967 when Turners finished third in the league behind Les Heaton's Esholt side and Holbeck Bethel and went on to complete a hat-trick of batting awards in the following two seasons. Like Fenton, he would join Bramley Sports in 1970, the season Turners' run in the Dales concluded — without a win in any of their 22 league fixtures.

26. THOS. WAIDES (1961–1962).

Waides Sports, as they were known in the Dales, played at Brownberrie Lane, Horsforth, in the league for two seasons without making much impact.

New Farnley's new home just across the road from where they started in the Dales in Farnley Park.

27. HOLBECK BETHEL (1965 to 1968), WEST LEEDS (1969-1973) and C.E.G.B. (1974-1977). Section B winners: 1965. Pool Paper Mills Cup winners: 1968.

Like many sides who have played in the Dales, Holbeck Bethel, who originally were members of the Yorkshire Central League, operated at Farnley Hall playing fields, Old Farnley and continued to do so when they merged with West Leeds from the 1969 season before becoming C.E.G.B. in 1974 when their home was at Beckwith Knowle at Harrogate.

The Holbeck side played in just four seasons in the Dales but won two trophies starting in overdrive in their first campaign by winning the B Section title with 50 points, losing just two of their 20 fixtures. They had a formidable attack with Ken Belsham, Don Foulkes and Douglas Thornton claiming the first three places in the division's bowling averages taking 135 wickets between them at a combined average of just 4.91 runs apiece. Belsham also finished fourth in the batting averages. The 1966 season saw them finish second in the top flight with their all-rounder Terry Drury having a vintage year by topping both the league's batting and bowling averages — the only time the feat has been achieved in the Dales though his team-mate Foulkes pushed him hard for the bowling award finishing just .6 of a run behind him in second place. "I remember that season well for I was captaining the side and it's still worth a glass or two nowadays when I see Terry and remind him that I made sure he bowled at the right end," said Belsham. "That's right," confirms Drury, "in fact, it was particularly important on the last day of that season when I needed seven wickets to top the league averages."

Holbeck finished runners-up again in the league in 1967 but claimed silverware in the final season in the Dales by winning the Pool Paper Mills Cup. As West Leeds they operated sides in both the A and B Sections for their first two seasons eventually losing their Section A status in 1972. They finished runners-up in B Section in the following campaign with Foulkes winning the divisional bowling award with an average of 4.80 and went into the top flight again as C.E.G.B. only to finish at the foot of the table in 1974. When they left the league three seasons later Drury signed off by finishing top of the Division B batting list with an average of 26.90 from almost 300 runs scored.

28. NEW FARNLEY (1966-1994 and 2000 onwards. League champions: 1968, 1969, 1972, 1983, 1992, 1994. B Section winners: 1991. D. Section winners: 1992, 2001. Pool Paper Mills Cup winners: 1980, 1983, 1992, 1993. Cawthorne Cup winners: 1992, 1994).

New Farnley can be justly proud of their record of 14 trophies from 1968-1994 in their first spell in the Dales followed up by a further championship in D Division soon after they rejoined the league by way of their third team at the opening of the new millennium. When you look at their splendid new home in Lawns Lane, New Farnley, it is easy to appreciate how far they have come as a club since they were founded in 1952 with money left from the Trustees of Farnley Iron Works CC (whose ground was lost due to subsidence). They joined the Barkston Ash & Yorkshire Central League in 1954 transferring to the Dales in the middle 60s where they soon became a force under the captaincy of their late president Barry Jackson who had the canny wicketkeeping skills of Harry Holmes and the pace bowling of Mick Holmes, John Ridley and Barry Finch to call upon. In fact, when the club retained the league championship in 1969, when their home pitch was in the far top corner of Farnley Hall park, the trio of top bowlers duly finished first, second and third in the league bowling averages.

The club has achieved the league and cup double on two occasions, in 1983 and then in 1992 when their second string also completed the D Division and Cawthorne Cup double in the same season to create a clean sweep for the 'club of the early 90s.' But in their run-up to their first double campaign they had to fight their way back into the top flight after relegation with fast bowler Alan Swarbreck, who won the league bowling award in 1981, one of their leading lights with both ball and bat.

Simon Lindsay picked up 82 wickets when New Farnley finished second in the league in 1989 to signal his arrival among the leading bowlers in the Dales and when they went down in 1990, he featured strongly in their promotion side of the following campaign. But it was in 1992 he really took centre stage taking the A Division batting and all-rounder awards and finishing second in the bowling averages to team-mate G. Hepworth as New Farnley swept the board at both first and second team level losing only one match between them with John Baldwin and J. Bentley taking the second teams' batting and bowling awards for good measure. Before leaving the Dales for the Central Yorkshire League they collected their sixth league title in 1994 with Lindsay signing off as the league's top all-rounder. Their second spell in the Dales was quickly highlighted by their title success in D Division in 2001 soon to be followed by Nick Oram's new A Division top score of 208 in a record partnership with Baldwin in 2003.

29. ARMLEY SAXONS (1968–1971).

Armley Saxons might not have been around long in the Dales but the name of their first ground was hard to forget — they played at The Butter Bowl on the Leeds Ring Road at Wortley. By their final campaign in 1971, however, they had moved on to Tyersal Park, Tyersal, having dropped the "Saxons" part of their name.

Holbeck Bethel's 1968 PPM Cup winning side. Back row l to r. Des Corcorran, scorer, S. Robinson, D. Foulkes, S. Maher, R. Waite, M. Wokes, D. Thornton. Front row. K. Worral, T. Lazenby, T. Drury, K. Belsham, G. Moss.

30. JOHNSON RADLEY (1968-1970).

Johnson Radley, who played at Throstle Nest, Farsley, spent three seasons in the Dales finishing at the foot of B Section in the first campaign and in mid table in their remaining seasons.

31. WIBSEY (1969-1984. B Sections winners: 1969, 1975).

Wibsey opened their account in the Dales by claiming the 1969 B. Section title with bowlers B. Yeadon (39 wickets at 4.56) and D. Shepherd (53 wickets at 4.64) leading the way for them. They played on Horsfall Playing Fields, Shelf, and soon introduced a bowler who was to make a big mark in the Dales in swing expert Keith Robertshaw. In June, 1970, he turned in an 8.4 overs, 5 maidens, 4 runs 9 wickets performance and followed that with 82 wickets at just 6.51 runs apiece to become the leading wicket taker in the Dales in 1971. It was the first of many lucrative seasonal returns in a career that took him via Oxford Place to Smith Sports and back to Wibsey. With Robertshaw departed, Wibsey went down in 1974 but bounced straight back the following season by a big margin with S. Brear topping the B Section bowling averages for them with 52 wickets at 6.84. It was relegation again in 1976 but with Robertshaw back they went up again in 1980, this time with their star bowling 357 overs to grab a staggering 97 victims at an average of just 6.60 and take the divisional bowling award. He hit a big century in 1982 to finish eighth in the batting averages besides topping the bowling list with 82 wickets at 7.74 with Wibsey finishing fourth. But after that they dropped down the table finishing at the foot of A Division in 1984 when they left the league.

32. FARNLEY HILL (1969-1971 and 1995 onwards. Cawthorne Cup winners: 1969).

Another team to play on the Farnley Hall park arena, they had a fine opening bowler in Colin Barraclough who topped the B Section averages in their first season in the Dales in 1969 with 66 wickets at 4.42. while their cultured opening batsman Derek Best matched the effort with an unbeaten 111 in his award winning average of 30.9. The Farnley side finished runners-up to Wibsey and a memorable first season in the Dales was completed by victory in the Cawthorne Cup. In their new surroundings in the A Division they again finished runners-up the following season with Barraclough once more topping the bowling averages, this time with 75 wickets at 6.77. They left the league after three campaigns when finishing in mid-table in 1971 to rejoin the Yorkshire Central League.

Nick Oram.

David Hunter.

Farnley Hill began life as a chapel team in the early 1920s when they were known as Farnley Hill Methodists playing friendly cricket until World War Two. They re-formed in the late 1940s and joined the Yorkshire Central League for the first time in 1958. Throughout the post war years and right through to and beyond the new millennium, synonymous with the name of the club was the name of Harry Lister. He first played for the then Farnley junior side in 1949 at the age of eight and was still playing some games in 2001 – a playing career covering 52 years with the Farnley side providing a proud record for both player and club.

Their 1980s side featured Lister, Mark Burns, Mick Newbound, Liam Walsh and Carl Best who were all league trophy winners but the club's most treasured award was the league's Sportsmanship Trophy in 1992. Back in the Dales three seasons later, they have continued to have their ups and downs but they have also continued to display the same principles upon which the club was founded – the ideals, which helped them to lift that 1992 trophy.

33. OXFORD PLACE (1970-1987. League champions: 1975. B. Sections champions: 1970, 1985. Pool Paper Mills Cup winners: 1977. Cawthorne Cup winners: 1970).

Oxford Place joined the instant champions club when they made their bow in the Dales in 1970 taking the B Section title and creating a new record along the way by completing their 22 fixtures without defeat, 18 of them in victory. It was a performance which saw them to the title by a massive 12 point margin with Brian Anderson top scoring in the division with 437 runs to finish second in the batting averages and Ernie Dufton second in the league bowling averages. And to underline their arrival in the Dales they picked up the Cawthorne Cup, to make it a debut double in the league.

Oxford Place, undefeated in 1970 when they won the B Section title and the Cawthorne Cup.
Back row l to r. E. Dibb, B. Eager, B. Paul, B. Brooke, E. Dufton, D. Quick, C. Smart.
Front row: J. Leybourne, D. Maltby, B. Anderson, R. Webster, W. Smart, P Rafton.

They consistently finished among the top sides in A Section, too, until they finally took the title in 1975 – again by a 12-point margin. Players like Brian Eager and David Benn who could take wickets and score runs, made them a tough proposition on their tiny ground at West Royd Park, Farsley, while Anderson and Dave Maltby set up a new league seventh wicket highest partnership in late August 1973 against Bramley Sports when they finished unbeaten with 109 on the board. But their title winning effort owed a lot to the wicket-taking skills of Harry Rider who finished the campaign by winning the league bowling award with an average of 5.79. Their cup success in 1977, however, proved to be their last touch of silverware for eight years.

Relegated in 1981, they gradually began to assert themselves again with fast bowler Lawrie Herbert regularly in the league averages and winning the bowling award in the 1983 campaign. But it was Peter Flint who took the award in 1985 when Oxford Place captured their final trophy – the B Section title.

34. PUDSEY CONGS. (1970-1978 and 1980 onwards. League champions: 1978, 1993. C. Section winners: 2000. D. Section winners: 1988, 1990, 1991, 1995, 1997. Pool Papers Mills Cup winners: 1972, 1974, 1975. Cawthorne Cup winners: 1975, 1987, 1988, 1989, 1990, 1991, 1993, 1996, 1997, 2004).

Pudsey Congs have a formidable record over their three decades in the Dales, particularly in the Cawthorne Cup which they have won no fewer than nine times with their run of five successive final successes the best consecutive return by any team in any of the Dales Council's competitions. They have had some of the league's top players through their ranks over the

Pudsey Congs Cawthorne Cup finalists of 2001: Back row l to r. A. Goodchild, C. Northrop, N. Strangeway, R. Kettlewell, S. Lynes, B. Newell, M. Edwards. Front row. S. Ford, K. Hall, C. Clifton, capt., G. Galvin, P. Gambles, scorer: Daniel Clifton.

years like Peter Marsh and Kevin Edwards with the most recent and most famous being England opening bowler Matthew Hoggard. But few have served the club and cricket in general both on and off the field with as much dedication as Ralph Middlebrook who, by the way, has done his bit in the media ranks, too. But in August, 2000, when the league made its 'live' debut on Radio Leeds he was also turning out for Congs at Mount Pleasant and so probably did not hear his link man back at the studio say: 'I can't talk to our man at the moment – he's out batting.'

However, he can take up Congs' story at this point for us: "The Crown and Anchor pub at Rodley was the unlikely starting place for the Congs adventure in the Dales. Of course, Congs members, who at times were expected to attend Chapel once a month, hardly dared let it be known they frequented pubs. Our first fixture was against West Leeds and when they reached 40 without loss certainly many Congs supporters were enjoying the possibility of being proved right – that we would not be good enough to compete in the higher standard – but we players were made of sterner stuff dismissing West Leeds for 70-odd, Congs winning by six wickets. We were strong enough playing wise, featuring in many cup finals – taking with the team approximately 100 spectators who contributed not only to the atmosphere of the match but ensured that our cricket club grew from one team to two and so on expanding on and off the field. Pudsey Congs always provided tough opposition, opponents always 'got a game', usually Congs ran out winners but great was the feeling as giants of the Dales such as Grove Hill, Smith Sports or Bramley Sports were overcome.

"Congs supplied players for the league X1, a captain even, eventually a president so the club contributed wholeheartedly in all league activities and made a reputation as a skilful, well organised club. My own memories include delightful enjoyable days playing cricket at Esholt, Farnley Estate, Pool Mills – taking a career best nine for 41 against Grove Hill at Queen's Park and the joy of beating (sometimes) our arch rivals Oxford Place. What battles.
"But principally, meeting so many genuine cricketing enthusiasts who put cricket and fun before everything else, working in difficult circumstances with little cash or facilities and making lasting friendships which endure to this day. Yes, I certainly enjoyed Pudsey Congs adventure in the Dales, long may it thrive." Ralph W. Middlebrook.

35. FARNLEY ESTATE (1971-1977. Cawthorne Cup winners: 1971).

Of all the away venues players in the Dales have enjoyed over the years, few places have matched Farnley Estate's ground in front of Farnley Hall with its wonderful views down the Wharfe Valley. For most teams, it was a bit of a trek to get to them up the side of the valley way beyond Pool-in-Wharfedale, but it was a beautiful spot on a warm, July afternoon. I had one bad memory there though taking a particularly fast delivery on my left ankle bone which left me unable to drive for over a week – I could not depress the clutch – and we were off on a family motoring holiday to Newquay the following day! The Estate side started life in the Dales by winning the Cawthorne Cup and finishing third in Section B with John Pullan second in the divisional batting list with 765 runs and David Pullan taking the bowling prize with 68 wickets. It was enough to win

Keith Robertshaw.

Dave Benn.

Brian Anderson.

promotion and in the top flight with Pullan, the bat, on the mark again (he won the league batting prize of 1972), the Estate side finished in a creditable fifth place in the table. The club enjoyed its best position in Section A when finishing runners-up to close rivals Otley Town in the 1974 campaign.

36. FARSLEY (1971-1972 and 1997-2003).

Like Oxford Place, Farsley, who initially had just two seasons in the Dales, played at West Royd Park, Farsley in 1971 and 1972. Eric Hargate, with 568 runs, topped the B Section batting averages for them in their opening campaign when they finished eighth in the 12-team division. He was second in the averages in the following season behind team-mate R. Giles, the pair of them sharing just over 1000 league runs but the Farsley side faired little better as a whole. They were effectively the third string of the village's Bradford League club and as such they rejoined the Dales again in 1997, playing at Priesthorpe School this time around and winning promotion to Division B in their first season.

37. RIVER AUTHORITY (1971-1973).

The River Authority club played for three seasons in the Dales B Section on Soldiers' Field, Roundhay, with a best league position of sixth in a 10-team division.

38. PHOENIX PARK (1973-1982. B. Division winners: 1973 and 1979).

Sadly, the ground Phoenix Park used, which overlooked a golf course at Thornbury, is now part of the car park for a multi-screen cinema complex. Like other teams before them, they started life in the Dales on a successful note winning the B Section championship in 1973 with J. Hudson leading the way for them with a batting performance, which saw him take the divisional batting prize. They finished a creditable fifth in the first season in the top flight but were relegated in 1977. They took the B Division championship with 99 points in 1979 only to finish second from the bottom three seasons later when they left the league after a ten year spell.

39. LEEDS Y.M.C.A. (1973-1988).

The YMCA side played at the association's sports ground off Otley Road at Lawnswood and while they did not get among the team trophies they had some fine players during the decade and a half they spent in the Dales. They included Ian Mortimer who hit an unbeaten 110 in the 1974 campaign when going on to take the divisional batting prize with an average of 42.83 as YMCA finished third in the B Section table. P.R. Fisher matched his effort in the following season when YMCA again finished in third place. They put a side in the second teams division in 1976 and five years later the second string topped the third section in the second elevens division while the first team gained promotion from Division B as runners-up to Leeds Zingari with Mortimer topping the batting averages for the second successive season. They lasted four seasons in the top flight without getting into the top half of the table before relegation. But they bounced straight back as runners-up to Lloyds Bank in one of the tightest finishes the league has known. That 1986 campaign also saw Bill Davis hit 763 at an average of 63.58 to win the B Division batting prize and along the way create a new highest season's batting average for the league - but after two more campaigns in the top flight the YM side left the Dales.

40. PUDSEY St. LAWRENCE (1974 onwards. Pool Paper Mills Cup winners: 1988).

You only have to get as far as the gates into their Tofts Road cricket ground to know that you have arrived at a special club. The Sir Leonard Hutton Memorial Gates open the way to the home of possibly Yorkshire's most famous cricket club after the county side itself. It was founded in 1845 and just to look down the list of players who have represented St Lawrence over the years is mind-boggling. But it is the club's relationship with the Dales Council which matters here.

Their third and fourth teams have played their part in the Dales over the last three decades starting with promotion as runners-up to Wibsey in B Section in 1975. In 1987 S. Worsnop topped the A Division bowling averages making it a double in the following campaign when St Lawrence also picked up the Pool Paper Mills Cup and finished third in the league. The 1989 campaign saw Stuart Camm as the league's top batsman with an average of 40.76 while Andrew Broadley was top wicketkeeper three years later. Keith Dickson picked up the batting award in the B Section when St Lawrence were again promotion winners in the runners-up slot in 1993 as Pete Langley went to the first of successive divisional batting awards in the second teams section. The 1997 and 2000 campaigns finished with Dave Threllfall and Paul Blackburn taking the B Division batting awards while Richard Bott was top bowler in the division in 2002, a feat repeated by Keith Marsden in the following campaign as the St Lawrence players continued to take the eye as prize winners while at the same time bringing on some of their talented young players under the guidance of older hands.

St Lawrence, like their neighbours Pudsey Congs down the road, have also played an important role for the league by allowing the use of their facilities for cup and representative fixtures not to mention the use of their clubhouse for League Committee and Umpires Association meetings. In all making up a happy relationship in the name of cricket.

The famous gates at the Pudsey St Lawrence ground.

Where batsmen batted and bowlers bowled once upon a time!

More than a dozen of the grounds loved by Dales Council players over the past 50 years are now no more. They are buried by a mixture of residential, parkland and commercial developments. Five much missed playing arenas were located at and around the scenes here:

Pheonix Park, now home of a cinema complex, once the home across the car park of English Electric.

Cricketers Green, Yeadon, once the home of Green Park.

Fyfe Crescent/Lane, Baildon, once the home of Butterfields.

Fieldway Avenue, Coal Hill Lane, Rodley, once the home of Smiths Sports.

Redwood Close, Yeadon, once the home of Ives Sports.

Chapter 14.
THE CLUBS:
Sides joining The Dales from 1975 - 1988.

41. CROMA (1976–1987. League champions: 1985,1987. B.Division winners: 1976).

Croma started their Dales life at Park Side School at Middleton but the majority of players remember them most for their days playing at Roundhay Park Oval where years before the Dales Council arrived cricketers like Australian demon fast bowler Ray Lindwall had played in one of the many celebrity games held there in the late 40s and early 50s. Even after that it was always a popular spot for the casual spectator to take in a game and one very hot Saturday afternoon playing there in the late 70s I remember having to stop on my run up when the Croma batsman pulled away distracted by around half a dozen teenagers who had decided the heat was just too much and were streaking through the extra cover area. The escapade brought ironic cheers from the scattering of people watching the match from the banking surrounding the playing area, a smile to everyone's face in the pavilion and outright laughing broke out there at the interval when the umpire asked my wife Margaret, who was scoring, just how she had managed to record the hold-up of several minutes in the scorebook.

Croma had by then swept to the B Section title in their opening campaign - with Scalebor Park five points behind them and the rest of the field no-where. They finished runners-up in the top flight in 1981 with Terry Fletcher, who was regularly in either the league batting or bowling averages in the early 80s, also taking the runners-up slot in the batting list. In the following campaign he took all ten wickets in Croma's fixture at New Farnley for 28 runs off 21 overs which included five maidens. But when Croma charged to the league title for the first time in 1985 with just a single defeat en route to a record 99 points, 30 clear of runners-up Eldwick & Gilstead, it was Peter Wiggins who spearheaded the way taking the league bowling award with 51 wickets at just 6.71 runs apiece. Then Mick Ashworth, with an average of almost 47, took the league batting award in 1987 when Croma signed off from the Dales as champions for the second time.

42. SCALEBOR PARK. (1976 to 1987. A Div champions, 1986)

Scalebor Park's first taste of league cricket came via The Dales Council. The club joined the league in 1976 and played in it for 12 seasons before going on to join the Leeds League. They played on one of the most pleasant grounds in the dales at the Scalebor Park Hospital and had patients as regular spectators at their games — and on one occasion they also had a television crew there and, along with the crew, one or two famous actors.

Scenes in the nuclear-based serial The Edge of Darkness were filmed at the hospital in the 1980's and club secretary Brian Jaques remembers the day the film crew wanted to include a cricket match in one shot. "It wasn't really cricket weather, it was done one Sunday in October and we even had to move the pitch round to fit in with the view from one of the hospital windows," he remembers. "It was a pretty long session, we were there through the morning and afternoon in order to get the right light and angle the television people needed but when the show, which featured Bob Peck, was shown you could see us playing away. They handed us £150 appearance money for our club's funds so it was worth it all and we keep seeing re-runs even now. The episode which featured us was on BBC3 not so long ago."

Scalebor openers George Baines, who was also an accomplished wicketkeeper, and Peter O'Brien, were both teachers at Middleton in Leeds. They established one of the best opening partnerships the league has known reaching a high point when they both hit centuries to create a new league highest opening partnership record of 225 in the 1981 campaign. O'Brien had joined the club one day after turning up to watch a friend playing. He had first been ushered into umpiring and then he asked if there was a chance of a game - and after that, as they say, the rest is history. In one run from 1978 to 1983 he topped the league batting averages four times, played for the league side and was a terrific fielder in the covers. "He was amazing, regularly hitting the stumps. He was our version of the famous South African cover fielder of the 1960's Colin Bland," said Jaques.

The club origins can be traced back to Leeds City Corporation Servicemen returning to the Parks Department at the end of the First World. They played on Soldiers' Field at Roundhay and it is reputed that Hedley Verity played one game for the club in the 1930s. But by 1959 the number of Parks Department employees in the team had dropped to one and shortly afterwards the club name was changed to Park CC. They got the chance of the hospital ground on condition they called themselves Scalebor Park in 1973 and with the recruitment of four or five of the Scalebor Park team a flourishing outfit developed. In1976 friendly cricket was left behind in favour of the Dales Council and promotion was gained in their first season in the league. Two seasons on only defeat in the final game stopped them taking the league title. But they finally landed the crown in1986.

43. BEN RHYDDING (1976–1986. B. Division winners: 1978. D. Division winners: 1986).

With the moors as the backdrop, it was always a pleasure to play at the big sports complex on the side of the main road to Ilkley that Ben Rhydding called home. In the season they pulled out of the Dales they finished at the foot of Division A but their second eleven took the Second X1, Section A title (now known as the D Division). They picked up their first silverware in the Dales in 1977 when M. Lockwood won the Second Teams batting award but in the following season there were trophies for the title winning B Section side and their batsman B. Wilson who topped the averages on 42.73 with an aggregate number of runs of 470. S. Rae and M. Wrigley won the second teams league batting award in successive seasons in 1980 and 1981 and in the B Section promotion campaign of 1983 when Ben Rhydding were elevated as runners-up to High Royds the division's batting prize was claimed by C. Jones. The 1985 season brought the League's batting prize for J. Clark while in the second team's competition, the bowling award was claimed by P. Bell who took all ten wickets (for 48) against Farsley Celtic in early July.

44. NEW WORTLEY (1976 onwards. League champions: 2001, 2002. C Division winners: 2001. D Division winners: 1993, 1999. Pool Paper Mills Cup winners: 2001. Cawthorne Cup winners: 2003).

Throughout the history of the New Wortley club one name stands out. Les Thompson was a founder member, captain, president and is now a life member. For a decade to the new millennium he was also president of the Dales Council and as

Croma players celebrate their 1985 title success.
Back: M. Addinall, A. Hunt, S. Wiggins, P. Wiggins, T. Clapham, E. Simpson, M. Ashworth, J. Ball.
Front: R. Webster, M. Groves, T. Fletcher, R. Townend (Capt.), R. Addinall, N. Hardy.

New Wortley's Cawthorne Cup winning side of 2003.

such was the initial inspiration behind this book. You can usually find him standing as an umpire at one of the league's games these days but his heart is very much with the club he has done so much for and when the second team pulled off a thrilling win to lift the Cawthorne Cup for the first time in 2003 he was a proud man when he handed over the trophy to Phil Worsnop and the man of match award to John Blackburn.

New Wortley, started in 1969 when several members of the Armley CC decided to breakaway and form their own club, play on Western Flatts Park, high above the Leeds Ring Road. Initially they operated in the Pudsey Sunday School league and after two particularly successful campaigns in 1974 and 1975 they were elected to the Dales. But it was tough going with re-election being sought in their first three seasons. New players were recruited and in 1980 a second X1 was formed but in their first season they were toppled out by Eldwick for just six, an unwanted record which was matched by New Farnley in 2002. The only way was up and there were successes in the Umpires Association Sportsmanship Trophy besides wins for Paul Smith (1990) and Stuart Kirk (1999) as the Young Cricketer of the Year. A. Arslan, a Leeds University mature student who had already achieved an all 10 feat back in Pakistan, joined the Dales all ten wickets in an innings club in 1988 conceding just 23 runs against Civil Service while at team level the second X1 picked up the club's first silverware as champions of D Division in 1993. By this point the running of the club was largely down to family involvement with the Thompsons, Bissetts, Becketts, Griffins, and Chambers in the forefront.

But it was the arrival of the new century which really saw the club take off. In 1999 the second team opened the door by taking the D Division title again going on to take the C Division championship in 2001. The first team, having battled against relegation from Division A for many years finally started to come good. Captained by Martin Knowles, the team finished runners-up in 2000 but then did the league and cup double in the following season. In 2002 they retained the league title and, although missing out in the cup, they still became the first side to break the 400 runs barrier when they hit 428 for six against Esholt in the first round on May 5 with Mark Hobson hitting a club record 164 not out.

45. OLICANIANS (1976-1987. B. Division winners: 1984. D. Division winners: 1985, 1987. Cawthorne Cup winners: 1981).

Under the shadow of the Cow and Calf rocks on the banks of the Wharfe at Ikley, the Olicanians play in idyllic surroundings. The club was originally formed in 1922 by the old boys of Ilkley Grammar School, the name originating from Olicana, the old Roman name for Ilkley. Cricket was then played on the recreation field adjacent to the Ilkley Tennis Club off Skipton Road but in 1926 the team lost the use of the ground, folded, but then re-formed four years later. They moved to a site next to their present ground, an area now covered by the open-air swimming pool, and after disbanding at the outbreak of war in 1939, resumed again in 1949 at the club's present home.

They joined the Dales in 1976 and after surviving an opening season in which they finished on the bottom of B Section, results improved to the point where they picked up four trophies in seven seasons from 1981. First came the Cawthorne Cup then the B Division title in 1984 and the D Division championship in 1985 and 1987. During this time in a first team game at Scalebor Park, Ron Middleton produced what must go down as one of the tightest spells of bowling in the league's history when he sent down 21 overs with 18 of them maidens taking four for four while in 1984 top awards in both the batting and bowling lists in the second teams competitions went to R. Hogarth and R. Dewhurst. Hogarth won the batting award again in 1986 with B. Moran taking the league bowling prize when the D Division title was secured in Olicanians final season in the Dales before joining the Leeds League from 1988.

46. KIRKSTALL FORGE   (1977–1979. B Division winners: 1977).

B section champions in their first season in the Dales in 1977, Kirkstall Forge played at the back of Cookridge Hall, Otley Old Road, Cookridge, climbing to third in the top flight in their final season in the league in 1979.

47. ADEL (1978 onwards. Pool Paper Mills Cup winners: 1986).

Founded in 1876, Adel cricket club played friendly cricket for most of the first century. The creation of the War Memorial Association after 1918 confirmed the club's present location and the picturesque old pavilion was purchased from Creskeld CC in 1948. Destroyed by fire in 1986, it was replaced the following year by the present pavilion which serves both the club's pitches.

Adel joined the Airedale & Wharfedale league in 1975 and also started a friendly X1 to bring on juniors and develop reserve strength. Friendly cricket failed to provide sufficient challenge or certainty of fixtures and so Adel joined the Dales Council in 1978, initially playing on the municipal grounds at Red Hall. In 1981 a second square was created at Adel, however, and the club has played Dales Council games 'at home' ever since. Promotion to the top flight came in 1985 and the club returned to Division A as B Division runners-up in 1996 to Jarvis Porter after relegation in 1993. The only team trophy has been by way of the 1986 victory in the Pool Paper Mills Cup but at player level it is a different story. Steve Shires captained the league side while other noteworthy players have included Les Fussey, who has regularly figured in the league averages and has cracked a few very rapid 50s in his time, and Reg Parker who joined Adel at the age of 56 in 1984 and opened the batting in the Dales from 1995 when he topped 800 runs at an average of 54.33 to finish runner-up in the B Section averages. He was top in the following campaign, this time with Fussey in the runners-up slot and with Shires taking the bowling award in the promotion winning side. Before retiring in 1998 he hit over 8,000 league and cup runs for the club.

48. RIDDLESDEN (1979–1982. Pool Paper Mills Cup winners: 1979, 1981, 1982).

Riddlesden, one of five clubs to join the Dales in 1979 from the Keighley area when the league had more than 40 teams in competition for the first time, played at Stockbridge, Keighley, on a tiny ground near the River Aire. D. Spragg topped B Division batting averages for them in their first season with a century in his aggregate number of runs of 622 as they gained promotion from fourth place in the table and won the Pool Paper Mills Cup. He finished runner-up in the top flight in the

Les Fussey.

Reg Parker.

following season and when Riddlesden left the league in 1982, it was on the back of another fine season. They had already proved their cup pedigree by winning the Pool Paper Mills Cup again in 1981 but they not only retained it in their final fling in the league but also finished runners-up in Division A and top of Section 2 in the second X1's competition with batsman S. Riddlough and bowler G. Emmett topping the league's second team averages. A short but very sweet journey in the Dales.

49. ELDWICK & GILSTEAD (1979-1988. League champions: 1981, 1988. Cawthorne Cup winners: 1982).

Handy for the famous Dick Hudson's moorside tavern and hard to beat on their sloping pitch at High Eldwick, Eldwick & Gilstead won the league title twice in their 10 year run in the Dales. They gained promotion in their first season and the league crown in the second season in the top flight. Stanford Robinson was the league's top bowler in 1983 when Eldwick finished runners-up to New Farnley and after going close on a couple of occasions they took the league title again in their final season in the Dales in 1988 when the top three batsman in the league averages were all Eldwick players — Roy Kilvington, John Smith and Kevin Tetley. Stalwarts of the club included wicketkeeper-batsman Donald Holmes, all-rounder Wilf Anderson and secretary Maurice Steele who would always find some kit in his car and make up the numbers when called upon. The club's second string picked up the Cawthorne Cup in 1982 but also achieved a handy league record when they bowled out New Wortley for just six runs two summers earlier with Anderson taking six wickets for two runs off 12 overs and Andy Maude three for none off 2.1 overs.

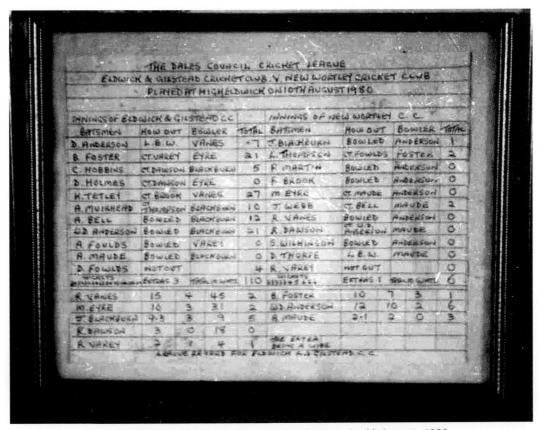

When Eldwick bowled out New Wortley for just six, 10 August, 1980.

50. MORTON (1979-1980).

Morton, whose stay in the Dales lasted just two summers, played at Brown Hill, West Morton. They topped Division B in the second team's competition in their debut season.

51. INGROW St. JOHN'S (1979-1987. Pool Paper Mills Cup winners: 1984).

Ingrow, who played at Marriner Road, Greengates, Keighley, won the senior knock out cup in their sixth season in the Dales. They had gained promotion to the top flight two seasons earlier in 1982 as runners-up to Pool Paper Mills in Section 1 of Division B and in1983 Dave Unwin was the league's top all-rounder with R. Howley top batsman in the second teams' competition. Unwin retained his all-rounder's title in Ingrow's cup year while in 1985 when their second string finished top of the Second X1s section 2, C Bottomley took the league's second team competition's batting award with an average of 37.10. Relegation for the first team in 1986 was followed by one more term in B Division before Ingrow left the Dales.

52. MORTON BANKS (1979-1987).

Morton Banks played at the back of the famous East Riddlesden Hall where a big hit could find the River Aire without too much trouble. They left the Dales after finishing 11th out of 15 in Division B in 1987 having been on the wrong end of three league records in the previous campaign. On May 4, 1986, the Adel pair C. Foord (176) and P. Allison (48 not out) shared a Pool Paper Mills Cup highest partnership against them of 224 for the second wicket, Foord's knock representing the highest in the cup at the time while in the second X1s competition P. Senior of Pudsey Congs scored 150 off their attack – the highest individual score in the competition.

53. MEANWOOD PARK HOSPITAL (1979-1988. Cawthorne Cup winners: 1985, 1986).

The Meanwood side played in the hospital grounds. They finished at the foot of Division B in their first campaign and managed to move up no more than a single slot in 1980. But in the 1985 campaign they picked up their first trophy when winning the Cawthorne Cup, retaining it in 1986 when they also won 12 of their 20 league games to finish top of Section

Home of Morton, high above Keighley at West Morton.

2 in B Division with bowlers P. Ruane and Graham Child sharing more than 90 victims to gain second and seventh places in the bowling averages. The 1987 season saw the B Division's batting prize claimed by P. Bagley who hit a century in his 418 aggregate. But after finishing eighth in the ten-team division the following season, they left the league.

54. CIVIL SERVICE (1980–1987).

It must have brought a smile at the time when the league tables for 1980 came out in the league handbook showing that in their first campaign in the Dales, Civil Service had apparently played more league games than any other side in a single season in the history of the league. They had finished 10th in the 14-strong Division B competition having taken part in 29 fixtures according to the 'matches played' column while every other side in the division had had 26 games to negotiate. Of course, the figure nine in '29' had somehow been printed upside down. In all, they played in the Dales for eight seasons without making much impact. They did, however, operate in one of the most picturesque areas of all the league's locations at the time next door to the locks on the Leeds and Liverpool canal at Hurst Lane, Saltaire.

55. LLOYDS BANK (1981–1987), HORSFORTH (1988–1991 and 1995–2000). (Division B winners: 1986).

With one of the keenest captains I have ever come across in all-rounder Martin Connolly and one of the best wicketkeepers I have bowled at in Peter Stebbings (who also matched the best of his time with the bat, too), Lloyds Banks had a couple of formidable cricketers in the spearhead of their mid-80s side. The club played at the ground just behind the Stanhope hotel and across the road from the site of the old Rodley railway station. They enjoyed their best campaign midway through their stay in the Dales in 1986, collecting the B Division crown in one of the tightest finishes to a season the league has known. They had started their Dales journey by winning B Division Section Two at the first time of asking in 1981 with Stebbings immediately making his mark. An unbeaten 82 in his 361 season's aggregate, which gave him sixth place in B Division's batting list, was backed up by picking up the league wicketkeeping prize with 26 victims. In the following campaign Bob Underwood's medium quick deliveries earned him top spot in the bowling averages. Stebbings was just a single short of his first century in the game at Civil Service in 1985 – but he finished the season with 668 runs and second placing in the B Division's averages. The title was then taken by losing fewer games than Leeds YMCA as both clubs finished on 62 points in 1986. The club merged with Horsforth from 1988 finishing at the foot of B Division in its last season in the Dales in 1991. Horsforth rejoined the Dales four seasons later for a further six campaigns making little impact this time around.

56. WORTLEY HIGHFIELD (1981–1983), YORKSHIRE SWITCHGEAR (1984–1986), DUNLOP & RANKIN (1987–1989).

The 1980s saw Wortley Highfield join the Dales Council from the Pudsey Sunday School League before evolving into the Yorkshire Switchgear side and finally becoming known as Dunlop & Rankin. They played, like many other sides over the years in the league, on the park at Farnley Hall, Old Farnley. The Wortley side managed just three seasons but in the first of those campaigns they had something to shout about – swing bowler Maurice Stead finishing eighth in the second teams' divisions bowling averages but top of the wicket-takers in the entire league, his 73 scalps costing him 8.26 runs apiece.

Though Yorkshire Switchgear's three year run in the Dales did not see them rise beyond the lower reaches of Division B they had an opening bowler in Dave Hardcastle capable of picking up his share of wickets and in their second campaign he finished runner-up in the divisional bowling averages with 53 victims costing him 8.06 runs apiece. Dunlop & Rankin closed the decade and the run by the three sides by finishing ninth of ten in Division B in 1989. The final game of their penultimate campaign

Meanwood's PPM Cup winning side of 1997. Back row, l to r. John Hamilton, scorer, M. Denney, I. Taylor, G. Walton, J. Shires, P. Dews, S. Shaw, R. Guthrie.
Front Row: R. Dobson, C. Roe, K. Bolton, capt., C. Dickinson, G. Child.

Lloyds Bank, champions of B Section in one of the tightest finishes in the league's history in 1986. Key players were leading bowler Malcolm Hall, back row, left, and captain Martin Connolly and wicketkeeper Peter Stebbings, front row, centre, and fourth from the left.

had, however, been noteworthy for J. Emmett who picked up all ten wickets in their clash with Cookridge for just 32 runs.

57. HIGH ROYDS (1982-1986. B Division winners: 1983).

High Royds played on the hospital ground at Guiseley which is now the home of Crompark. They ran out winners of B Division Section 2 in their first season in the league in 1982 with J. Barton hitting 428 runs and taking 42 wickets to finish the division's top all-rounder. Their encore was the B Division title in the following campaign when J. Broklebank's 37 victims gave him the league's wicketkeeping trophy. But it was in their final year in the Dales in 1986 when they really took off with the help of a couple of cricketers from Down Under. Chris Cumberland was the league's top batsman with 514 runs at an average of 46.73 with Simon Stirling runner up and also top all-rounder and top bowler with 60 wickets costing him just 6.37 runs apiece. Their efforts played a major role in steering the side to the runners-up slot in Division A.

58. NATIONAL WESTMINSTER BANK (1983-1999. Pool Paper Mills Cup winners: 1996).

The Bank side operated from Woodhall Playing Fields and had their first trophy winner in their first promotion season of 1988 when David Bottomley finished top of the B Division's batting averages. Once they arrived in the A Division, Paul Slater began to appear in the league bowling averages but it was as a batsman that he would hit the real heights. Before that though Gary Edwards would make his mark in 1995 hitting an unbeaten 166 against New Wortley in early July to set a new highest individual scoring record before going on to top the league batting list with a new league record average of 68.40. Slater was fourth, the pair of them hitting a total of 1200 runs, 684 provided by Edwards. With John Patrick and J. Henderson collecting 129 wickets between them, Nat West finished runners-up to Tong.

The following year saw the Bank lift the Pool Paper Mills Cup but then 1997 was Slater's year. He hit 774 runs to top the league averages on 55.28, finished eighth in the bowling averages and carried off the Division A all-rounder's prize. The trophy he won that was really special though was a new one presented by the then league president Les Thompson at the league's annual dinner to mark the first double hundred hit in the Dales – against Jarvis Porter in late August. Henderson had the last word for the Bank side, however, topping the league bowling averages in the club's final campaign in the Dales in 1999.

59. SANDMOOR (1985-1989).

Sandmoor played at the Alwoodley Recreation Ground in Alwoodley and first came to prominence in the 1986 season. It was then when they were runners up in the Division B Section 2 and two seasons later, by which time Division B had become a single competition of 10 teams, they were runners-up again with J. Wilkes topping the divisional bowling list for them with 74 wickets at an average of 7.63 runs apiece. Life in the A Division in their final season in the league saw them finish second bottom of the table but they had a great day on Whit Monday at Cookridge when Wilkes turned in the bowling performance of the season by claiming all ten wickets for 20 runs.

60. MEANWOOD (1987 onwards. League champions: 1998. D. Division winners: 1989, 1994, 2003. Pool Paper Mills Cup winners: 1989, 1994, 1997, 1998, 2002, 2003. Cawthorne Cup winners: 1995).

Of the sides to have joined the Dales in the last 20 years, Meanwood rank among the most successful, particularly hard to beat on their little ground at the back of the Myrtle Inn in Meanwood and particularly dominant in the league's premier knock-out competition, the Pool Paper Mills Cup.

Since joining the league in 1987 and winning promotion from B Division at the first attempt with Rob Guthrie and Pete Langley scoring almost 1,000 runs between them and Langley also picking up 43 wickets, the club's two sides have picked up team trophies into double figures (including the Pool Paper Mills Cup six times). In addition, the club finished level on points with the 2001 champions New Wortley and has suffered defeat in one cup final and tasted defeat in a further four semi-finals.

One of Meanwood's strongest features has been the progression of young players through the ranks and, in the cup final sides in 2000 and 2002, they had nine players who had been with the club since their teenage years. The club also boasts some of the league's most consistent performers with Guthrie one of the leading runmakers currently playing in the Dales Council. Former Meanwood junior Matthew Dyson is also a prolific all-rounder. With the ball, father and son Mick and Paul Dews have both been consistent wicket-takers for the club while the long-serving Graham Child's time at Meanwood covers the whole of the club's run in the Dales. The 2003 campaign brought him the league's second teams top batting average of 78.60, a season that also saw Stewart Dobson set a new bowling record with his 10 for four return against Shipley Prov. Regularly top five finishers in the A Division, Meanwood have built up some healthy rivalries, Dews, the younger and a former colleague of mine on the sports writing circuit, points out. "New Farnley, cup final scalps in 1989, were one of the club's first foes before the senior side moved into the Central Yorkshire League while Tong were another side Meanwood enjoyed some epic battles with," he said.

61. THORITE (1987-1993) LAWNS PARK (1994-1997). (B. Division winners: 1993).

Thorite, who also played in Farnley Hall park, finished sixth in Division B in their opening season in 1987, but gained promotion anyway. In their second campaign in the top sphere, Gary Sowden finished in the runners-up slot in the league batting averages having hit 577 runs while Mark Harrison and David Palmer shared 85 wickets as the team moved up to a comfortable mid-table position in Division A in 1990. The 1991 campaign then proved to be their most successful when they finished runners-up to champions Leeds Civil Service with Sowden, probably the cornerstone of the club's time in the Dales, and Mark Scaife sharing almost 900 runs to cement Thorite's season. But in the following campaign they went down only to bounce back as champions in 1993 with a massive 111 points, more runs from Sowden and a B. Division bowling prize for David Arundale, whose 69 wickets cost him just 5.84 runs apiece. Third in the bowling list was Harrison (the divisional all-rounder of the year) who claimed 82 wickets to underline the power of the Thorite attack.

In 1994 as Lawns Park, the club finished fourth in Division A with Sowden fourth in the league batting list but they left the league three years later after finishing at the foot of Division A with just three victories in their 22 games.

62. LEEDS CIVIL SERVICE (1988-1993. League champions: 1989, 1991. B Division winners: 1988).

The Leeds Civil Service club started life in 1948 as the Leeds Inland Revenue cricket club. Founded by the club's secretary of over 30 years John Gibson and Bert Charnley, the club played friendly cricket initially, went into the Barkston Ash league and from there joined the Dales Council. They played at Newton Road, Chapel Allerton, during their six years in the Dales and from the off in 1988 moved into over-drive by running away with the B Division title by a clear 11 points – a performance which was backed by a string of individual efforts which earned places in the averages.

Phillip Allinson, who had followed his father Bernard into the side, was runner-up in the B Division batting list with 416 runs at an average of 27.73 with Paul Merrick and captain Trevor McDonnell narrowly behind in third and fourth slots. Graham Simister was their leading wicket-taker finishing third in the bowling averages but there was more to come. The 1989 campaign brought the league title with Ian Hanley, a cousin of the famous Ellery, hitting over 500 runs to finish third in the batting averages and Kevin McGuinness running out top bowler with 81 wickets at an average of 6.93. He did it again in 1990 (79 wickets at 8.32) but his side suffered the heartache of missing out on the title by the narrowest of margins when both Cookridge and Civil Service finished on 77 points, Cookridge taking the trophy by virtue of winning the most games. There was no such close call the next time around as the Leeds Civil Service side went to their second league title in three seasons by seven clear points with Ian Long grabbing 40 wickets to top the league's bowling averages. But in 1992 they finished fourth in the table slipping to 11th out of Division A's 12 teams in their final season.

63. COOKRIDGE (1988 onwards. League champions: 1990. C Division winners: 1996. Pool Paper Mills Cup winners: 1990).

Formed in 1933, the Cookridge cricket club developed as a section of the Cookridge Sports Club which had been founded a little earlier for the benefit of local residents. Roots were put down in Smithy Lane in 1934 and 12 months later the cricket section became an independent self-financing body. During the Second World War the club's facilities were made available to the local Home Guard detachment with serious cricket resuming in 1946 when Norman Bradley was appointed secretary.

The Dales Council Cricket League — Match Report Sheet

Phone Result before 8.30pm to 0113 257 9963

Home Team: MEANWOOD v SHIPLEY PROV — Date: 2nd August 2000

FULL NAMES OF ALL PLAYERS MUST BE ENTERED ON THE REPORT SHEET

Name of 1st Batting Side: MEANWOOD

	Batsman	How Out	Bowler	Runs	FOW	
1	R. Guthrie	Ct & Bowled	Bull	54	1	184
2	G. Walton	Bowled	Walsh	120	2	197
3	M. Dyson	Bowled	Bull	18	3	239
4	D. Fletcher	Ct Belcher	Bull	24	4	248
5	M. Zubar	Ct Bull	Patterson	32	5	285
6	J. Monkhouse	Bowled	Bull	12	6	285
7	M. Lone	Not Out		2	7	291
8	S. Shaw	Ct Symcox	Bull	6	8	294
9	C. Dickinson	Bowled	Belcher	2	9	294
10	P. Dews	Bowled	Belcher	0	10	
11	S. Dobson	Not Out/Bowled	Belcher	0		

Time commenced 2.02 — Time completed 4.35 — Extras 24 — Total 294 — Wkts 9

Name of 2nd Batting Side: SHIPLEY PROV.

	Batsman	How Out	Bowler	Runs	FOW	
1	D. Belcher	Bowled	Dobson	4	1	8
2	S. Marsden	Not Out		6	2	8
3	J. Symcox	Ct Monkhouse	Dobson	0	3	12
4	P. Dearing	Bowled	Dobson	0	4	12
5	D. Burton	Bowled	Dobson	0	5	20
6	R. Beatley	Bowled	Dobson	2	6	24
7	C. McNulty	Bowled	Dobson	0	7	24
8	S. Horrell	Bowled	Dobson	0	8	28
9	W. Bull	Bowled	Dobson	0	9	28
10	G. Walsh	Bowled	Dobson	0	10	29
11	D. Pattison	Bowled	Dobson	0		

Time commenced 5.04 — Time completed 5.55 — Extras 17 — Total 29 — Wkts 10

Bowling Analysis (Meanwood)

	Bowler	Overs	Mdns	Runs	Wkts
1	D. Patterson	15	3	53	1
2	G. Walsh	11	-	72	1
3	W. Bull	15	1	103	5
4	J. Symcox	3	-	55	-
5	D. Belcher	1	-	2	2

Bowling Analysis (Shipley)

	Bowler	Overs	Mdns	Runs	Wkts
1	S. Dobson	6.1	5	4	10
2	P. Dews	5	3	8	-
3	S. Shaw	1	-	1	-

Notable Performances (all 50s to be timed and recorded)

G. Walton 50 in 60 minutes
R. Guthrie 50 in 80 minutes
S. Dobson 6.1-5-4-10 (League Bowling Record)

Umpires' Section — Time of Signing 6.10

	Name of Club	Total	Wkts	Overs
1st Innings	Meanwood	294	9	45
2nd Innings	Shipley Prov.	29	10	12.1

Comments (late starts etc)

Club	Fielding Point	Wicketkeeper	Fax Sheet to:
Meanwood	J. Monkhouse	C. Dickinson	0113 257 9963
Shipley Providence	D. Patterson	S. Marsden	

Signatures: ...... (16) S. Stafford (14)

Scorecard covering Stewart Dobson's 10 for four feat.

There was a major setback in 1971 when the pavilion was destroyed by fire but led by Barry Richardson, members and friends rallied round and the present buildings were ready for use by the start of the following season. After surviving threats from developers, the ground's freehold was purchased outright in 1979. The club joined the Dales Council in 1988 gaining promotion at the first attempt with long time servant Ron Mackenzie finishing fourth in the B Division bowling averages with 73 wickets at 8.49 runs apiece.

Robin Dewhirst topped the league's second elevens batting averages in the following season but it was 1990 when Cookridge hit the jackpot. After winning the Pool Paper Mills Cup they went to the double in one of the tightest finishes the league has known grabbing the league title by winning 15 of their 22 games against 13 won by Leeds Civil Service with both clubs finishing on 77 points to take the prize by virtue of most games won. Alan Perring and Andy Commery took 101 league wickets between them to spearhead the successful assault. Relegation in 1992 and 1995 (even though Neil Bonnington was B Division's top all-rounder that season) put Cookridge in C Division but they responded by taking the divisional title in 1996. The 1998 campaign brought the B Division bowling prize for Ian Lee, an effort matched by Mackenzie in the second team in D Division in the following season. Franklin Williams then claimed a place in the record book for second X1s in 2000 by smacking an unbeaten 186 against New Farnley in mid August but 2001 saw Cookridge finish second from the foot of B Division and at the foot of C Division and moving into the 2002 season with just one side.

64. TONG (1988–1999. League champions: 1995. Pool Paper Mills Cup winners: 1995).

League and Cup double winners in 1995, Tong played behind the Greyhound Public House in the village. Promotion from Division B came in their second season in the Dales when they were runners-up to Otley in 1989 and though they finished some distance behind the club from Wharfedale they did produce a league record seventh wicket partnership of 148 undefeated against them in mid June courtesy of Mick Holmes and Steve Burnhill. Then in a successful first season in the top flight they finished third to double winners Cookridge with Mike Rankin hitting 400 runs to be runner up in the batting league averages and K. Bradford cracking the fastest 50. Dave Hornby and Robert McCutcheon gave Tong another place in the record book with their ninth wicket unbroken stand of 126 against Crompark in 1994 and in the following campaign it was Tong's turn to join the list of league double winners. After lifting the knock-out cup they surged to the league title to win it with101 points, 13 clear of their nearest rivals Nat. West Bank. Paul Hudson hit 546 runs and Darren Holmes took 80 wickets in 1996 and Tong collected 102 points but they had to bow to Rodley in the league title race with the rest of the field a long way behind and the same placings persisted in 1997. Bridesmaids again for the third successive season in 1998 with three of their batsmen, Darren Holmes, Gareth Bottomley and Dave Rule in the top five in the league averages must have been especially hard to take but they soldiered on and in their final season in the league finished mid table to the latest double winners Mount.

65. NEW ROVER (1988–1997. B Division winners: 1995).

With the backing of the Richmond family and their keen club members, the New Rover club went from strength to strength in the 90s. But the club can trace its origins back to 1931 and youngsters playing in Potternewton Park, in the Chapeltown district of Leeds taking its name after a Rover Scout camp and playing its first game at Soldiers' Field, Roundhay, in mid June 1934 – winning against Belgrave C.C. For the next 50 years the club continued almost completely unchanged playing friendly cricket on the same pitch. But in the 80s the club had a thriving junior section and near the end of the decade the decision was taken to go into league cricket via the Dales Council. Ambitious plans to become a force in local cricket saw a sub-committee formed to find a suitable site for the club and by May, 1993, a 7.5-acre sloping cornfield in Adel was transformed into what is now one of the best local cricket grounds in the county. The club quickly made its mark in the Dales and in 1995 swept to the B Division championship with Michael Richmond, the son of the club's chairman Geoffrey Richmond, creating a batting record which it is difficult to see being overtaken. He hit almost 600 runs at an average of 97.50 to easily claim the divisional batting award while Richard Stevens weighed in with 99 wickets at an average of 7.84 as the title was taken with 105 points, nine ahead of runners-up Rodley. In 1998 the club moved on to play in the Leeds League and two years later went into the Wetherby League but members still retain fond memories of their time in the Dales. Meanwhile the ground, known as the Richmond Oval, was blossoming, too. In 1999 a partnership with the county side was set up with Yorkshire's academy squad using the club as its mid-week base. Keith Boyce, one of the top groundsmen in the game, was appointed as the club's full time groundsman; Yorkshire's first and second team squads now use the ground's superb facilities and already international sides have played at New Rover. It is all a far cry from those days in 1931, but the Dales Council can feel well satisfied that another of its clubs has enhanced the name of cricket.

*Keith Boyce working on the pitch
at New Rover.*

*Meanwood captain Kevin Bolton with
PPM Cup, 1997.*

Chapter 15.

EDWARDS - A MAN FOR ALL SEASONS
WITH A TEAM FOR ALL SEASONS

IN most cases in cricket it takes a day to set up a new record, in some cases it takes a season. Most records are vulnerable every weekend yet there is one in the Dales Council that will never be matched.

It belongs to wicketkeeper~batsman Mike Edwards who has been a fixture in the league since it started by playing in every season since the first in 1956. Most seasons it has been for the full nine yards though in recent times his knees have dictated the number of matches in which he has been able to play. However, he has always made at least the odd token appearance to maintain the sequence while still supporting the league in the middle as an umpire.

But as a player in the Dales it all started for him as a 13-year-old and now he looks back over the100s of games he has played for Wilson and Mathiesons, Leeds Zingari, Crompark and Pudsey Congs with great pride and pleasure. "Cricket in the Dales Council has been a way of life for me over the years. It has brought many wonderful memories and great times and I have played with and against many terrific players," he said.

He made his debut for W&M in the same season England beat Australia at Headingley for the first time – the game in which England had recalled Lancashire veteran Cyril Washbrook (who hit 98 in England's innings and 42 run victory) at the age of 41, 28 years older than the teenaged Edwards. "Even 23-year-olds in our team seemed old men to me when I first started never mind a forty-something playing for England," he recalls.

But after he had captained W&M to the B division title in the 1971 season it looked as though the run of 16 consecutive seasons playing in the Dales was over for him for he decided to go and live in Australia. The lure of Yorkshire (and maybe the Dales Council), however, was too strong and by the following July he had returned – just in time to keep his record going in the league he loved.

When W&M folded he joined Zingari in 1973 and stayed with them until 1990 when he moved on to Crompark before finally joining Pudsey Congs where his younger brother Kevin is still a formidable player. In 1995 he picked up the league's wicketkeeper's prize and still remembers well his top score (in 1991) in the Dales of 88 not out. "Those were the days," he smiles now.

But Edwards' remarkable run in the Dales has put him in a unique position in terms of remembering the players who have graced the league over the years and so I felt it fitting that if anyone should choose a team for all seasons it should be the league's player for all seasons. He points out that his team of teams will not be everyone's choice – "It's a personal choice of the players I have known, played with and against and respected. It has taken a bit of selecting but I just feel if somehow it had been possible to get them all together at their best they would have made up a team that in our class of cricket would have been invincible," he said.

So here, with selection thoughts in his own words, is the Edwards All Stars X1 (in batting order)

1. Peter O'Brien and 2. George Baines, Scalebor Park.

Peter was the more stylish of the two, very strong through the offside and generally a superb driver. George was much more unorthodox but they complemented each other well and their running between the wickets was second to none. There have been many other opening batsmen who were their equal, amongst them Jack Stones (W&M), Don Baker (Grove Hill, later to become Otley Town) and Peter Bullock of Leeds Zingari but I have chosen Pete and George because they were a pair.

3. David Pearce, Smiths Sports.

Although I didn't always see eye to eye with Dave (and most opponents didn't) his record speaks for itself.

4. Billy Russell, W&M

Mr Russell was my first hero in local cricket. My memories are not too clear because he was in the first Wilson's team I played in all those years ago but I remember a man with sleeves rolled down, shirt collar up, who seemed to hit the ball a mile. He bowled quickly, with a slingy action off a short run, similar to Craig White. I only knew him for a short while when I was very young because he died at an early age. Billy was part of a W&M team which included Jack Stones, Harry Moxon (a fairly rotund man who tied up his trousers with a neck-tie) George Harris, a Cockney, Cyril Mudd, a ginger haired fast bowler and Ronnie Dixon, who mended my first bat!

5. Peter Seaman, W&M

Peter was a top-class all-rounder – a destructive batsman, medium pace or off spin bowler and an exceptional fielder. He played in a W&M team which included Jimmy Lawrance, later of Leeds Zingari and Otley Town, Keith Cowgill, who went on to make a name in the Bradford League but who sadly passed away recently, and Jeff Walton, who could have gone on to be one of the best.

6. Kevin Edwards, W&M, Leeds Zingari & Pudsey Congs.

What can I say? Our kid! Who is still scoring runs and taking wickets.

7. **Kenny Booth, Smiths Sports and Farsley Celtic.**

Ken was a superb player, extremely quick when he was young and he could hit the ball as hard and as far as anyone. Yet another cricketer and friend who passed away much too early.

8. **Chris Cartmell, Leeds Zingari.**

Chris could be as quick as anyone in the Dales Council and was also a tremendous hitter. I would have loved to have seen both Kenny and Chris   batting and bowling together. I reckon a few sparks might have flown.

9. **David Hunter, Leeds Zingari.**

I have never met a braver cricketer, nor one I respected more, than David. He could have batted at No 4 in my team but I have chosen him because of his skill as a left arm spinner.

10. **Roy Webster, Oxford Place, Smiths, Farsley Celtic and Croma.**

Well, I couldn't pick me! So I've gone for the best wicketkeeper I played against in the Dales.

Kevin, left, and Mick Edwards.

Vince Edwards.

11. Vince Edwards, W&M.

Maybe I should have picked another spinner to balance my team but instead I chose my late father who could break partnerships and slog a bit. But my best memories are of his fielding. He was one of the best I saw and he could catch the proverbial swallow. So my dad can be captain.

Of course, the selection of a team like mine can be questioned. Why did I not pick Keith Smith of Turners Sports and Bramley Sports who surely could have played for Yorkshire had he gone to the Bradford League earlier, or Dave Benn of Smiths Sports as one of my fast bowlers, or even Eddie Fox of W&M. I could have picked two or three teams really. My selection in the end was based on ability, of course, but also on enjoyment of playing with and against the players I have chosen – and a little bit of sentiment, too!

Mike Edwards, 2002 season.

Leeds Zingari of the early 80s, Back row l to r. A. Pullsikis, K. Edwards, C. Cartmell, M. Edwards, D. Brannan, D. Hunter. Front row: P. Tate, D. Boscow, P. Bullock, C. Tate, D. Finn, S. Cartmell, M. Finn.

Chapter 16.
THE CLUBS:
Sides joining The Dales from 1989.

66. OTLEY (1989-1999. B. Division winners: 1989).

The latest of the sides from Otley to compete in the Dales carried the name of the town and played at the Prince Henry Grammar School grounds. They picked up the B Division title in their first season in the league by the massive margin of 20 points, losing only one of their 20 fixtures with T. Henry hitting more than 300 runs to finish third in the divisional batting awards and J. Hunt and R. Gardner sharing 64 wickets to claim places in the bowling averages.

But it was in Otley's second season in the top grade that they produced a record-breaker. In the tradition of the great players to represent teams from the area, Australian Peter Lewis, who had been just too late to register for Otley's Aire-Wharfe sides, took the A Division bowlers to task and hit 851 runs in 19 visits to the crease at an average of 50.06 to lift the league's 1991 batting award and set a new highest aggregate for a season in the Dales which is still standing. D. Dalby, with 72 wickets in the following campaign, then gave notice of his skill with the ball and in 1993 when Otley achieved their highest position in A Division in finishing runners-up to Pudsey Congs, he topped the league's bowling averages with 62 wickets at an average of 8.87, seeing off the challenge of three bowlers from champions Pudsey Congs, one of which was the blossoming Matthew Hoggard. Otley left the Dales in 1999 after finishing at the foot of A Division with 20 defeats in their 22-match league season.

67. WHITEHALL (1989 onwards. B Division winners: 1997. C. Division winners: 2002).

The Whitehall club, whose home is at Becketts Park, Headingley, was originally formed just after the Second World War by three brothers, Stan, Roly and Fred Bissett and their families and went under the name of Bissetts Mission, a small Sunday school near Armley Jail. After merging with Whitehall Road Methodists, the club played in the Leeds Sunday School League. From there it was the Leeds Combination League then the Barkston Ash League. They have played at Brown's Filed, Armley Park, Soldiers' Field, Farnley Park and Templenewsam before finding their way to Beckett's Park in 1986 and the Dales three years later.

Promotion came in 1992 as runners-up in B Division to Crompark with Ron Brady leading the way, hitting just one run short of 700 to give him a divisional winning average of 53.77. They finished in mid-table in their first campaign in A Division but Paul Rainford hit 743 runs to top the league averages with a record breaking average of 67.55. In the following campaign, however, the club finished at the foot of A Division and to compound their misery at the bottom of the second elevens' table, too. But with 100 points, they took the B Division title to claim their first team silverware in 1997 with A. Mandreker finishing runner-up in the divisional batting awards with four team-mates taking up the next four slots in the averages. David

Crozier claimed third position in the batting list to go with top prize in the bowling averages and the B Division's all-rounder award and, to round off a fine season for the club, Brady picked up the D Division's batting prize, too. But it was relegation again in 1998 though Mandrekar and Brady walked off with the batting awards in Divisions B and D in the following campaign. The club reverted to a single side playing in C Division in 2000 and in 2002 took the title with 18 victories in 22 games which produced 109 points and the divisional batting and all-rounder trophies for Zeb Jaffary.

68. OLD MODERNIANS (1989 onwards).

The Old Modernians club has its roots in the Leeds Boys Modern School founded in 1845. Some 50 or so years later following the formation of an Old Boys Union, a sports section was introduced though the cricket section remained nomadic until 1961 when the present ground in Cookridge Lane was acquired. They joined the Leeds League in 1978 and in 1991 a new changing room complex was erected by the Old Modernians Sports Association at a cost in excess of £50,000 to cater for the football and rugby sections as well as the cricketers. In the meantime the club entered a side in the Dales which now plays down the road at Bedquilts. Relegation from B Division in 1995 was followed by promotion in the following campaign when they finished in third spot in Division C and in 2000 they introduced a second side into the Dales.

69. CASTLEHILL (1990 onwards. B Division winners: 1990, 2003. Pool Paper Mills Cup winners: 1991).

The Castlehill club was formed in 1975 as an offshoot of Armley C.C. and took its name from the building society where the wife of Steve Prince, who ran the club, was employed. Two years on, there were sides in the Barkston Ash and in the Pudsey League and in 1990, when playing at Queen's Park, Pudsey, entry into the Dales was achieved with sides in the B and second elevens' divisions, the senior eleven taking the B Division title at the first attempt with Gary Edwards picking up the divisional

Whitehall at the turn of the millennium. Back row l to r. Ray Keeling, umpire, D. Redfearn, A. Calvert, D. Johnson, E. Taylor, M. Wood, D. Elsey. Front row: S. Mace, A. Mandraker, T. Lewis, D. Nash, D. Crozer, scorer, Les Green.

all-rounder's trophy. They struggled in the league in their initial season in A Division and went down with Pudsey St Lawrence but it was not all downhill for they beat Nat West Bank in the final of the Pool Paper Mills Cup at Esholt and in the seconds there was an unbeaten first wicket stand of 279 by M. Mills and Robert Keane against Whitehall while H. Thompson turned in a nine for 14 performance against Rodley. Edwards picked up the B Division all rounder's award again in 1992. But the loss of several experienced players had its effect in 1994 with relegation from Division B and re-application of league status required. A new venue at Corinthians Rugby Union club in South Leeds was organised and in 1996 promotion back to B Division was achieved as C Division runners-up with captain Steve Gautrey collecting the bowling award with 49 wickets at under 10 runs apiece. Runners-up again and promotion again in 1997 gave Castlehill a taste of life at the top and though they struggled they hung on to a Division A place. The league bowling prize was won by captain Dave Fenton in 2000 but following the loss of players and financial problems it was decided to close the second eleven and seek league permission to drop back into B Division. Hard times, but the club battled on winning on the last day of the 2001 campaign to stay up and in 2003 the smiles returned with the B Division title and runner's up spot in the batting averages for Fenton who included a big century in his 700-plus aggregate which gave him an average of 46.73. His runs also included 39 sixes over the campaign and with no previous record of season totals for six hitters in the league, a new slot in the league's record book was opened.

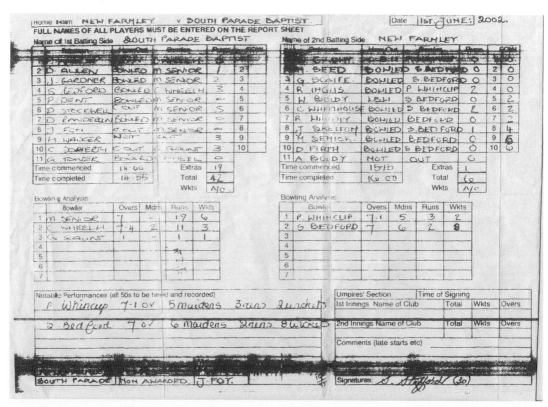

Scorecard covering South Parade Baptist's record equalling dismissal of New Farnley for six on June 1, 2002.

70. ARTHINGTON (1990-1998).

Amongst the most beautiful locations the league has enjoyed during its 50 years is at Arthington where matches are played in the shadow of a lovely country church on one side, a pond on the other and with the valley of the Wharfe stretching out into the distance beyond the ends of the wicket. Arthington started life in the Dales by gaining promotion as runners-up to Castlehill in their opening campaign in 1990 with David Samuel (575 runs) and Andrew Nichols (53 wickets) picking up the divisional batting and bowling awards. They reached third spot in the 1993 campaign when Mark Pennington, elder brother of their present captain Chris, was the league's top all-rounder. But they went down two seasons later and left the Dales to join the Nidderdale league after the 1998 campaign. Their ground, which has been used for cricket since 1864, is still played on in the Dales by Hawksworth.

71. ILKLEY (1991-1997. B Division winners: 1994).

The Ilkey club played at the Ilkley Grammar school ground at Ben Rhydding sweeping to the B Division title in 1994 unbeaten with 113 points from their 22 fixtures. They had three bowlers in the top four in B Division with C. D'Arcy taking the trophy with an average of 7.61. But their stay in the top flight was brief and after two more seasons in B Division they left the Dales.

72. ST CHAD'S BROOMFIELD (1992-1997).

The St Chad's side played at the Tetleys Sports Ground at Weetwood and made their first impact via the all-round skills of Alf Hull who finished second in the B Division batting averages in the 1994 season besides taking the divisional all-rounder's trophy. They remained in the B. Division during their six seasons in the Dales leaving in 1997 when they finished in 10th place in the 12 team division.

73. NORTH LEEDS (1994-1997).

North Leeds played at Roundhay School gaining promotion to the top flight in their first season in 1994 as runners-up to Ilkley. But after three seasons in the A Division during which they failed to get into the top half of the table they left the league.

74. JARVIS PORTER (1995-1997. Division B winners: 1996. Division C winners: 1995).

Jarvis Porter lasted just three seasons in the Dales. They played at Middleton Clearings and Gypsy Lane opening their account by winning C. Division in 1995 by 14 clear points with a total of 109 and the batting and bowling awards going to K. Frankland (623 runs) and Dean Simister (92 wickets). To underline their domination of the division John Metcalfe finished runner-up in the batting averages with 539 runs and Mick Walworth was third in the bowling averages with 47 wickets. The side did it all over again in the following campaign, too, this time with 112 points and a 12 point margin with Simister weighing in with 86 wickets in the runner's-up slot in the bowling averages. They left the league after the 1997 campaign during which they finished ninth out of 12 in Division A.

75. ALWOODLEY (1995-1997).

Yet another club with a three-year life span in the Dales, Alwoodley played at Stonegate Road playing fields and Cragg Lane, Alwoodley. During their brief stint they managed a best position of fifth in B Division in their final campaign in 1997.

76. HAWKSWORTH (1995 onwards).

Hawksworth beat the Dales to the golden milestone by three years. The club started life in Odda Lane, Hawksworth but had to leave the village in 1970 playing all their games away for a number of years. They moved in when Grove Hill left their park ground in Otley but after celebrating their 25th anniversary there they had to move once more when the Otley by-pass was built and eventually finished up at Yarnbury's grounds at Horsforth. They joined the Dales in 1995 playing at Bedquilts and then moved on once more to share Arthington's ground. Club president Keith Dibb, looking back on the club's formative years during the golden anniversary celebrations, recalled that some of the club's early matches played on Sundays had to finish at 6pm after a complaint from the local vicar. "He wanted matches to finish early so that players could go to Evensong. But it did not seem to make much difference to the size of the congregation," he said. "When we played at Hawksworth the wicket was fenced off with barbed wire and we had to remove all the cow claps before we could play." Captain Chris Yewdall, the only remaining Hawksworth-raised player in the team at the time of their golden year, immediately found his way into the batting averages in the club's first campaign in the Dales and has remained a regular fixture there most seasons since winning the C Division prize with 660 runs at an average of 36.66 in 1996. With 105 points in 2002 Hawksworth moved into B Division as runners-up to Whitehall with Terry Townsend claiming the C Division bowling prize with 50 wickets at 7 runs apiece and Yewdall runner-up in the batting awards.

77. MOUNT (1997 onwards. League champions: 1999, 2000. Division B winners: 1998. Division C winners: 1997. Pool Paper Mills Cup winners: 1999, 2000, 2004). MOUNT B (Division C winners: 1998. Cawthorne Cup winners: 1998, 1999, 2000, 2001). MOUNT PLEASANT (1999–2001. Division B winners: 1999).

Mount quickly found a top place in the Dales hall of fame by achieving the league and cup double feat in successive seasons after moving quickly up the divisions from the off. But to underline the power of the club, Mount B had also achieved a double by taking the C Division title and Cawthorne Cup in 1998 – the first of four successive cup successes.

The club started life in the Dales at Queen's Park, Pudsey, before giving their visitors a bit of a gallop to reach their home in the middle of the Pontefract Racecourse. Then, after three seasons, it was back to Batley and their present home at Hyrstland Park. The club was founded in the town in 1976 by Hanif Mayet, Farid Karolia and Yusuf Kathrada. "There was no opportunity for us to play as it was difficult for our youngsters to break into other teams so we decided to form a team of our own," said Mayet, chairman and captain at the club, who has been nicknamed Mr Mount after many years at the helm. Success in the Dewsbury and District League followed including victory in the Sheard Cup in 1981, when the club was still in Section B. As the first Asian side to win the trophy, they were now on the map and more success was to follow, not least the all ten wicket haul achieved by Yunus Patel against Ruddlesden in 1991. By 1997, Mount had moved on so much that they entered teams in the Dales, the Wakefield Warrior Second Division and the Barkston Ash Leeds League (two sides). Their run in the Dales was one of trophy after trophy as the millennium approached and then on into the new century they continued to be the team to beat. In 2002 their first team went to play in the Leeds West Riding League but as Mount Pleasant their second team finished fourth in the Dales A Division and their third eleven third in B Division.

78. RAMGARHIA SIKH (1997–2001), LEEDS SIKH (2002 onwards).

As Ramgarhia Sikh, the club started life in the Dales at Farnley Park before moving on to Solders Field at Roundhay. Promotion, as runners-up to the powerful Mount side, was achieved at the first attempt in 1997 with the C Division batting and bowling prizes lifted by A.S. Ryatt (with 305 runs at an average of 33.88) and J. Bharj (36 wickets at 7.80 runs apiece).

They moved up to the top flight the following season after taking joint second place in Division B with Farnley Hill with D.S. Ryatt taking the divisional batting prize this time after hitting 630 runs at an average of 70.00. They hung on in Division A initially, but moved up to finish in a respectable fifth position in 2001 by which time they had introduced a second eleven into the league with G. Makwana taking the under 18 all-rounder award – and retaining it in 2002 by which time the club had become Leeds Sikh. For the 2003 campaign the club moved on to play at the Leeds YMCA ground at Lawnswood.

79. SKELTONS WOOD (1997–2001).

Skeltons Wood had a brief run in the Dales playing at Skeltons Lane, north Leeds. They won promotion in 1999 as runners-up in Division C to Carr Manor with Ronnie Rainford topping the divisional bowling averages for them with 46 wickets at 6.13 just ahead of team-mate Kevin Duckworth who picked up 75 wickets with an average of 6.96 runs apiece. Their second eleven finished runners-up in Division D to give the club a promotion double. The 2000 campaign saw Rainford again as divisional top bowler, this time in B Division with Mark Burton following suit in C Division. Both sides finished in mid table positions in their final campaign.

80. BAILDON METHS. (1998 onwards. League champions: 2003. Division B winners: 2001. Cawthorne Cup winners: 2002).

One of the league's success stories of the years in the run-up to our golden anniversary, Baildon Meths went to their first league championship title in 2003 with 108 points. After claiming promotion in their first campaign in 1998 with sides in C and D Divisions, they introduced a third team in 1999 with their chairman and long time servant Don Butterfield hitting 633 runs to become the divisional top scorer of the season in B Division as his side climbed to the runners-up slot behind Mount Pleasant. They could manage no more than 11th position in the 12 strong A Division in 2000 but responded to relegation in the most spectacular fashion claiming the B Division championship in 2001 with a record 114 points with Butterfield averaging over 52 to take the batting prize and their paceman Mohammed Nawaz becoming only the second bowler in the league's history to go through the 100 league wickets in a season mark to top the divisional bowling list. For good measure, too, they reached the final of the Pool Paper Mills Cup. They then finished third in A Division in 2002 with their second team runners-up in B Division besides winning the Cawthorne Cup in a tight final with Crompark while the league batting prize went to the younger Butterfield, James, with an average of 44.30. Then came the big prize in 2003 when the league title was taken.

The club was formed in 1947 joining the Bradford Sunday School league in 1948 and plays at Sandal School, West Lane, Baildon, a ground with stunning views down the Aire Valley and across Bradford but it can be pretty cold there on a long afternoon in the field when the wind blows off the nearby Baildon Moor. They have two pitches at the school, the first and second teams play on the senior ground where the club pavilion is located while the third team share the second ground with Esholt. In addition to the three Saturday sides, the club also has an Under 17 side playing in the Bradford Central Junior competition plus a further side, which plays in the Bradford Evening League, both midweek teams playing on Wednesdays.

81. SHIPLEY PROVIDENCE (1998 onwards).

Surviving floods and the heavy loss of players in the early part of the millennium, Shipley Providence bounced back to put two sides out once more in 2004. Anyone who witnessed the devastation caused by the overflowing River Aire in 2000 must have wondered what the future held for clubs like the Shipley outfit as water from the river submerged their entire ground at Coach Road – and all but the roof of their pavilion, too. Then in 2003, the departure of players left them having to pull their second eleven out of the league in mid season while their forces struggled on conceding some big records but manfully keeping their heads above water, in a manner of speaking. To their credit they kept going and were rewarded with a new influx of players during the winter making possible the re-introduction of their second eleven for the following campaign.

Both their sides won promotion in their first season in the Dales in 1998, as runners-up in C Division and by finishing in third place in Division D with Don Pattison turning in the performance of the campaign when he took eight wickets for just one run (including five in an over with seven of his eight victims bowled). Third place in 2000 in B Division was enough for a place in the top flight but after two seasons in the penultimate spot at the foot of the table followed by their troubles of 2003 when they finished at the bottom of Division A there were then signs of a revival of fortunes. Throughout, however, the club has been well served by long standing members. As our league anniversary approached Syd Marsden, secretary since 1968, was still a playing member; Colin White joined the club in 1969 and had a run as chairman in the 80s before settling in as treasurer; Peter Lee joined in 1961, Barry Thorp, the late 60s, Chris McLaren, mid 70s and Pattison, the late 70s. Pattison has operated mainly in the second eleven regularly picking up in excess of 50 wickets over much of the quarter of a century to and beyond the millennium. The club's history can be traced back to the 1930s playing in the Shipley Churches League with the re-birth after the war years in 1945 largely down to Bill Lupton who just about on his own reclaimed the square which had become a pasture used by grazing cattle. In 1948 the club changed leagues to join the Bradford Mutual Sunday School League where they stayed until moving to the Dales.

Mount's Cawthorne Cup winning side of 2001.

82. CARR MANOR (1998–2002. Division C winners: 1999).

With sweeping views down the A1, watching and playing cricket at the Carr Manor ground had a lot to offer. They played at Bowcliffe Hall, near Bramham, and they picked up their first team silverware in the Dales in 1999 when they carried off the C Division title with a record at the time of 112 points which included 17 consecutive wins. They were 19 points clear of their nearest rivals Skeltons Wood with John Batty hitting 710 runs to win the divisional batting award for the second successive season with a new record average of 54.62. Runners-up to Farsley Celtic in 2000, they then moved up to the top flight while at the same time having introduced a second eleven in which P. Waring made his mark by carrying off the D Division bowling prize. Mohammad Yousef claimed 55 wickets to finish seventh in the bowling list in 2001 but Carr Manor left the Dales after the following campaign when finishing in 10th place in the 12 strong A Division. They had started life as Meanwood Methodist Church CC and became Carr Manor CC in the early 1950s. Interestingly their name was adopted because the club's home pitch was then on Stonegate Road, Meanwood, near the Manor House of the Carr Family which, in turn, gave its name to the Carr Manor Housing Estate. Over the years the club also played at the Red Hall playing fields off Wetherby Road and Soldiers' Field, Roundhay.

83. MOTIVATORS (1999–2000).

Just two seasons in the league, yet they have left their mark via the record book. They played at the Prince Philip Playing Field off the Leeds Ring Road at Meanwood gaining promotion after finishing in third place in the C Division table of 1999 but left the league after the following campaign when they were 11th out of 12 in Division B. In that first campaign, however, Terry Bowler picked up the divisional all-rounder's award besides playing his part in a new league record third wicket stand of 262 with Jonathan Collier against Shipley Prov. But the really special part of that early May afternoon was Collier's hitting which eventually brought him an unbeaten 253 and the league's highest individual scoring record. It was his first three figure score for the side and it included an astonishing 19 sixes and 18 fours. "Everything he hit just went. I think we lost about 12 balls and had to use old ones in the end," the captain Malkeet Singh said later.

84. CHURWELL (1999 onwards. Division C winners: 2003).

Churwell, who started life in the Dales sharing the ground at Throstles Nest with Farsley Celtic before moving on to Farnley Park, picked up their first team trophy in 2003 when they took the C Division title. It was a tight contest for much of the campaign with Esholt, Rodley and Kirkstall Educational all in the hunt before Churwell captured the crown with the batting

Don Butterfield.

Baildon's wicket-machine Mohammed Nawaz.

of Ian Dawson, who hit 385 runs to top the averages on 38.50, a key factor. There were placings in the bowling averages, too, for Mally Singh and Kevin Haley.

85. WIBSEY PARK CHAPEL (2000 onwards).

The first new club to join the Dales in the new century, they played their first season at the Bradford University grounds at Woodhall Lane, Calverley, before moving on to their Wibsey headquarters at Haycliffe Lane. The club was founded in 1887 as Park Chapel CC and joined the Bradford Mutual Sunday School League in 1908 playing there until 1998. At that time the club was the oldest surviving member of the league having missed just one season since joining. Originally the club members were drawn from the membership of Park Methodist Church in West Bowling and although that is not the case these days, the club still retains links with the church through a number of both playing and non-playing members. The club is proud of a record of 16 league titles in the Sunday School league playing in the top divisions of the league for most of the time. In 1999 the club modified their name to reflect the area in which they now operate. At the same time the club was accepted into the Bradford Central League where their two main sides played. A third eleven was retained in the Sunday School League before the move into the Dales with two sides in 2000.

In that first campaign their D Division academy side had the pleasure of seeing Tim Hanley top the batting averages with an unbeaten 99 in his 277 aggregate for the season with Colin Simons repeating the feat in the following campaign with almost 400 runs to his credit. The C Division side won promotion as runners-up to New Wortley with Andy Hirst leading the way by taking 46 wickets at 8.36 runs apiece to top the bowling list and it could have been even better for the swing bowler. He was robbed of the chance of taking all ten wickets at Crompark in early May when the home side were a man short. Hirst, 38, who had played from school with the club had had an eight for six, six years earlier but his analysis of 10.3 overs, 4 maiden, 16 runs and 9 wickets that day was all the more impressive because he had just got back in the side after hamstring and a double hernia problem. In their home fixture with Crompark in 2002 there was another noteworthy happening, too, when Peter Briggs made his league playing debut in the Dales where he was already well-known as an umpire of some standing. At 7ft 2 ins in height you could hardly miss the Wibsey player that day but it did cause a moment or two of smiles all round when the tallest man in the team, indeed in the league, was joined at the crease by Wibsey's tiniest player in 4ft 8 ins tall Gary Low. The club has an enviable crop of youngsters and they continue to progress - in 2003 the league's under 18 batting prize went to Matthew Walsh who hit 419 runs at an average of 38.09.

86. GARFORTH (2002).

Garforth, who played at Church Lane, Garforth, had just one season in the Dales finishing fifth out of 12 in Division B in 2002 with C. Field runner-up in the divisional batting awards with an average of 36.00. Cricket in the village can be traced back for more than 125 years with the Garforth Gentleman being formed in 1877.

87. SOUTH PARADE BAPTISTS (2002 onwards).

It took South Parade Baptists just over a month to find a place in the Dales Council record book. They went to New Farnley for an inter-divisional match on June 1, 2002, and after managing just 42 then whipped out the home side for six with Steve Bedford picking up eight wickets for two runs, six of his seven overs being maidens. The effort matched that of Eldwick back in 1980 who had dismissed New Wortley for the same score. P. Whincup, who picked up the other two wickets for three runs in the blitz, finished runner-up in the C Division bowling averages with 51 wickets at 7.31 apiece as the club gained promotion by finishing third in the table at their first attempt. They followed that by claiming the runners-up place in B Division in 2003 with Bedford topping the batting averages with 459 runs at 51.00, taking the runners-up spot in the bowling list with 33 victims at 9.09 and the divisional all-rounder's award. The part in the club's upward surge played by Dominic Allen was noteworthy, too, for he finished third in the bowling averages after bowling almost 300 overs to claim 63 wickets at 11.87 runs apiece.

The club was formed in 1946 by members of the South Parade church in Headingley, and played at various grounds in Headingley and Meanwood before settling down at Bedquilts in Adel in 1954. A junior team was started in the early 60s and after an initial setback there was an influx of young players and when they combined with others from the church there was a fine junior side playing on Saturday mornings which in turn improved the senior side. Over the years teamwork has been important at the club from the tea ladies to the opening batsmen with Edna Robinson picked out by the club for special mention for her work at teatime. In 1996 the club had their square re-laid, helped by donations from their 50th anniversary, while a year earlier the Carr Manor Cup was won with the Joe Dews Trophy claimed in 1999 and 2001 before the club moved on into the Dales.

88. KIRKSTALL EDUCATIONAL (2003 onwards, B Div. Champions 2004).

After making the early running, Kirkstall Educational finished in fourth position in Division C in their first campaign with S. Mahmood taking the runners-up slot in the bowling averages. The 2003 season was special at the club which was formed on April 4, 1853, their new venture in introducing their third Saturday X1 in the Dales helping to mark the club's 150th anniversary. A group of young men from the Kirkstall Educational Society, a literary club attached to St Stephen's Church school, conceived the idea of starting the club all those years ago and after four years at Kirkstall Abbey fields a move was made in 1857 to the club's present ground, then part of the Kirkstall Grange Estate.

Kirkstall became a founder member of Leeds Second Class League in 1893 and four years later moved to the Yorkshire Central League. The club has also played in the Yorkshire Council and joined the Leeds League in 1929. In 1999, the club's final season in the Leeds League, the first X1 finished as champions of Division One also reaching the final of the Hepworth Cup and in 2000 were champions of Division C in the Airedale & Wharfedale League. In the same year the club started a third X1 who play on Sundays while in 2002 their Under 13s were North Zone champions. The Dales side operates at Bedquilts and in 2004 set a new league points record of 122pts.

89. HALIFAX DIRECT CC (2004 onwards, C Div. Champions 2004).

One of two new sides for our final season before our golden anniversary year, Halifax Direct play at Bedquilts and was started by former players at Old Modernians, sharing their Dales team's pitch.

90. BURLEY PARK CC (2004 onwards).

The newly formed side started life at the Bradford University grounds at Woodhall, Pudsey. Many of the players had previous experience of playing in the Dales, notably at Whitehall. The club lifted the total number of clubs over the years in the Dales Council to a nice round figure of 90 but including all the clubs that have merged with others in the league during the first 50 years, there has been 115 different outfits in the Dales up to the start of the league's golden campaign in 2005. And we trust that by our 100th year in 2055 that number will have grown much higher.

Cricket lovely cricket
or WEATHER to play or not

All cricketers know about R.S.P. afternoons but floods and snowstorms? That's not cricket. Yet those who look after Dales grounds in the Aire valley, featured here, know all about tricky weather conditions.

The flooding River Aire engulfs the Shipley Prov ground in 2000 and almost submerges their pavilion. Welcome to the 21st century.

January 1, 1995, and county and local cricketers brave the snow at Esholt to launch Ashley Metcalfe's Yorkshire benefit year.

Five years later the Esholt ground is under water as the nearby River Aire bowls a googly.

AT THE DOUBLE......No 8.

Cricket, lovely cricket.... and when it matters to be Yorkshire-born

In a Grandstand finale to our AT THE DOUBLE features, the BBC Look North Presenter Harry Gration reveals just how much cricket means to him.

I AM the proud owner of two new twin boys. Well, there'd hardly be three would there? But their birth presented me with the realisation of just how much cricket meant to me.

The date was May 11th. I was covering a football match for Grandstand, the last match of the season, featuring Everton and the champions Manchester United. My wife was showing signs of starting labour but we thought it was a couple of days away. Anyway, to be on the safe side she accompanied me to the match, dutifully sitting in the car park waiting for my return. After the match I had to interview that nice Sir Alex Ferguson. To cut a long story short he kept me waiting ages before telling me "NO!". Unbeknown to me the missus was enjoying five minute contractions. Now the predicament – a Lancastrian birth.....or a race to Leeds. It had to be Leeds because I wanted them to play for Yorkshire. I was then reminded that Michael Vaughan was born in Lancashire and the birth qualification doesn't apply anymore. But to me it does matter.

I learnt my cricket at two great schools. Leeds Grammar and St Peter's School, York. The latter, in particular, was heaven for me. My mentor was the former Leicestershire captain David Kirby and my coach, an old Bradford League player called George Curry. It was George who introduced me to the Bradford League. My dad had played for Pudsey Britannia (I think) in the old days. He was a wicketkeeper. I was an opening bowler and bat. Very slow. Batsman that is. My trial in the second team was back in 1968 producing a haul of 5-46 and 32 not out. Then I played my next game. I came up against a brilliant West Indian batsman who proceeded to hit my first four deliveries for 4-4-6-2.....I ended up with 0 for 60 in four overs! It taught me a lot though.

Harry Gration.

Arnie Beech.

Peter Snape.

The sad thing about cricket these days, however, is that outside the leagues it is hardly being played. I did a survey only a year ago trying to find out how many schools in the Leeds area played competitive inter school matches. Only four. It's a similar story in many of the other areas in this great county, the home of cricket. League cricket, I am delighted to say, keeps the sport alive. I know of many clubs who run teams from under 7's through to under 16's. The problem though is trying to keep them after the age of 16. If you look at the cornerstones of league cricket they are made up of the likes of Barry Foster. They can be defined thus: once had ability, think they still have, and make themselves captain so they can't be dropped! But would any of us want it any other way?

Harry Gration, October, 2003.

At the double partner.................................Arnie Beech.

Few cricket people I have known can match the affection for the sport that was held by my former Yorkshire Post colleague Peter Snape who sadly is no longer with us. His features on local cricket and local cricket personalities in the newspaper were much loved and among them was one he put together on one of the Dales Council's most consistent bowlers, Arnie Beech. Beech is among the league's all-time leading wicket-takers and as such well qualifies to be included with the players featured alongside our personality writers in our AT THE DOUBLE series. It seems fitting, therefore, as we round off the series to re-print, with the kind permission of the Yorkshire Post, the article that appeared in the newspaper on June 15, 1979.

Beech achieves bowler's dream

ARNIE BEECH, 50 in December and troubled by arthritis in knee and elbow, achieved a lifetime's cricketing ambition on Saturday and did not realise he had done it. When he pushed the ball through a bit quicker to have the last Olicanian batsman stumped he was surrounded by his Smith's Sports colleagues congratulating him for taking all ten wickets for 25 runs.

"I didn't realise I had taken the first nine. I tend to lose track of statistics when I am concentrating on my bowling," he said.

"Suddenly they all crowded round me and I realised I had achieved the bowler's ultimate after more than 35 years striving for it.

"I was so tired it didn't really sink in on Saturday but the captain Keith Brattley is having the ball mounted for me and it will be my most treasured possession. I had had hat-tricks, eights and a 6-0 but never all ten." Of the ten, four were bowled, two caught, one stumped, one lbw and two caught and bowled. "One was wide of mid-on but I charged after it and caught it. I wasn't going to let it go – if the not out batsman had not been dropped I would have taken 11," he smiled.

A career spanning hundreds of wickets for Whitwood, Methley, Pudsey Britannia and the last 12 years for Smith's in the Dales Council has seen him drop from a 25-yard run to a gentle nine paces in which he tries a bit of everything with constant variation. This season he voluntarily stepped down to the second team even though the seniors still want his services. "Unless you give the youngsters a chance sooner or later you are a team of old men. That's no way to encourage youth to develop. Besides the first team has plenty of good bowlers."

A man who frankly admits he has no time for "fancy cap" cricketers still plays it as hard as ever. "I have no time for friendlies. I always aim to win," he points out. "I have seen matches lost by saying 'Their last man is only a little lad; let's give him a chance' and he has hit us all over the field. Youngsters have got to learn the hard way but that doesn't mean there is no room for a joke on the field. Nobody ever drops a catch on purpose."

Humour is an integral part of Beech's cricketing philosophy. "I remember at Methley the team was captained by the local vicar Ralph Emmerson who went on to become Bishop of Knaresborough. He was a lovely batsman but he was nonplussed when he complained of having water on the knee to a collier in his team. 'I can't understand you. Do you do much kneeling?'," was the reply. He looks at his arthritis in the same spirit. "The doctor tells me it is a sign of a mis-spent youth bowling fast in the Yorkshire Council. It was a little embarrassing two years ago when at the league dinner for I was due to go up to receive the bowling prize from Geoff Cope only to find my knees lock as I tried to get out of the chair."

LEAGUE CRICKET
Peter Snape

Although he does not rate his batting abilities, he scored an unbeaten 32 on Saturday as Smith's topped 200. "When I was a lad I rigged up the big room in my father's pub at Whitwood with mirrors to help me practice. Nevertheless I have always found bowling a more fascinating challenge." After the ultimate is there anything left? "Everyone will be gunning for me now so I'm going to gun for them. I shall be trying for all ten again every Saturday starting with Pool Paper Mills on Saturday. I want to play as long as I possibly can. When I get to 65 I might switch to left-arm over and they'll have to push my wheelchair up to the wicket before I'll give up."

A special moment for Ashley Metcalfe and in Yorkshire's history. It is August, 1983 at Park Avenue, Bradford, and with Geoff Boycott at the other end, the 19-year-old former Dales Council player is cracking the ball through the covers for the boundary against Nottinghamshire that takes him to a century on his debut, only the third player to achieve the landmark for the county.

Matthew Hoggard never faced anything like this when he was playing for Pudsey Congs. It is the last day of the 2nd Test against Pakistan, June, 2001, at Old Trafford and he is surrounded by Pakistan's finest having gone in to try and help Darren Gough. He survived the last ball of Saqlain's 47th over but England, having lost eight wickets for 60 runs after tea, fell in the next over to a hardly expected 108 runs defeat.

PLAYERS from the DALES COUNCIL who have gone on to play or be selected at COUNTY or NATIONAL levels

Name	Dales club	County	National side																	
				1	2	3	4	5	6	7	8	9	10	11	12	13	14	15	16	17
Matthew Doidge	Pudsey St Lawrence	Yorkshire																		
Matthew Hoggard	Pudsey Congs	Yorkshire	England																	
Ashley Metcalfe	Esholt	Yorkshire, Notts. Cumberland																		
David Leatherdale	Pudsey St Lawrence	Worcestershire																		
Des Finn	Leeds Zingari	Yorkshire																		
James Middlebrook	Pudsey Congs	Yorkshire, Essex																		
Gareth Clough	Pudsey St Lawrence	Notts.																		
Paul Hutchinson	Pudsey St Lawrence	Yorkshire, Sussex																		
Geoff Cope	Leeds Zingari	Yorkshire, Lincolnshire	England																	
Peter Whiteley	Pool Paper Mills	Yorkshire																		
Phil Carrick	Smiths, Pudsey Congs.	Yorkshire																		
Matthew Duce	Pudsey Congs	Trials with two counties																		
Katherine Leng	Pudsey St Lawrence	Yorkshire	England																	
Chris Taylor	Pudsey St Lawrence	Yorkshire																		
James Smith	Pudsey St Lawrence	Yorkshire																		
Paul Heaton	Esholt	Spain																		
Malcolm Franks	Esholt	*Spain																		

* selected. Did not play

Chapter 17.
Dales Record Breakers
The ten out of ten achievers

RIGHT from the moment Pool Paper Mills bowler Ken Wilkinson took three Netherfield wickets in successive deliveries during the first programme of matches of the then infant Dales Council on 28 April, 1956, the league has had record breaker after record breaker.

The 400 runs barrier has been blown apart at team level, batsmen have breached the 200 mark four times, a couple of bowlers have gone through the 100 league wickets in a season milestone and one bowler, with a spell of 10 wickets for no runs, hit a peak which is as good as it gets, almost.

Midway through the 2003 season Stewart Dobson shattered the league's best return with 10 wickets for four runs, a feat which in itself sits in the top handful, if not at the top, of cricket's greatest all time bowling performances in competitive league games anywhere. But add to that the fact that the four runs came BEFORE the first wicket was taken and you have figures, which cannot be beaten.

An amazing achievement really by the Meanwood all-rounder yet, of course, there have been many, many other notable performances by teams and individual players which have also added immeasurably to the fabric of the Dales Council's golden years – so many that to include them all would just about fill another book. But the record of the pick of those records has to start somewhere and the summer of 2003 proved to be a more appropriate time than most in our 50 years.

It was a scorcher: a special time for all kinds of reasons. Temperatures in England sizzled through the 100f mark for the first time as double hundred hitter Graeme Smith devoured the international record books - and England bowlers - when he led South Africa from the front on the national scene while at local level, as we already know, more than a little was stirring in the Dales.

In fact, in the space of 70 days in mid season, first two 25-year-old all-rounders, Dobson and Nick Oram, charged through the two top individual performance high water marks with ball and bat with unforgettable displays, then Mount produced a new highest league score. The three massive new records were all established in games against the same side, too, Shipley Providence finding few comfort zones as they battled through a campaign in which little went their way.

"We lost three players before the season opened and our captain during the week it started so we went into the campaign with 16 players including two 12-year-olds for our two sides. We tried but we soon had to withdraw our second team from the league," said Shipley's secretary of 35 years,

Syd Marsden. "Basically we had what amounted to a C Division side operating in the A Division and when the season finished we were just pleased to have got through it without having to give a match away. It was tough but we got home in the end."

First, New Farnley's Oram gave the Shipley bowlers a torrid afternoon as he blasted his way to a new Division A highest score cracking 158 in boundaries on the banks of the River Aire in his total of 208. In early August it was the turn of Shipley's batsmen to suffer as Dobson demolished them with his unbelievable 10-wicket spell on Meanwood's homely little patch behind the Myrtle Public House. The only runs he conceded turned out to be the boundary clipped through the slips in his first over and after that no one could lay a meaningful bat on his deliveries. As if that was not enough, however, before August was spent Mount then tore into Shipley's attack once more by the river to finish within a whisker of the 400 mark with just three wickets down.

Reviewing the individual performances, Dobson's achievement has the look of a once in a lifetime effort with the ball. But Oram was not far behind for while his top innings was the high point of his season, the New Zealander went on to finish with 750 league runs to top the league batting list with an average of 62.50 besides taking his share of wickets with a final haul of 50 at 14.72 runs apiece. And for good measure he picked up the top all-rounder award, too.

Oram, from Christchurch, had arrived in England the previous November. "I was always coming to Leeds to play because one of the lads who played here at New Farnley came down to NZ and played in the team I was captaining in Wellington. He made it clear that when I made it to England I should pop up to Yorkshire. After all, Yorkshire is cricket – that's the way we think about the county on our side of the planet," he said at the end of the season.

"It's been a great season for me personally but I'll always remember that particular innings. I think I managed to put about six in the river but I knew from early on it was going to be one of those special days. I got the first boundary right in the screws as we say and with our chairman John (Baldwin) at the other end, I was able to play my shots," said Oram whose cousin Jacob was playing in the New Zealand one day side at the time.

The Farnley side lost opener Mark Seed to a first ball duck but Oram and Baldwin then re-wrote the record for the league's second wicket highest partnership held by Smiths pair David Pearce and Tony Metcalfe for 26 years. Baldwin stroked 67 in the stand of 239 while Oram was collecting 23 fours and 11 sixes in his record effort, bringing up his 200 with one six into the river. "It was an outstanding innings by Nick, I just stood at the other end and applauded. He's a super lad to have at our club, it doesn't matter what job he's doing for us he just gets on with it. He's a great all round character," said Baldwin.

But to their credit Shipley did not buckle under the weight of a New Farnley declared total of 310 for four. Their all-rounder David Belcher led the way for them by following up his 17 over stint with a knock of 80 in their draw-earning 164 for 2. Belcher, in fact, went on to hit 500 runs in Shipley's unhappy season finishing a creditable ninth in the league batting list with an average of 33.33.

Seven weeks on, Dobson's day was the prelude to yet another big weekend for Meanwood who went on to win the Pool Paper Mills Cup the following afternoon in a one sided game against

A mock-up on the New Farnley scoreboard of the detail of the record second wicket stand of Nick Oram and John Baldwin with the pair on hand to celebrate.

Phone Result before 8.30pm to 0113 257 9963   **The Dales Council Cricket League**   Match Report Sheet

Home Team SHIPLEY PROVIDENCE v NEW FARNLEY   Date 14·6·03

FULL NAMES OF ALL PLAYERS MUST BE ENTERED ON THE REPORT SHEET

Name of 1st Batting Side NEW FARNLEY

	Batsman	How Out	Bowler	Runs	FOW	
1	J. BALDWIN	B. ATKINSON	W. BULL	67	1	3
2	M. SEED	B MARSDEN	D. BELCHER	0	2	242
3	N. ORAM	CT + BWLD	C. WARD	208	3	310
4	W. PINNOCK	NOT	OUT	17	4	310
5	I. SIMPSON	LBW	C. WARD	0	5	
6	R. GRIMES	NOT	OUT	0	6	
7	G. SOWDEN				7	
8	B. COOPER				8	
9	D. SANDERSON	D.N.B.			9	
10	K. IRWIN				10	
11	N. BULLOCK					

Time commenced	2·00	Extras	18	
Time completed	4·22	Total	310	DEC
		Wkts	4	

Name of 2nd Batting Side

	Batsman	How Out	Bowler	Runs	FOW	
1	J. SYMCOX	W. PINNOCK	G. SOWDEN	32	1	112
2	D. BELCHER	K. IRWIN	G. SOWDEN	80	2	140
3	C. WARD	NOT OUT		30	3	
4	R. ATKINSON	NOT OUT		1	4	
5	D. WARD				5	
6	C. McNULTY				6	
7	W. BULL				7	
8	S. MARSDEN	} D.N.B.			8	
9	S. HORRELL				9	
10	D. ATKINSON				10	
11	J. ATKINSON					

Time commenced	4·42	Extras	21	
Time completed	7·00	Total	164	
		Wkts	2	

Bowling Analysis

	Bowler	Overs	Mdns	Runs	Wkts
1	D. ATKINSON	17	1	128	—
2	D. BELCHER	17	2	100	1
3	W. BULL	4	—	48	1
4	C. WARD	4	—	24	2
5				294	
6				16	BYES
7				310	

Bowling Analysis

	Bowler	Overs	Mdns	Runs	Wkts
1	N. ORAM	13	5	23	—
2	D. SANDERSON	13	4	29	—
3	I. SIMPSON	3	—	17	—
4	B. COOPER	4	—	9	—
5	K. IRWIN	6	—	31	—
6	G. SOWDEN	5	—	16	2
7	W. PINNOCK	2	—	8	—
8	R. GRIMES	1		16	

149
15 BYES +L/B 76
164

Notable Performances (all 50s to be timed and recorded)

N. ORAM 208 HIGHEST INDIVIDUAL SCORE A DIVISION
N. ORAM + J. BALDWIN 239 PARTNERSHIP 2ND WICKET
(NEW LEAGUE RECORD)

Umpires' Section		Time of Signing	
1st Innings Name of Club	Total	Wkts	Overs
NEW FARNLEY	310	4	42
2nd Innings Name of Club	Total	Wkts	Overs
SHIPLEY PROVIDENCE	164	2	48
Comments (late starts etc)			

Club	Fielding Point	Wicketkeeper	Fax Sheet to:
SHIPLEY PROV	D. WARD	S. MARSDEN	0113 257 9963
NEW FARNLEY	K. IRWIN	M. SEED	

Signatures:

The scorecard recording the Oram-Baldwin records for New Farnley of 2003.

Crompark. While he watched Rob Guthrie take the individual honours with an unbeaten 82 in the cup triumph, Dobson reflected on his moment of glory. "I'd taken over as skipper because Gary Walton, our captain, had injured a foot while batting through the innings and didn't go out to field with the cup final coming up. He needed to rest the injury," said the 10-wicket man.

Meanwood had managed 294 for nine with Walton helping himself to a century before Dobson got to work with his fast medium deliveries. He quickly conceded four but then it was all downhill as he claimed nine of his victims by bowling them, the second wicket falling to a catch in the gully. The Shipley side managed just 29 with Marsden finishing as their top scorer - unbeaten on six but never having to face the whirlwind.

"I did feel a bit sorry for them and since I was acting captain I was debating whether to bring myself off after I'd taken about six wickets but the lads would have none of that insisting I should be using the spell to get ready for today's final," said Dobson whose final analysis was 6.1 overs, five maidens, four runs and 10 wickets. With Shipley picking up 17 of their runs in extras as eight of them fell without scoring, it was a day to forget for them.

It was Dobson's first ten-wicket haul and the first time any bowler had managed it in the Dales Council without conceding at least double figures. The Meanwood born accountant's previous best return had been eight for 17 while playing for Highbury seconds against Garforth in the Leeds League. Like Oram, he has cricket Down Under to thank for developing some of his game, too, for in a seven-month spell playing in Australia with Tatura, a Melbourne club, he finished their campaign as leading wicket taker with 26 victims.

But Shipley's misery was far from over after the big two had done their damage for up stepped Mount to inflict more torment - their 398 for three total on August 23 topping their own record of five years earlier against Arthington by 22 runs. It was still 30 runs shy of the highest cup innings of 428 for 6 hoisted in 40 overs by New Wortley against Esholt fifteen months earlier but the best in 45 league overs mainly due to an unbroken partnership of 202 by H. Javed and N. Khan.

Michael Richmond.

Stewart Dobson.

"Against Meanwood we simply did not have the batting to cope with Dobson on a green wicket; Oram just hit everything, he looked far too good for our league and we made the mistake of putting Mount in on a very hot day in the hope of making a game of it. But they chased the record," explained Marsden.

It was hard on Shipley Providence but the shattering of a trio of major records gave the summer of 2003 – which also saw Graham Child (Meanwood) create a new highest second teams' batting average of 78.60 - a special place in the league's annals. Yet many of our seasons have found other luminaries of rare standing and maybe now we can move them into focus – like the nine clubs to have achieved the league double of champions and Pool Paper Mills Cup winners.

Green Lane became the first double winners in 1960 to be followed by Otley Mills, Smiths Sports, New Farnley, Cookridge, Tong, Meanwood, Mount and New Wortley. In 1992 New Farnley became the first club to carry off all three top league trophies in the same campaign when they added the Cawthorne Cup to their double achievement and seven years later Mount did the same, doing it again the following season to underline their dominance of the Dales at the turn of the millennium.

The first side to achieve over 100 points in a season was the Bramley Sports team in 1980 when they took the Division B title with 102 points from 26 games. At that time it was 5 points for a

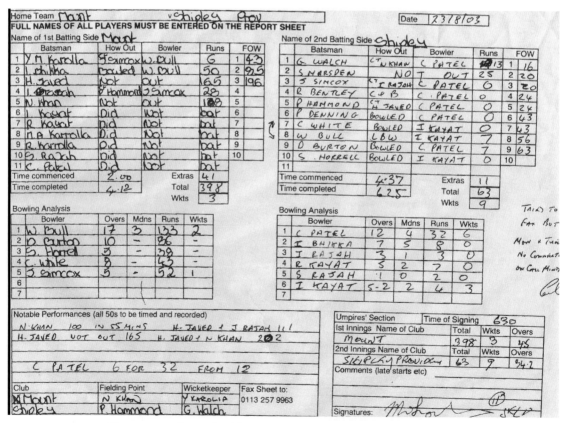

The scorecard covering Mount's record highest league total in 2003.

win but in addition to the 95 points they claimed from 19 victories and the five they collected from three drawn games they also picked up two points from a tied game. Croma, with 19 wins in 22 games in 1985, set a new record for most points in a season in Division A with 99 points but following the introduction of six points for a victory it became a regular occurrence for clubs to go through the century mark in league points.

In fact, in 2002 three clubs in the same division all collected more than 100 points, Whitehall winning the Division C title with 109 points from Hawksworth (105) and South Parade Baptists (101). The best haul though is held by Kirkstall Eds. who won the Division B title with 122 points (19 wins from 22 matches and no defeats) in 2004.

Meanwood (297 for 8) and New Wortley (300 for 4) combined a year earlier to create the record aggregate for one match, just three short of 600, while the 10 managed by Netherfield Sports against Crompark in 1957 remains the lowest score by a side in a first team game. In second eleven league games the lowest score against a full eleven stands at six – by New Wortley (against Eldwick in 1980) and New Farnley (against South Parade Baptists in 2002). In 1965, however, Netherfield managed just eight when they had only eight men in a match against Esholt and three years later Leeds Zingari were dismissed for five when they had only nine players when facing Otley Mills.

Michael Richmond is the only batsman to have broken the 60-plus average mark for the season twice with his astonishing average of 97.5 for New Rover in 1995 the highest yet recorded. He followed that up 12 months later with an average of 62.81 but the first batsman to break the 60-plus barrier was John Mortimer who clocked in with 61.13 in 1981 for Leeds YMCA.

Malcom Dibb, the Green Lane opener, was the first to go through the 700 mark when the league was in its fourth season in 1959. Since then a further 14 batsmen have managed more than 700 runs, three of them topping the 800 mark. It was 1991 before Australian Peter Lewis, in a one-off season for Otley, became the first member of the 800 club when his 851 league runs took him to the still standing highest season's aggregate. Reg Parker, showing you cannot keep a good old 'un down, scored 815 in 1995 when he was a mere 70 years old and Akhlaq Ahmed of New Wortley then accumulated 807 in 2001 – and at one point in 2003, it looked like Oram would top the lot. But it was not to be.

Richmond's magical season coincided with the league's ruby anniversary campaign. It was a time when Dales Council bowlers rarely got him out – in fact he was unbeaten in eight out of 14 league visits to the crease as he built up an average which might have gone through the three figure mark had Bradford City not been part of the calculations!

The teenager needed just a further unbeaten 15 runs with one league game left to finish the season with a landmark few cricketers have achieved wherever the game has been played – an average of 100 – but he gave up the opportunity to follow City. New Rover had already made sure of the Division B title with their game at Wibsey still to play. "I decided to follow City down at Wrexham instead of playing cricket. Dad (Geoffrey) was chairman at City but I was a fan and wanted to be there at all costs," he said.

"It would have been nice to have achieved the 100 average and I suppose I'm very unlikely to get another chance at it but I was still at school and just keen to see all City's games at that time. It would have been even more difficult for me if we had still been going for the championship at New Rover. But while individual awards are great, they are very much of secondary importance – being part of the team comes first and, after all, we had the title in the bag," said the young Richmond whose aggregate of 585 runs included a top score of 90.

Sidney Newton, with an unbeaten 107, for Ross Mills in May, 1956, was the league's first centurion while David Pearce, with 11,809 runs to his name, holds the record for the highest aggregate in all competitive Dales Council matches. The highest average for a season in Division A is held by Nat West batsman Gary Edwards who had an unbeaten 166 in his 684 runs in 1995. It secured him an average of 68.40, some way below Richmond's B. Division effort in the same campaign, but some way above anyone else in the top sphere that season.

John Batty (Carr Manor) with an average of 54.62 in 1999 holds the record in Division C while the highest innings in Division B stands at 157 and was hit by D. S. Ryatt for Ramgarhia Sikh in 1998 when he was on his way to an average of 70.00 while scoring 630 runs in nine knocks. (A minimum of eight visits to the wicket was required that season in B Division to qualify for the averages). The highest average for second elevens is held by Graham Child (Meanwood) with 78.60 in 2003 while the highest individual score for second elevens stands at 186no, hit by F. Williams in the Cookridge v New Farnley game in 2000.

In cup cricket the unbeaten 183 by Paul Kirby in Crompark's game with Otley in May, 1996, tops the list. "I'd had a bad spell and could barely hit a run so I decided to go for it and it came off," said Kirby later. "I have to admit though the gods were with me, we were playing a pretty young side and they dropped me around five times so I just kept hitting. It was one of those days when everything went my way though the following innings when I managed a century against Meanwood was far more satisfying because I managed it without giving a really clear chance."

Oram's 208 in 2003 gave him the highest individual score in A Division cricket. It was the fourth double hundred hit in the league following Paul Slater's 200 for Nat West against Jarvis Porter in 1997, the unbeaten 253 from Motivators' Jonathan Collier against Shipley Providence in 1999 (which still stands as the highest score hit by anyone in the league and obviously the top score by a Division C batsman) and Neil Kettle's 206 not out for Rodley against New Wortley in 2000. Collier's astonishing innings saw him lose 12 balls on his way to 18 fours and 19 sixes in a league record third wicket partnership of 262 with Terry Bowler. He was 24 at the time and played in just

Mick Wright.

Ralph Middlebrook.

Terry Drury.

one campaign in the Dales. On the issue of six hitters, a new slot in the league records was introduced in the 2003 season with Dave Fenton, the Castlehill batsman, finishing with a total of 39 for the campaign.

Paul Renton of English Electric was the first bowler to manage an average for a campaign of less than four runs per wicket when he returned figures of 3.85 in 1958 but that was when the qualification mark in the lower division was 25 wickets and he collected 27. Tony Imeson's 87 wickets in 1961 cost him only 3.77 runs apiece when the qualification factor had settled into its present day target of 30 wickets for the campaign but that was clipped by .06 by Wilson and Mathiesons' bowler Eddie Fox five years later when his haul of 63 wickets cost just 3.71 runs each.

Exceptional weather conditions saw the qualification figure reduced for a one off time in 1998 to open the door for the all time low return from Rodley's veteran Mick Wright when he topped D section's bowling figures with his tricky slow stuff with a staggering average of just 2.84 after conceding just 71 runs in the season and taking 25 wickets.

But there has never been a bowling effort to match that managed by Gordon (Gloss) Sample in the first season of the league when he claimed 111 league wickets. Mohammed Nawaz, with 101 league scalps in 2001 is the only other bowler to break the century mark in the league though when it comes to career aggregates the Smiths, and later Farsley Celtic pair, Kenny Booth and Arnie Beech take some matching claiming over 2,100 wickets between them.

Their team-mate through much of his prime at Smiths, Roy Webster stands out as the master wicketkeeper of the Dales. He holds the record for victims in a single season of 52 (40 in the league) in 1976 and counts 500 dismissals to his credit in all his Dales Council outings. The final blow when it comes to records though has to go to Rodley's Ian Dobson who, in 1985, became

Bramley Sports D Division title winning side of 1981 celebrate.
Back row l to r. J. Paterson, I. Dobson, M. Kay, E. Taylor.
Middle row: C. Vorley, S. Fenton, M. Brown, H. Speight.
Front row: S. Tempest, M Knapton, J. Fenton, capt. Four years later
Ian Dobson (then with Rodley) and Mick Knapton (Farsley Celtic)
would face each other in the six sixes in an over episode.

Paul Kirby.

the only league player so far to smash six sixes in one over – ironically off the bowling of a former Rodley player Mick Knapton who was then playing for Farsley Celtic and who can still smile about those torrid few minutes! Dobson went on to 97 before being run out - and for good measure the all-rounder picked up five wickets that afternoon, too.

Highest partnerships for each wicket

1st.	233	R. Guthrie & M. Lone.	Meanwood v. Crompark.	5.5.01
2nd.	239	J. Baldwin & N. Oram.	New Farnley v.Shipley Prov.	14.5.03
3rd.	262	J. Collier & T. Bowler.	Motivators v. Shipley Prov.	1.5.99
4th.	190	R. Shuttleworth & M. Franks	Esholt v. Tong Park.	1957
5th	182	P. Blackburn & G. Sharpe	Pudsey St Law. V. Motivators	17.6.00
6th	141*	L. Fussey & G. Brown	Rodley v. Adel.	23.6.84
7th	148	M. Holmes & S. Burnhill	Tong v. Otley	24.6.89
8th	127	J. Petty & B. Horner	Farsley v. Hawkesworth	2.8.97
9th	126*	D. Hornby & B. McCutcheon	Tong v. Crompark	1994.
10th	93*	P Shires & N. French	Adel v. Crompark	17.6.89
Cup	224	C. Ford & P. Allinson	Adel v. Morton Banks	4.5.86

First tied game in the league

June 23, 1956 when Netherfield and Pool Paper Mills both hit 63 in a second elevens' fixture.

Players who have topped batting and bowling averages in the same season

Section A: T. Drury (Holbeck Beth), 1966.   **Section B:** R. Middlebrook (Pud Congs), 1970.

Players who have taken 10 wickets in an innings: G. Sample (Green Lane v Ross Mills 10-28, 1957); P. Hargreaves (W & M v R Gaunts 10-36, 1959); J. Sharpe (Leeds Zingari v Smiths 10-23, 1961); A. Imeson (Bramley S v R Gaunts 10-16, 1963); A Beech (Smiths v Olicanians 10-25, 1979); A. Kingett (E & Gilstead v N Farnley 10-31, 1980); T. Fletcher (Croma v N Farnley 10-28, 1982); P. Bell (B Rhydding v Farsley C 10-48, 1985); A. Arslan (N Wortley v C Service 10-23, 1988); P. Dwyer (Pudsey C v Sandmoor 10-22, 1988); J. Emmett (Dun & R v.Cookridge 10-32, 1988); J. Wilkes (Sandmoor v Cookridge 10-10, 1989); S. Dickens (Rodley v Castlehill 10-32 , 2000); S. Dobson (Meanwood v Ship. P 10-4, 2003).

Players who have carried their bat throughout an innings: E. Gill (Smiths v Crompark 22 no and v W & M 9 no, both 1958); J. Mahoney (PPM v Turners 72 no 1964); L. Heaton (Esholt v R Gaunts 46 no 1964); D. Elsworth (Bramley S v N Farnley 47 no 1967 and for Rodley v B Rhydding 82 no 1983); B. Rhodes (Smiths v Crompark 137 no 1972); T. Morton (Pudsey C v Bramley S 46 no 1978); R. Turner (Leeds YMCA v Pud S L 32 no 1980); M. Wright (Rodley v Thorite 15 no 1988); M. Connolly (Horsforth v Rodley 9 no 1988); M. Brown (Rodley v Castlehill 54 no 1990); N. Bonnington (Cookridge v Rodley 15 no 1995).

Team with best points total: With the league's 50th year opening just under a month away, fittingly, Kirkstall Educational completed the 2004 campaign on a new league record number of points of 122 out a possible 132 with 19 victories and no defeats

2005
CALENDAR

Farnley Park, over the years home for three Dales sides most Saturday afternoons.

The Dales Council Cricket League's
Golden Anniversary Year
1955 to 2005

JANUARY, 2005.

Esholt with a light covering of snow to start the New Year.

S	M	T	W	T	F	S
						1
2	3	4	5	6	7	8
9	10	11	12	13	14	15
16	17	18	19	20	21	22
23	24	25	26	27	28	29
30	31					

FEBRUARY, 2005.

Meanwood with Spring almost in the air.

S	M	T	W	T	F	S
		1	2	3	4	5
6	7	8	9	10	11	12
13	14	15	16	17	18	19
20	21	22	23	24	25	26
27	28					

MARCH, 2005.

Cookridge – and stalwart Gerry Redshaw goes for a mighty cut shot.

S	M	T	W	T	F	S
		1	2	3	4	5
6	7	8	9	10	11	12
13	14	15	16	17	18	19
20	21	22	23	24	25	26
27	28	29	30	31		

APRIL, 2005.

Pudsey Congs, scene of many Dales Council Cup finals.

S	M	T	W	T	F	S
					1	2
3	4	5	6	7	8	9
10	11	12	13	14	15	16
17	18	19	20	21	22	23
24	25	26	27	28	29	30

MAY, 2005.

Olicanians, under the shadow of the famous Cow and Calf rocks.

S	M	T	W	T	F	S
1	2	3	4	5	6	7
8	9	10	11	12	13	14
15	16	17	18	19	20	21
22	23	24	25	26	27	28
29	30	31				

JUNE, 2005.

Arthington, one of the gems of cricket in Wharfedale.

S	M	T	W	T	F	S
			1	2	3	4
5	6	7	8	9	10	11
12	13	14	15	16	17	18
19	20	21	22	23	24	25
26	27	28	29	30		

JULY, 2005.

Bedquilts, Adel. Plenty of space for hitting hundreds.

S	M	T	W	T	F	S
					1	2
3	4	5	6	7	8	9
10	11	12	13	14	15	16
17	18	19	20	21	22	23
24	25	26	27	28	29	30
31						

AUGUST, 2005.

Shipley Providence's Don Pattison seen in action from the banks of the River Aire.

S	M	T	W	T	F	S
	1	2	3	4	5	6
7	8	9	10	11	12	13
14	15	16	17	18	19	20
21	22	23	24	25	26	27
28	29	30	31			

SEPTEMBER, 2005.

Pudsey St Lawrence, looking towards the Sir Leonard Hutton Memorial Gates.

S	M	T	W	T	F	S
			1	2	3	
4	5	6	7	8	9	10
11	12	13	14	15	16	17
18	19	20	21	22	23	24
25	26	27	28	29	30	

OCTOBER, 2005.

Tong Park, one of the country's most beautiful settings for a cricket ground.

S	M	T	W	T	F	S
						1
2	3	4	5	6	7	8
9	10	11	12	13	14	15
16	17	18	19	20	21	22
23	24	25	26	27	28	29
30	31					

NOVEMBER, 2005.

New Rover, good enough for county and international players these days.

S	M	T	W	T	F	S
		1	2	3	4	5
6	7	8	9	10	11	12
13	14	15	16	17	18	19
20	21	22	23	24	25	26
27	28	29	30			

DECEMBER, 2005.

Eldwick and Gilstead, next door to the well-known Dick Hudson's hostelry and beneath the moor in mid winter.

S	M	T	W	T	F	S
			1	2	3	
			1	2	3	

S	M	T	W	T	F	S
			1	2	3
4	5	6	7	8	9	10
11	12	13	14	15	16	17
18	19	20	21	22	23	24
25	26	27	28	29	30	31

The leading sides of the 50s & 60s

Green Lane, the first champions of the Dales Council. Back row l to r. Scorer A. Luty, E. Lennon, B. Coutlass, B. Graham, G. Marshall, J. Tolliston J. Driver. Front row: M. Dibb, R. Lawson, D. Exley, G. Yeadon, N. Cousins.

Otley Mills Cup winning side of 1966. Back row l to r. Stan Handford, president, P. Ward, G. Perkins, S. Renner, G. Bona, D. Norris, S. Danskin. Front row. A. Tomlinson, I. Wilson, W. Mason, cap., J. Hamer, G. Ives. Scorer, Geoff Wolfenden.

THE DALES COUNCIL — Clubs from the opening season to 2005

League champions	Cup winners	Nos.	Clubs	From	To. Inc.	Ground	Location
		1	Butterfield Sports	1956	1958	Fyfe Lane	Charlestown, Baildon.
57,		2	Crompark	1956	1956	Back Ln, Netherfield, High Royds	Guiseley / Menston
		3	David Brown Tractors	1956	1956	Canal Bank	Rodley
		4	English Electric	1956	1963	Phoenix Park	Thornbury
59, 62, 65, 67, 84.		5	Esholt	1956	1984	Esholt Lane	Esholt
56, 58, 60, 61.	57, 59, 60,	6	Green Lane	1956	1961	Green Lane	Yeadon.
		7	James Ives Sports	1956	1968	New Scarboro'	Yeadon
		8	Netherfield Sports	1956	1965	Netherfield Road	Guiseley
63, 64, 66.	66	9	Otley Mills	1956	1968	Grove Hill Park	Otley
		10	Otley Wesley	1956	1966	Wharfe Meadows Park	Otley
	58,	11	Pool Paper Mills	1956	1986	Pool Paper Mills	Pool-in-Wharfedale.
		12	Ross Mills	1956	1960	Canal Bank	Rodley.
		13	Smiths Sports (Rodley)	1956	1961	Coal Hill Lane	Rodley.
		14	Thackley	1956	1958	North Hall, Ainsbury Av.	Thackley.
		15	Tong Park	1956	1958	Low Springs.	Tong Park, Baildon
		16	Laisterdyke	1956	1959	Broad Lane	Laisterdyke
	61,	17	International Harvesters	1956	1962	opp. Stansfield Arms	Apperley Bridge.
	63, 64, 65.	18	Wilson & Mathieson's	1956	1972	near Stanhope Hotel	Rodley.
		19	Newlands	1957	1957	Canal Bank	Rodley
		20	Leeds Zingari	1957	1990		
73	70	21	Bramley Sports	1958	1980	Canal Bank	Rodley
		22	Illingworth St Mary's	1958	1961	The Ainleys, Whitehall Rd.	Illingworth
	62	23	Reuben Gaunts	1958	1968	Throstle Nest	Farsley
		24	Sowerby Bridge	1958	1960	Walton Street	Sowerby Bridge
		25	Turner Sports	1961	1970	Swinnow Lane	Bramley
		26	Thos. Waides	1961	1962	Brownberrie Lane	Horsforth
71, 76, 80.	67, 69, 73, 76.	27	Smiths Sports (2nd spell)	1965	1980	Coal Hill Lane	Rodley
	68	28	Holbeck Bethel	1965	1968	Farnley Hall	Old Farnley
68, 69, 72, 83, 92, 94.	80, 83, 92, 93.	29	New Farnley	1966	1994	Farnley Hall	Old Farnley

Yr.	Clubs/teams
1956:	18. 24.
1957:	18. 26.
1958:	22. 32.
1959:	19. 30.
1960:	18. 29.
1961:	18. 28.
1962:	15. 24.
1963:	13. 17.
1964:	12. 16.
1965:	14. 19.
1966:	14. 20.
1967:	13. 19.
1968:	15. 22.
1969:	15. 23.
1970:	17. 24.
1971:	18. 24.
1972:	16. 22.
1973:	16. 22.
1974:	17. 23.
1975:	17. 23.
1976:	22. 30.
1977:	22. 32.
1978:	21. 32.
1979:	26. 41.
1980:	26. 42.
1981:	27. 44.
1982:	28. 46.
1983:	27. 44.
1984:	27. 44.

League champions	Cup winners	Nos.	Clubs	From	To. Inc.	Ground	Location
		30	Armley Saxons	1968	1971	The Butter Bowl, Leeds Ring Road	Wortley
		31	Johnson Radley	1968	1970	West Royd Park	Farsley
	71	32	Grove H (form. Otley Ms.)	1969	1973	Grove Hill Park	Otley
70		33	Wibsey	1969	1984	Horsfall Playing Fields	Odsal, Wibsey.
		34	West Leeds (form H Beth)	1969	1973	Farnley Hall	Old Farnley
		35	Farnley Hill	1969	1971	Farnley Hall	Old Farnley
75	77	36	Oxford Place	1970	1987	West Royd Park	Farsley
78	72, 74, 75.	37	Pudsey Congs	1970	1978	Queen's Park	Pudsey
		38	Farnley Estate	1971	1977	Farnley Hall	Farnley Hall, Otley
		39	Farsley	1971	1972	West Royd Park	Farsley
		40	River Authority	1971	1973	Soldiers' Field	Roundhay
		41	Phoenix Park	1973	1982	Phoenix Park	Thornbury
		42	Leeds YMCA	1973	1988	Otley Road, Lawnswood.	Lawnswood
74, 77, 79	78	43	Otley T (Otley M/Gr. Hill)	1974	1979	Grove Hill Park	Otley
		44	CEGB. (form W Lds/H B)	1974	1977	Beckwith Knowle, Otley Road.	Harrogate
	88	45	Pudsey St Lawrence	1974		Queen's Park	Pudsey
		46	Wil & Math (2nd spell)	1974	1976	near Stanhope Hotel.	Rodley
85, 87.		47	Croma	1976	1987	Park Side Sch. & Roundhay Oval	Middleton/Roundhay
86		48	Scalebor Park	1976	1987	Scalebor Park Hospital	Burley-in-Wharfedale
		49	Ben Rhydding	1976	1986	Leeds Road, Ben Rhydding	Ben Rhydding
2001, 2002.	2001	50	New Wortley	1976		Western Flatts Park	Wortley
		51	Olicanians	1976	1987	Denton Road by Ilkley swim pool	Ilkley
		52	Kirkstall Forge	1977	1979	Back of Cookridge Hall	Cookridge
	86	53	Adel	1978		Red Hall then Church Lane, Adel.	Whinmoor/Adel
	79, 81, 82.	54	Riddlesden	1979	1982	Stockbridge	Riddlesden
81, 88.		55	Eldwick and Gilstead	1979	1988	High Edlwick near Dick Hudson's	Eldwick
		56	Morton	1979	1980	Brown Hill	West Morton
	84	57	Ingrow St John's	1979	1987	Marriner Road, Greengates	Keighley

Yr.	Clubs/teams	
1885:	26.	41.
1986:	27.	43.
1987:	26.	41.
1988:	22.	32.
1989:	22.	29.
1990:	23.	33.
1991:	23.	34.
1992:	23.	34.
1993:	24.	35.
1994:	24.	35.
1995:	28.	38.
1996:	28.	38.
1997:	31.	43.
1998:	27.	40.
1999:	29.	43.
2000:	28.	45.
2001:	26.	43.
2002:	26.	40.
2003:	25.	38.
2004:	25.	36.

Nos.	Clubs	From	To. Inc.	Ground	Location	Yr. Clubs/teams	Cup winners	League champions
58	Morton Banks	1979	1987	East Riddlesden Hall	Riddlesden			
59	Meanwood Park	1979	1988	Meanwood Park Hospital	Meanwood			
60	Civil Service	1980	1987	Hurst Lane	Saltaire			
61	Pudsey Congs (2nd spell)	1980		Queen's Park	Pudsey			93
62	Bramley (form. Bram Sp.)	1981	1982	Canal Bank	Rodley			
63	Farsley Celt (form Smiths)	1981	1987	Throstles Nest	Farsley		85, 87.	82
64	Lloyds Bank	1981	1987	near Stanhope Hotel (Sandoz)	Rodley			
65	Wortley Highfield	1981	1983	Farnley Hall	Old Farnley			
66	High Royds	1982	1986	High Royds Hospital ground	Guiseley / Menston			
67	Rodley (form Bram/Br S)	1983		Canal Bank	Rodley			96, 97, 2004
68	Nat. West Bank	1983	1999	Brad Univ Woodhall Playing Fields	Calverley, Pudsey		96	
69	Yorks Switch (form W Hi)	1984	1986	Farnley Hall	Old Farnley			
70	Sandmoor	1985	1989	Alwoodley Recreation Ground	Alwoodley			
71	Esholt (2nd spell)	1986		Brad Univ. W'dhall PF& West Lane	Calv.,Pudsey/Baildon			
72	Meanwood	1987		Parkside Road by The Myrtle	Meanwood		89, 94, 97, 98. 2002, 2003.	98
73	Thorite	1987	1993	Farnley Hall	Old Farnley			
74	Dun & R (form WHi/YSw.)	1987	1989	Farnley Hall	Old Farnley			
75	Horsforth (form Lloyds B)	1988	1991	near Stanhope Hotel (Sandoz)	Rodley			
76	Leeds Civil Service	1988	1993	Newton Road	Chapel Allerton			89, 91.
77	Cookridge	1988		Smithy Lane	Cookridge		90	90
78	Tong	1988	1999	By the Greyhound Public House	Tong		95	95
79	New Rover	1988	1997	Old Park Road & Smithy Mills Ln	Roundhay / Weetwood			
80	Otley	1989	1999	Prince Henry Grammar School	Otley			
81	Whitehall	1989		Becketts Park	Headingley			
82	Old Modernians	1989		Tetley Spts.gd. & Bedquilts	Weetwood / Adel			
83	Castlehill	1990		Queens Pk. & Corinthians RUFC	Pudsey/Middleton		91	
84	Arthington	1990	1998	Arthington (across from the church)	Arthington			
85	Green Lane (2nd spell)	1990	1997	Yarnbury, Priesthorpe & Weeton CC	Horsf'th, Pudsey, Otley			
86	Ilkley	1991	1997	Ilkley Grammar School ground	Ben Rhydding			

League champions	Cup winners	Yr. Clubs/teams	Nos.	Clubs	From	To. Inc.	Ground	Location
			87	St Chads Broomfield	1992	1997	Tetley Sports ground	Weetwood
			88	Otley Town	1993	1997	Pool-Harewood Rd	Arthington
			89	Lawns Park	1994	1997	Farnley Hall	Old Farnley
			90	North Leeds	1994	1997	Roundhay Sch. Old Park Rd.	Roundhay
			91	Jarvis Porter	1995	1997	Middleton Clearings & Gipsy Ln	Beeston
			92	Farnley Hill	1995		Farnley Hall	Old Farnley
			93	Alwoodley	1995	1997	Stonegate Rd. PF & Cragg Ln.	Meanwood/Alwoodley
			94	Hawksworth	1995		Yarnbury RUFC then Arthington	Horsforth/Arthington
			95	Horsforth (2nd spell)	1995	2000	near Stanhope Hotel (Sandoz)	Rodley
99, 2000.	99, 2000, 2004		96	Mount	1997		Ponte Racecourse & Hyrstland Pk	Pontefract/Batley Carr
			97	Ramgarhia Sikh	1997	2001	Soldiers Field, Roundhay Park.	Roundhay
			98	Farsley	1997	2003	Priesthorpe, Sandoz, Red Lane	Farsley/Rodley
			99	Skeltons Wood	1997	2001	Skeltons Wood off Skeltons Lane.	Seacroft
2003			100	Baildon Meths	1998		Belmont, now Sandals School.	Baildon
			101	Shipley Providence	1998		Coach Road.	Baildon
			102	Farsley Celtic (2nd spell)	1998	2001	Throstles Nest, Newlands.	Farsley
			103	Carr Manor	1998	2002	Bowcliffe Hall	Bramham
			104	Mount Pleasant (Mount)	1999	2001	Ponte Racecourse & Sands Ln.	Pontefract/Dewsbury
			105	Motivators	1999	2000	Prince Philip PF Scott Hall Avenue.	Meanwood
			106	Churwell	1999		Throstle Nest then Farnley Hall	Farnley/Old Farnley
			107	New Farnley (2nd spell)	2000		Farnley Hall	Old Farnley
			108	Wibsey Park Chapel	2000		Haycliffe Lane	Wibsey
			109	Braml S B (form Sm/FCel)	2002	2003	Brad Univ. Woodhall Playing Fields	Calverley, Pudsey
			110	Garforth	2002	2002	Church Lane	Garforth
			111	Leeds Sikh (form Ram.S)	2002		Soldiers Fld./Leeds YMCA	Roundhay/Lawnswood
			112	South Parade Baptists	2002		Bedquilts	Adel
			113	Kirkstall Educational	2003		Bedquilts	
			114	Halifax Direct	2004		Bedquilts	Weetwood
			115	Burley Park	2004		Brad Univ. Woodhall Playing Fields	Calverley, Pudsey

Two of the Dales Council's Double winning sides

Smiths Sports double winning side of 1976. Back row l to r. R. Long, K. Booth, A. Longley, D. Benn, C. Janney, I. Parker, W. Stott. Front row: D. Pearce, P. Worsnop, B. Cooke, R. Webster, K. Robertshaw, B. Bennett, J. Fisher.

New Wortley's double winning side of 2001. Back row l to r. J. Lee, K. Blackburn, D. Creasey, Liz Chambers, scorer, K. Pickles, F.Smith, M. Hobson. Front row: S. Kirk, Akhlaq Ahmed, Kala Khan, Mohammed Arif, M. Knowles, capt., K. Tompkinson.

The Dales Council's Trophy Cabinet.

OVER the years as the number of clubs and teams they generate have grown or fallen the Dales Council management committee has found it necessary to introduce differing formats to accommodate numbers in any given season. This practice has involved using a number of different names for divisions but they all add up to first, second, third and fourth divisional competitions.

Back in 1956 when the Dales got off the ground with 18 clubs there was a 1st Elevens competition made up of the original 18 clubs and a 2nd Elevens competition for the second teams of six of the founder clubs. Since then the various titles used to identify the different divisions of the league have included 1st Elevens, 2nd Elevens, Section A, Section B, Division A, Division B, Division C and Division D.

In this history of the league I have printed the given name of any particular division as it was used in its original format when preparing the league tables in the records section, and, where necessary in the text. It seemed right to identify divisions with the names used at the time.

However, in an effort to give the Dales records some uniformity from 1998 it was decided that the divisions would appear simply as Divisions A, B, C and D with the winners of Division D, in general terms, being the winners of the second elevens' competitions over the years and so on. So, for instance, the champions of the 2nd Elevens competition in 1956, Wilson & Mathiesons, are traced in ongoing league handbooks as winners of D Division.

In a nutshell, the league competitions have evolved as follows:

League champions (winners of A Division) – THE JACK SHUTTLEWORTH CUP.

B Division champions – THE WILLIAM HILL TROPHY.

C Division champions - THE JOHN COLLINS TROPHY.

D Division champions – THE HOLMES WHITELEY TROPHY.

Winners of **the senior cup knock-out competition** – THE POOL PAPER MILLS CUP.

Winners of **the cup knock-out competition for lower division sides and second teams** – THE CAWTHORNE CUP.

There are also trophies for **Fair Play** (senior sides The UMPIRES ASSOCIATION SPORTSMANSHIP TROPHY) and (lower division and second teams THE LES BULMER TROPHY) and trophies presented by the Yorkshire Evening Post for **the top youngsters and the top umpires** (JOHN MORGAN'S YOUNG CRICKETER OF THE YEAR AWARD and JOHN MORGAN'S UMPIRES AWARD) besides all the usual individual awards for players.

Chapter 18.

THE ESSENCE OF CRICKET

IN 50 years of ups and downs there have been endless examples in the Dales Council of why cricket holds such an enduring fascination for all those who know and love the game and, no doubt, there will be any number of Dales players, past and present, who would argue they could turn to a better example of the essence of cricket than the one which follows.

But of well over 1,000 games I have been involved in over nearly half a century of playing in local cricket in Yorkshire there was one in particular which emphasised the magic of the game for me like none before – and I thought looking back at it, it was the kind of fairy tale of a cricket game that might round off the thousands of words that make up the Dales Council story.

We are talking about a modest little fixture (yet nonetheless important on the day to both sides) played on a pleasant if unimpressive pitch at Becketts Park, Leeds. Crompark's C Division team were visiting Whitehall with both sides deep in relegation trouble on the second Saturday of August, 2001.

Crompark had struggled to raise eleven all season, a major reason for their predicament of the moment, and on this day, sitting as they were on the bottom of the table, the situation was almost as bad as it gets. Holidays and work calls, injuries and other, seemingly flimsy reasons, at that moment in time left Crompark with just nine men.

I was in charge and knew we somehow had to get a result against a team just above us to have much of a chance of salvaging a campaign that had started with such promise after winning the D Division title just 11 months previously. But what could we expect with two men short?

To compound a bad situation I lost the toss for the sixth successive time and, quite rightly, my opposite number asked us to bat on a very green track. Inside three overs we were three down with just one run on the board....effectively five down for one when you take into account our missing team-mates. It seemed that the fat lady had just about finished her song but as the saying goes it is not all over until she has actually finished singing.

We had reached one of those cometh the moment, cometh the man times and our vice-captain Andy Halliday, a centurion twice over in the previous 12 months, decided to try and take the game to Whitehall. He was put down twice as he went for the jugular but his bold hitting suddenly began to brighten a gloomy afternoon for Crompark. Paul Stamp kept his nerve at the other end and as the runs came, one by one, four by four and six by six on the tiny ground, the pair breathed new life into what had seemed a dead cause.

Halliday's crash, bang wallop style and Stamp's resistance worked to such an extent that the pair put on a century stand to pluck the initiative from what had been a confident Whitehall side. The magic was working but then the game took another twist to underline that you can never take Lady cricket for granted.

Stamp went after making 18 in a stand of 113 but when Simon Mace rejoined the Whitehall attack it was not long before Halliday went to a catch at slip, the first victim of a hat-trick for Mace. Suddenly Crompark had lost five wickets in adding just 13 to finish on 126 thanks mainly, of course, to Halliday's effort which had seen him smack 103 in 118 minutes.

But we knew that with two fielders short the inevitable gaps in the field would still leave the odds in Whitehall's favour. And with their captain Mick Wright taking them to 99 for four with a half century and with still plenty of overs remaining it looked all over for Crompark, especially since the threat of a heavy downpour had receded.

Yet from somewhere I conjured up five wickets in seven deliveries without conceding a run to turn the contest on its head once more. Wicket, wicket, dot ball, wicket, wicket, dot ball, wicket and Whitehall crumpled from 99-4 to the brink of an unlikely defeat. The rush of wickets took me to eight for 40 and, fittingly, Halliday took the last wicket (and fielding point) and Whitehall were beaten by 17 runs after losing their last six wickets for just 10 runs.

The fat lady, almost out of breath I suspect, had finally finished. She had been good to Crompark after all – but what a game of ups and downs, just what cricket is all about.

Andy Halliday.

Barry Foster.

Sponsors, Subscribers & one-in-50 years dedications

Our main Sponsor:

A. Baldwin & Co (Builders) Ltd., Morley. £1000.
(John Baldwin, chairman, New Farnley C.C.)

Our Sponsors:

Les Thompson,	*Dales Council Life Member,*	£100
Peter Marsh,	*Dales Council Life Member,*	£100
David Smith,	*Dales Council Chair/Hon Treasurer,*	£100
Alan Wardle,	*Dales Council Hon Secretary,*	£100
Robert Kibble,	*Crompark CC President,*	£100

Turning Back the Clock

Wilson & Mathieson's ground at Rodley, scene of some of the Dales Council's earliest contests.

Ross Mills, one of the original 18 clubs in the Dales Council, with Sidney Newton, the first player to hit a century in the league, fourth left on the front row. The team group also includes Cyril Chapman, (third left front row) well known as an administrator and umpire in the league in later years, and Geoffrey Tempest, (back row third left) who went on to play in the Bradford League for many years.

International Harvesters' ground at Apperley Bridge, a Dales Council ground from day one of the league.

One of the first Dales Council league representative sides, with Dales umpires and believed to be from 1957/8 campaigns. Back row l to r. Umpire C.J.E. Sladen, M. Franks (Esholt), N. Hartley (Int. Harv.), unknown, M. Dibb (Green Lane), H. Stead (Tong Park), G. Sample (Green Lane), umpire Jack Toothill. Front row: unknown, E. Thornborrow (Esholt), R. Shuttleworth (Esholt), E. Barker (Esholt), A. Pickard (PPM).

WHARFEDALE & AIREDALE OBSERVER

HAT-TRICK STARTS RECORDS IN NEW DALES COUNCIL

Low Scoring Games on Opening Day

FIRST day for the new Dales Council was more a trial for the officials than the clubs and players, most of whom were simply playing their first match of the season. For the officials, however, it was a test of the league machinery which was in full motion for the first time.

On the surface there is no difference between matches in this new league and the company in which the clubs and players were last season but there is a difference, an exciting one.

All start from scratch and all clubs and players, have a chance to make history in the shape of records of being the first in.

And first home is K. Wilkinson, of Pool Mills, who registered the first hat-trick. There will be others later but this is a record that cannot be improved on. And so it will be with other feats. They will go on record and will stay there to long as the Council exists.

With this proviso, however. The feats must be noted in the score sheets or they may be missed. So clubs should make it a duty to see that their score does his job properly and records interesting features which often are not provided for in scoresheets complex though these are these days.

CLOSE FINISHES

It was a steady start, one on which the teams can build. Scoring was on the low side, reflecting the damp wickets and the dominance bowlers were able to exercise on them.

For excitement the match at Laisterdyke took first place. Esholt rent in their last man, wanting 14 to win, and got him, T. Walker (29 not out) being the match-winner.

Butterfields Sports went down by only 6 runs at Smiths (Rodley), and English Electric won by only 3 wickets although they put Ives Sports out for 44. For M. Ives foundered on the bowling of J. Gate who took 8-11, but one of Ives' men, P. Parkinson, went home pleased. He had taken 5-9.

ALL-ROUNDER

One of the best performances of the day was that of W. Russell, of

INTERNATIONAL HARVESTERS

FINAL LEAGUE TABLES, 1956

1st ELEVENS

	P	W	L	D	Total Pts.
Green Lane	21	17	2	2	53
Wilsons & Mathiesons	21	14	3	4	46
Tong Park	21	12	4	5	41
David Browns Tractors	21	11	7	3	36
Smiths (Rodley)	21	9	6	6	33
Laisterdyke	21	9	7	5	32
Crompark	21	8	7	6	30
James Ives Sports	21	8	7	6	30
Butterfields	21	7	8	6	27
Ross Mills	21	7	10	4	25
Otley Mills	21	6	9	6	24
Pool Paper Mills	21	6	9	6	24
English Electric	21	6	9	6	24
Esholt	21	6	10	5	23
Thackley	21	5	11	5	20
International Harvesters	21	5	12	4	19
Netherfield Sports	21	4	13	4	16
Otley Wesley	21	3	11	7	16

2nd ELEVENS

	P	W	L	D	Total Pts.
Wilsons & Mathiesons	20	14	3	3	45
Green Lane	20	13	4	3	43
Esholt	20	8	9	3	27
Pool Paper Mills	20	7	9	4*	26
Otley Wesley	20	4	12	4	16
Netherfield Sports	20	2	12	6*	13

* Denotes tie—2 points awarded.

42

The league positions at the end of the Dales Council's first season, 1956.

DALES CRICKET COUNCIL WIND UP A NOTABLE FIRST SEASON

111 Wickets for Sample but No Prize

GREEN LANE finished like champions, with a 9 wickets' win against one of their chief rivals. And their star bowler, Gordon Sample, also finished with a flourish, taking 6-24. With an amazing aggregate of 111 wickets to his credit, it seems ironical that G. Milner, with 32 wickets for 100 runs.

Two matches were cancelled because 3-16, and R. Haywood 2-19, putting the ball of set grounds and the putting the Mills out for 32 positions are. After they had put Thackley out for 77, Butterfields Sports won by 6 wickets.

RESULTS

Ross Mills 52 (E. Worrall 4-16, R. Haywood 3-15); *Laisterdyke 53-4 (J. Hartley 31).

Thackley 77; *Butterfields Sp. 184-4 (J. Dixon 29).

Netherfield Sp. 45 (S. Barrett 4-21); *Pool Mills 46 (M. Tankard 27, R. Boller 7-20).

Smiths Sports v. Otley Wesley: Cancelled, Ground unfit.

*English Electric 75 (G. Parry 4-28); International Harvesters 68 (A. Swallow 4-9).

*David Brown Tractors 62 (J. Robinson 2-16); Rawdon 43-6, Lewis 4-16, J. Balter 4-21.

Crompark v. Wilson & Mathieson—Cancelled, ground unfit.

Otley Mills v. Ives Sports.—Cancelled, ground unfit.

Second Teams

Wharfedale & Airedale Observer records the first day's fixtures of the new Dales Council league in April, 1956.

Wharfedale & Airedale Observer's report of the final day's play of the league's first season, September, 1956.

Our Subscribers:

Keith Smith
Kevin Tomkinson
Mike Willoughby
Michael Richmond
Joyce Pearce
Graham Chambers
Rob Driver
Reg Parker
Barrie Turner
Arnold Beech
David Bissett
Andy Halliday
Mark Shaw
Jeremy Jones
Barrie Crighton
Donald Holmes
Gerry Redshaw
Cliff Barker
Derek Leadley
Dom Allen
Bill Beckett
Brian Bonnington
Ernest Brady
Brian Brown
Gerry Dove
John Farrar
Green Lane CC
Stuart Horrell
Michael Knight
Ron Mackenzie
Rod Marwood
Ralph Middlebrook
Otley CC
Steve Raistrick
Harry Rifer
David Shuttleworth
Dave Stockwell
Simon Twine
John Whitney

Malcolm Dibb
Bill Robinson
Melvyn Reuben
John Webb
Christine Booth
Derek Elsworth
Les Fussey
Bob Webb
Ray Gambles
Barry Gill
Richard Wilkinson
Peter Clark
Nick Lawson
David Robinson
Martin Grant
C Geoffrey Fryers
Martin Young
Richard Colledge
Martin Ashworth
Jamie Allen
Chris Beckett
Stephen Bradbury
Ron Brady
Colton Cricket Club
Mark Dufton
Geoffrey Fowler
Jeremy Harris
Raymond Keeling
Peter Langley
Syd Marsden
David Mawn
Brian Newall
Richard Owen
Dan Randerson
Edna Robinson
Graham Shuttleworth
Geoffrey Tarbatt
Brian Wall

Adrian Carr
Geoffrey Jones
Wibsey Park Chapel CC
Allister Booth
Helen Lambert
Rick Vanes
Mike Sanders
David Bean
Brian Wrigglesworth
Alistair Wilson
John Toft
Robert Pritchard
Phil Cooper
Steve Thompson
Brian Rhodes
Stephen Wood
Lawrence Young
Derek Hawley
Stephen Bedford
Jacques Allen
Derek Best
James Bradbury
Peter Briggs
Keith Dibb
Mick Edwards
Graham Gaunt
Michael Hirst
Bill Kelso
Mick Lockwood
Jack Marshall
Andrew McLaughlin
Olicanian CC
Anne Pantall
Derek Reason
Darren Shotton
Stan Stafford
Brian Tearle
Colin White

GOLDEN YEARS OF THE DALES COUNCIL

Players, umpires, officials, clubs and friends sponsor their special year in the league's first 50.

1956 Crompark C.C. the only Dales club with 50 years unbroken league membership
1957 Kirkstall Eds celebrate 100 years of cricket at their Queenswood Drive ground, Leeds.
1958 Marking the formation of the Dales Council Umpires Association.
1959
1960 Les Heaton – a longstanding loyal supporter of the Dales Council
1961 Bramley Sports double champions (B&D divs.) repeated as Rodley in 1996 (A&D divs).
1962
1963
1964
1965
1966 Terry Drury, only player to top the League batting & bowling averages in same season
1967
1968
1969
1970
1971
1972
1973 Wicketkeeper John Fenton hits the boundary that takes Bramley Sports to the League title
1974
1975
1976 Roy Webster, season's top wicketkeeper & captain as Smiths win League/Cup double
1977
1978 Pudsey Congs CC become League champions for the first time
1979
1980
1981 Eldwick & Gilstead, A Division champions of the Dales Council in 1981 & 1988.
1982 Keith Brattley is captain of the League champions Farsley Celtic.
1983
1984 Esholt win their fifth league title to span their only year in 50 out of the Dales as champions.
1985 Croma achieve record 99 pts. In memory of George Pearson, Trevor Clapham & Paul Newton.
1986 Adel find a place on the trophy-winning table by lifting the PPM Cup.
1987 Umpire and former Smith Sports all-rounder Alan Wardle takes over as League secretary.
1988
1989 Meanwood lift the PPM Cup to start the Dales' most successful cup-winning sequence.
1990 Cookridge are League and Pool Paper Mills Cup double champions
1991
1992 Double Champions New Farnley also capture PPM & Cawthorne Cups to sweep the field.
1993 Rodley's loyal club member Cyril Chapman awarded umpire of the year accolade.
1994
1995 Michael Richmond sets record 97.50 batting average in New Rover's B Division title success.
1996
1997
1998 Hawksworth CC : Remembering Gordon Hay for his enthusiasm, skill and sportsmanship.
1999 In memory of Michael Holmes, 1945-1999, who played for New Farnley and Tong.
2000 Wibsey Park Chapel CC marking the first year of the Wibsey Park Chapel Academy
2001
2002 In memory of Keith Duckett, captain, Crompark D Division champions & Cup finalists
2003 Baildon Meths follow up their record points total of 114 in 2001 with their first league title success.
2004 Marking the Whiteley family's support for the Dales Council from the league's formation
2005 Dales Council Cricket League in celebration of our 50th anniversary year.

ACKNOWLEDGMENTS AND THANKS

IT IS difficult to know where to start when it comes down to thanking people for their help in making this account of the Dales Council's first 50 years possible. Someone, somewhere, who provided that important item that, without its addition, makes the whole less plausible or at least much less complete is bound to have been overlooked but anyway, thanks to everyone who helped though, of course, it would be inappropriate not to mention a few people in particular.

The league's former president Les Thompson is easy to put ahead of the rest. It was his brainchild as much as anyone to put this book in motion in the first place. Then there are people like Roy Webster, Derek Hawley, John Whiteley, the league's officers both ancient and modern, particularly Alan Wardle, Steve Raistrick and David Smith and not forgetting the umpires, club officials and players who helped with the histories of the clubs and stories half forgotten. Mick Edwards, Malcolm Franks, Mick Wright, Steve Bradbury, Harry Dean, Gordon Sample, Malcolm Dibb, Tony Metcalfe, Keith Smith, John Fenton, Terry Drury, Les Fussey and many others who spared time to talk about days gone by also deserve thanks along with copy reader Peter Taylor. Then there is a special thank you to the guest writers who have given freely of their talents to add what I regard as a distinctive extra feature to the whole and to Neil Priscott, the MCC Communications Officer, not to mention help on the pc side from Wildman Computers of Baildon.

It would be an omission, too, not to remember the "invisible" people who helped to put together the league handbooks over the years for the statistics therein have provided a major source of information for this story. The figures, particularly in some of the league tables, did not always add up but where possible corrections have been made. In addition, long distance memories/inquiries have not always come up with the first name that fits an initial and so rather than leave out 'A. Brown', for instance, because it could not be determined whether he was Arthur, Alan or Andrew, merely 'A. Brown' has been used. On the question of long distance memories, there may also be the odd point that has been recalled with some embellishment by sources and, of course, responsibility cannot be accepted for the accuracy of such recollections — but rest assured every effort has been made to check out the memory banks.

Turning to other avenues of information, a great debt is also due to the local newspapers, particularly the Wharfedale and Airedale Observer, the Ilkley Gazette and its deputy editor Alan Birkinshaw and the Shipley Times & Express, Telegraph and Argus, the Yorkshire Post and the Yorkshire Evening Post for their help with news items and photographs. In addition there are the many other supporters of the cause who have helped with illustrations like photographers/journalists Colin Gadsby, Bruce Greer, John Fisher, Raymond of Baildon (now Lillian Light of Yeadon) and Tony Fickes. Exhaustive efforts have been made to trace copyright holders of all photographs used, of course, and an apology is due for any acknowledgment omissions, which are unintentional. Obviously, the Dales Council would be pleased to include an appropriate acknowledgment in any subsequent edition.

Finally, without all the above ingredients, and the patience of my wife Margaret who not only put up with me while I was spending maybe too much of our "retirement" researching and writing but was also the book's chief copy reader, this project would have been a non starter.

Barry Foster, November, 2004.